*Very Short Reflections
through the Liturgical Year*

Very Short Reflections

—for Advent and Christmas, Lent and Easter,
Ordinary Time, and Saints—

through the Liturgical Year

MARK G. BOYER

WIPF & STOCK · Eugene, Oregon

VERY SHORT REFLECTIONS
—for Advent and Christmas, Lent and Easter, Ordinary Time, and Saints—
THROUGH THE LITURGICAL YEAR

Wipf & Stock
An Imprint of Wipf and Stock Publishers
199 W. 8th Ave., Suite 3
Eugene, OR 97401

www.wipfandstock.com

PAPERBACK ISBN: 978-1-7252-7107-4
HARDCOVER ISBN: 978-1-7252-7108-1
EBOOK ISBN: 978-1-7252-7109-8

Manufactured in the U.S.A.   08/13/20

Dedicated to

St. Joachim High School Class of 1968:

Marilyn Bone (Pinson)

JoAnn Bone (Kelly)

John Boyer

Michael Coleman

Jerry DeClue

Robert Finch

Wayne Koch

James Pashia

Mary Ann Politte (Pratt)

Geraldine Sampson (Willert)+

Kenny Sansoucie+

Catherine Singer

George Wall+

+ = deceased

"Advent has a twofold character, for it is a time of preparation for the solemnities of Christmas, in which the first coming of the Son of God to humanity is remembered, and likewise a time when, by remembrance of this, minds and hearts are led to look forward to Christ's second coming at the end of time. For these two reasons, Advent is a period of devout and expectant delight."

—"Universal Norms," par. 39.

"... [T]he Church has no more ancient custom than celebrating the memorial of the Nativity of the Lord and of his first manifestations, and this takes place in Christmas Time."

—"Universal Norms," par. 32.

"Lent is ordered to preparing for the celebration of Easter, since the Lenten liturgy prepares for celebration of the Paschal Mystery [by] ... the faithful, who recall their own Baptism and do penance."

—"Universal Norms," par. 27.

"... [T]he sacred Paschal Triduum of the Passion and Resurrection of the Lord shines forth as the high point of the entire liturgical year."

—"Universal Norms," par. 18.

"The fifty days from the Sunday of the Resurrection to Pentecost Sunday are celebrated in joy and exultation as one feast day, indeed as one 'great Sunday.'"

—"Universal Norms," par. 22.

"Besides the times of year that have their own distinctive character, there remains in the yearly cycle thirty-three or thirty-four weeks in which no particular aspect of the mystery of Christ is celebrated, but rather the mystery of Christ itself is honored in it fullness, especially on Sundays. This period is known as Ordinary Time."

—"Universal Norms," par. 43.

Contents

Abbreviations

ca.	circa, around
cf.	confer, see by way of comparison
CE	Common Era (same as AD, *Anno Domini*, in the year of the Lord)

CB (NT)	**CHRISTIAN BIBLE (NEW TESTAMENT)**
Acts	Acts of the Apostles
Col	Letter to the Colossians
1 Cor	First Letter of Paul to the Corinthians
2 Cor	Second Letter of Paul to the Corinthians
Eph	Letter to the Ephesians
Gal	Letter of Paul to the Galatians
Heb	Letter to the Hebrews
John	John's Gospel
1 John	First Letter of John
Luke	Luke's Gospel
Mark	Mark's Gospel
Matt	Matthew's Gospel
Phil	Letter of Paul to the Philippians
Rev	Revelation
Rom	Letter of Paul to the Romans

| 2 Tim | Second Letter to Timothy |
| Titus | Letter to Titus |

HB (OT)   HEBREW BIBLE (OLD TESTAMENT)

1 Chr	First Book of Chronicles
Deut	Deuteronomy
Exod	Exodus
Ezek	Ezekiel
Hag	Haggi
Isa	Isaiah
Jer	Jeremiah
Lam	Lamentations
Mal	Malachi
Ps(s)	Psalm(s)
Prov	Proverbs
Zech	Zechariah

OT (A)   OLD TESTAMENT (APOCRYPHA)

Bar	Baruch
Sir	Sirach
Wis	Wisdom (of Solomon)

| par(s). | paragraph(s) |
| +(with a year) | year of death |

Notes on the Bible
and *The Roman Missal*

THE BIBLE

The Bible is divided into two parts: The Hebrew Bible (Old Testament) and the Christian Bible (New Testament). The Hebrew Bible consists of thirty-nine named books accepted by Jews and Protestants as Holy Scripture. The Old Testament also contains those thirty-nine books plus seven to fifteen more named books or parts of books called the Apocrypha or the Deutero-canonical Books; the Old Testament is accepted by Catholics and several other Christian denominations as Holy Scripture. The Christian Bible, consisting of twenty-seven named books, is also called the New Testament; it is accepted by Christians as Holy Scripture. Thus, in this work:

- Hebrew Bible (Old Testament), abbreviated HB (OT), indicates that a book is found both in the Hebrew Bible and the Old Testament;

- Old Testament (Apocrypha), abbreviated OT (A), indicates that a book is found only in the Old Testament Apocrypha and not in the Hebrew Bible;

- and Christian Bible (New Testament), abbreviated CB (NT), indicates that a book is found only in the Christian Bible or New Testament.

In notating biblical texts, the first number refers to the chapter in the book, and the second number refers to the verse within the chapter. Thus, HB (OT) Isa 7:11 means that the quotation comes from Isaiah, chapter 7, verse 11. OT (A) Sirach 39:30 means that the quotation comes from Sirach, chapter 39, verse 30. CB (NT) Mark 6:2 means that the quotation comes from Mark's Gospel, chapter 6, verse 2. When more than one sentence appears in a verse, the letters a, b, c, etc. indicate the sentence being referenced in the verse. Thus, HB (OT) 2 Kgs 1:6a means that the quotation comes from the Second Book of Kings, chapter 1, verse 6, sentence 1.

In the HB (OT) and the OT (A), the reader often sees LORD (note all capital letters). Because God's name (Yahweh or YHWH, referred to as the Tetragrammaton) is not to be pronounced, the name Adonai (meaning *Lord*) is substituted for Yahweh when a biblical text is read. When a biblical text is translated and printed, LORD (cf. Gen 2:4) is used to alert the reader to what the text actually states: Yahweh. Furthermore, when the biblical author writes Lord Yahweh, printers present Lord GOD (note all capital letters for GOD; cf. Gen 15:2) to avoid the printed ambiguity of LORD LORD. When the reference is to Jesus, the word printed is Lord (note capital L and lower case letters; cf. Luke 11:1). When writing about a lord (note all lower case letters (cf. Matt 18:25) with servants, no capital L is used.

THE ROMAN MISSAL

The Roman Missal is the book of prayers used by a priest or bishop when celebrating the Eucharist, commonly referred to as saying Mass. In 1970, following the close of the Second Vatican Council, Pope Paul VI issued a new Roman Missal in Latin replacing the one issued by Pope Pius V in 1570 after the close of the Council of Trent. The Missal of Paul VI was emended in 1971 and issued in English in 1974. In 1975, a second edition in Latin was issued by Paul VI; it was issued in English in 1985. A third edition of *The Roman Missal* was issued in Latin by Pope John Paul II in 2002 and emended in 2008; however, it was not until 2011 that *The Roman Missal* was issued in English. Thus, all references made to *The Roman Missal* in this book refer to the 2011 English edition listed in the bibliography of this work.

In alphabetical order, here are some terms used in *The Roman Missal* with which the reader may not be familiar:

Advent Season = The Advent Season begins on the First Sunday of Advent, the Sunday closest to November 30. The First Sunday of Advent is calculated by counting backward from whatever day of the week December 25 falls. The Sunday before December 25 is the Fourth Sunday of Advent, the Sunday before that is the Third Sunday of Advent, etc. The First Sunday of Advent is always between November 27 and December 3.

Christmas Season = The Christmas Season begins after 4 p.m. on December 24 and lasts until the Baptism of the Lord, usually the second Sunday of Janaury, which falls between January 7 and 13.

Collect = This is the opening prayer of the Eucharist (Mass) introduced by the priest or bishop with "Let us pray." It collects all the prayers of the congregants into one general, all-inclusive prayer.

Common = For some celebrations all the parts of Mass texts are not given in the Proper of Saints section of *The Roman Missal*; the celebrant is referred to a Common: Common of the Dedication of a Church, Common of the Blessed Virgin Mary, Common of Martyrs, Common of Pastors, Common of Virgins, and Common of Holy Men and Women. The Common not only presents several selections from which to choose the missing Mass texts, but it is also subdivided. For example, the Common of Pastors is divided into five subsections: I. For a Pope or for a Bishop; II. For a Bishop; III. For Pastors; IV. For Founders of Churches; and V. For Missionaries. The subsections are often further divided; for example, subsection IV. For Founders of Churches is subdivided into two subsections: A. For One Founder and B. For Several Founders. Subsections of subsections may provide more than one set of Mass texts; these are indicated by 1, 2, 3, etc. Thus, the reader may find in this book the following: Common of Martyrs, A. For Several Martyrs, 2. The Mass texts missing from the Proper of Saints are taken from the Common of Martyrs, subsection II. During Easter Time, subsection A. For Several Martyrs, subsection 2. In the text of this work, the reference is listed as Common of Martyrs, II. During Easter Time, A. For Several Martyrs, 2.

Communion Antiphon = This is the communion song of the Mass. Often, it consist of a biblical verse or a gloss on a biblical verse; a gloss is an interpretative application of a biblical verse regardless of its historical context. In some instances, several parts of biblical verses are combined to form the antiphon, which often enhances the theme of the specific Mass and of the season. Usually, the antiphon is sung in between verses of a psalm.

Easter Season = This is a season that lasts for fifty days, beginning with Easter Sunday and ending with Pentecost Sunday. Easter is calculated according to the phases of the moon. It is the first Sunday after the first full moon after the spring equinox. Thus, Easter may be on any Sunday between March 22 and April 25.

Entrance Antiphon = This is the opening song of the Mass. Often, it consist of a biblical verse or a gloss on a biblical verse; a gloss is an interpretative application of a biblical verse regardless of its historical context. In some instances, several parts of biblical verses are combined to form the antiphon, which often sets the theme of the specific Mass and of the season. Usually, the antiphon is sung in between verses of a psalm.

Lenten Season = This is a season that begins with Ash Wednesday and lasts until the beginning of the Sacred Paschal Triduum on Holy Thursday evening. Because its beginning is calculated backward from Easter (see above), it may occur on any Wednesday from February 6 to March 10. The best way to know when Lent begins is by consulting a liturgical calendar.

Ordinary Time = The Season of Ordinary Time is divided into two parts. The first part occurs from the Monday after the Baptism of the Lord (the end of the Christmas Season) and ends on Tuesday before Ash Wednesday. The second part begins on Monday after Pentecost and ends on Saturday before the First Sunday of Advent. The word *Ordinary* does not mean *usual* or *customary*. The name comes from the word *ordinal*, meaning counted Sundays and weeks. Thus, in the Season of Ordinary Time there are thirty-three or thirty-four numbered Sundays (Weeks), such as the Third Sunday in Ordinary Time.

Prayer after Communion = This is a concluding prayer said by the priest or bishop after communion—the sharing of the body and blood of Christ—has finished.

Prayer over the Offerings = This is a prayer said by the priest or bishop after the gifts of bread and wine have been prepared, presented to God, and set on the altar.

Prayer over the People = This is a solemn form for blessing people. It is required on the Sundays of Lent and is recommended for the weekdays of Lent. At the priest's discretion, a Prayer over the People may be used at any time during the liturgical year.

Preface = This prayer, introduced with dialogue between the priest or bishop and the congregants, praises and thanks God for something specific, such as the coming of Christ in glory or his nativity. It begins the Eucharist Prayer and concludes with the Holy, Holy, Holy Lord acclamation. When several choices are provided, they are numbered, such as, Preface I of Advent, Preface II of Advent, etc.

Saints = Days in honor of men and women of the past are assigned to various days throughout the liturgical year. These are ranked according to importance. The highest importance after the Sacred Paschal Triduum (see below) are most Sundays, followed by solemnities, followed by feasts, followed by memorials, followed by optional memorials. Very few optional memorials are treated in the chapter on saints. It is best to check a liturgical calendar to see when saints' days are celebrated and when they are omitted because, for example, they come into conflict with a Sunday.

In this book, the saints (chapter 7) are divided into categories: Saints during Advent, Saints during Christmas, Saints during Ordinary Time: Part I, Saints during Lent, Saints during Easter, and Saints during Ordinary Time: Part II. These are general categories. Because the beginning of the liturgical seasons changes from year to year, the category the saint is in may not be accurate for a given year. For example, in most years the Feast of St. Andrew (November 30) is in Advent (where it is placed in this book), but there are years when it is in Ordinary Time: Part II. In most years, the Memorial of St. Scholastica (February 10) is in Ordinary Time: Part I (where it is placed in this book), but there are years when it falls in Lent. A liturgical calendar, either in paper form or online, will show the season in which the saint's day is celebrated.

Sacred Paschal Triduum = The high point of the Liturgical Year are the three—triduum—days which begin on Holy Thursday evening and last until Easter Sunday evening. Since liturgical time is counted from evening to evening, Holy Thursday to Good Friday is one day; Good Friday to Holy Saturday is one day; and Holy Saturday to Easter Sunday is one day. Thus, the three days mark the Last Supper, Jesus' death on the cross, and his resurrection from the dead.

General Notes

All prayers of any kind in *The Roman Missal* are specified for every day of the liturgical year. Thus, in this book one may find a reference to Monday of the First Week of Advent; this means that a set of prayers for the Eucharist on Monday of the First Week of Advent is provided. A set consists of an Entrance Antiphon (opening song), Collect (opening prayer), a Prayer over the Offerings (prayer over the gifts of bread and wine), a Preface (specific thanksgiving), a Communion Antiphon (song during communion), and a Prayer after Communion (concluding prayer). During Lent, a Prayer over the People (extended blessing) is provided for each set. And on Sundays and some Solemnities and Feasts a Solemn Blessing may be recommended. The Collect, the Prayer over the Offerings, and the Prayer after Communion are usually addressed to God through Christ in the unity of the Holy Spirit. For those interested, a footnote indicates the page or pages where a set of prayers can be found in *The Roman Missal* edition used in the writing of this book.

When commemorating saints, a rank is presented: Solemnity, Feast, Memorial, or Optional Memorial. A solemnity, a feast, and a memorial often take precedence over an Advent, Christmas, Lent, Easter, and Ordinary

Time weekday, but not over an Advent, Christmas, Lent, Easter, or Ordinary Time Sunday; it is best to check a liturgical calendar to be sure what is being celebrated on a given day. When saints' days fall on an Advent, Christmas, Lent, Easter, or Ordinary Time Sunday, they are usually omitted for that year. An optional memorial is one that is not required but may be chosen at the discretion of the individual.

Not all of the reflections in this book will be used in any single liturgical season. For example, the days of December 17–24 take precedence over the last days of the Third Week of Advent, but not the Fourth Sunday of Advent. When December 26 through 31 occurs on a Sunday, that day is replaced with the Feast of the Holy Family of Jesus, Mary, and Joseph. In some years, when the Solemnity of the Epiphany on a Sunday is followed on Monday with the Feast of the Baptism of the Lord, some of the days from Monday through Saturday Before/After Epiphany are omitted. When March 19 or March 25 falls on a day of Holy Week, the solemnity is moved to the second Monday after Easter. When August 15 or November 1 falls on a Sunday in Ordinary Time, the solemnity is celebrated, and the Sunday in Ordinary Time is omitted. The best way to determine what day is being marked in the liturgical year is to use a liturgical calendar, either in a print edition or online.

Introduction

TITLE

The title of this book, *Very Short Reflections—for Advent and Christmas, Lent and Easter, Ordinary Time, and Saints—through the Liturgical Year*, accurately describes its contents. Chapter 1 presents a short reflection for every day of the Advent Season. Chapter 2 does the same for every day of the Christmas Season. Lent is covered in chapter 3, the Sacred Paschal Triduum in chapter 4, and the fifty days of the Easter Season in chapter 5. Chapter 6 covers Ordinary Time. And chapter 7 presents a short reflection for every solemnity, feast, and memorial of saints, whose special day falls during the liturgical year.

The short reflections are based on sets of Mass texts—Entrance Antiphon, Collect, Prayer over the Offerings, Preface, Communion Antiphon, Prayer after Communion, and Prayer over the People—presented for every day of Advent and Christmas, Lent and Easter, Ordinary Time, and Saints in *The Roman Missal*. The reflection identifies the theme of the day and presents how it is manifested in the Mass texts. Usually, reflections for Advent and Christmas and Lent and Easter are based on the biblical texts assigned for every day. However, a little known fact is that reflection may be based on the Mass texts for a given day.[1] These short reflections are designed to expose the liturgical spirituality that emanates from the Mass texts.

The focus of the first two weeks of Advent is on the second coming of Christ in glory. Only on December 17 does the focus change to immediate preparation to celebrate Jesus' birth, even though his return in glory continues to permeate the Mass texts through the remainder of Advent and

---

1. "General Instruction," par. 65.

into the Christmas Season. During the two to three weeks of Christmas, the focus begins with his birth, moves on to his manifestation or epiphany, and concludes with his baptism. The liturgical spirituality that flows from these six weeks gives us unexpected delight.

Lent is focused on penance and baptism; it is a time of retreat, when people prepare to celebrate the Sacred Paschal Triduum and the Easter Season. Beginning with Easter Sunday the Easter season lasts for fifty days; it concludes with Pentecost Sunday. Its seven weeks are considered to be one joyful and exultant feast day celebrating Christ's resurrection.

The thirty-three or thirty-four weeks remaining in the liturgical calendar are referred to as Ordinary Time; they are divided into two parts: the five to nine weeks between the end of the Christmas Season and the beginning of Lent, and the seven to thirty-three or thirty-four weeks between the end of the Easter Season and the beginning of Advent. Also, throughout the liturgical year, there occur special days in honor of saints.

LITURGICAL SPIRITUALITY

The word *spirituality* attempts to capture "the heart of what it means to be in relationship with God."[2] Liturgical spirituality fosters that relationship through the Mass texts assigned to the seasons and saints throughout the year. According to White, "The Christian spiritual path has at its center the opening up of our hearts to the Spirit of God, so that rooted in the Divine mystery, we may fall more and more in love with the source of life."[3] Of course, reflective prayer of any kind plays a central role in spirituality—especially liturgical spirituality—because it brings us into "the transforming presence of an all-embracing God."[4] Throughout the liturgical year, the Mass texts connect us and keep connecting us in deeper and deeper levels, helping us to realize that God is "all in all" (1 Cor 15:28).

The goal of all spirituality—personal transformation that flows from the individual out into the community—begins with our awareness that we are already one with God. By listening to another—in this case reading my words—the seeds for further transformation are planted. As they take root and begin to sprout, the reader delves ever deeper into liturgical-year spirituality as it is presented in *The Roman Missal's* Mass texts.

2. White, "Liturgical Spirituality," 244.

3. White, "Liturgical Spirituality," 244.

4. White, "Liturgical Spirituality," 245.

My hope is that you, the reader, will grow in liturgical spirituality throughout Advent and Christmas, Lent and Easter, Ordinary Time, and Saints as you read the short reflections recorded in this book. My prayer is that you will finish the spiritual journey of Advent and Christmas, Ordinary Time I, Lent and Easter, Ordinary Time II, and Saints enriched for having spent time with these very short reflections.

MARK G. BOYER
February 26, 2020
Ash Wednesday

1

The Advent Season

FIRST WEEK OF ADVENT

Sunday: Dare to Hope[1]

The liturgical texts for the First Sunday of Advent are focused on hope. The Entrance Antiphon employs the first three verses of Psalm 25 imploring God to let no one who hopes in him to be put to shame. The Collect asks God to grant all the resolve to complete life's race to meet Jesus' second coming with a basket of righteous deeds; the basket contains all the right things we have done because they were the right things to do! Those righteous deeds, according to the Prayer over the Offerings, will win the prize of eternal redemption for us as, and according to the Prayer after Communion, we walk in the midst of passing things now and hope for what endures as we wait in hope for Christ's coming again in glory. Since the earliest days of Christianity, believers have stood with heads raised waiting for this to oc-cur. Jesus' return in glory permeates the liturgy. Thus, while participating in prayer—privately and communally—at all times we are waiting for Christ to return in glory.

---

1. *Roman Missal*, 139.

Monday: Our Savior Will Come[2]

The Entrance Antiphon's words about our Savior's coming are a gloss on the words of the prophet Isaiah: "Here is your God. He will come and save you" (Isa 35:4c, e). Isaiah offers hope to the Israelite captives in Babylon; God, he declares, will bring them back to Judah to rebuild Jerusalem. The same hope for deliverance is found in the Collect for today; we pray that God will keep us alert during Advent as we walk in the midst of passing things and hold fast to what endures (Prayer after Communion). By remaining watchful through prayer, we will be prepared to greet Christ when he comes in glory. While we await this event, we pray the Communion Antiphon, which petitions the Lord to visit us now in peace. "Remember me, O LORD, when you show favor to your people; help me when you deliver them," is our individual prayer (Ps 106:4). Or, it may be this one: "Remember now, O LORD, I implore you, how I have walked before you in faithfulness with a whole heart, and have done what is good in your sight" (Isa 38:3a). Either petition reminds God to remember that we await his Son's glorious return.

Tuesday: Consoled by Presence[3]

Today's Collect presents an oxymoron for reflection. After asking the LORD God to show us his compassionate help in our trials, we state that we are consoled in the presence of Christ even as we await his coming. In other words, we are presented with the contradiction of Christ's presence and his absence. The Entrance Antiphon, a gloss from two verses from the prophet Zechariah, emphasizes the LORD's coming with his holy ones (Zech 14:5b) on a day when even evening will be light (Zech 14:7). Likewise, the Communion Antiphon is a gloss on a verse from the Second Letter to Timothy in which the author refers to the Lord, the righteous judge, who will bestow a crown of righteousness on those who long for his appearing (2 Tim 4:8). Thus, because we cannot save ourselves, we rely upon God's mercy to rescue us and to teach us to judge wisely while we live on earth in order to be admitted to heaven when Christ comes in glory (Prayer over the Offerings, Prayer after Communion). We experience the consolation of Christ here while awaiting its fullness hereafter.

2. *Roman Missal*, 140.
3. *Roman Missal*, 141.

Wednesday: Prepared Hearts[4]

In one understanding, the heart of a person is the individual's center; it is a way to speak about his or her totality. Thus, today's Collect asks God to prepare our hearts using his divine power that we may be prepared for the coming of Jesus Christ. Because the biblical perspective is that the LORD is in charge of everything, all humankind can do is pray that God will make us ready. So, we implore God's mercy in the Prayer after Communion. Even the Entrance Antiphon, based on a passage from Paul's First Letter to the Corinthians, is focused on the heart: ". . . [D]o not pronounce judgment before the time," writes the apostle, "before the Lord comes, who will bring to light the things now hidden in darkness and will disclose the purposes of the heart" (1 Cor 4:5a). Paul's "purposes of the heart" refers to the intentionality that only each person knows flows from within his or her totality. In other words, the heart reveals the true self of a person. We hope to be found integrated (*hearted*) in order to enjoy the banquet of eternal life when, in the words of the Communion Antiphon, "the Lord GOD comes with might" (Isa 40:10a).

Thursday: Merciful Grace[5]

Contrary to popular thinking, grace is not a thing (noun); grace is an action (verb). It describes the action of God giving himself to people. Today's Collect asks that God rouse his power and come to help us with the grace of his mercy. While waiting in the midst of passing things (Prayer after Communion), we stand with arms outstretch and hands open to receive this gift which overwhelms our sins and endures to eternal life. The verse from Psalm 119, which forms the Entrance Antiphon, refers to grace as the LORD being near (Ps 119:151). Since God actively shares himself with us, how can he not be near to us? Our response to grace is "in the present age to live lives that are self-controlled, upright, and godly, while we wait for the blessed hope and the manifestation of the glory of our great God and Savior, Jesus Christ," according to the Communion Antiphon (Titus 2:13–14). The fullness of the prize of eternal redemption (Prayer over the Offerings) is ours because the LORD has come to help us with the mighty strength of his grace (Collect).

---

4. *Roman Missal*, 142.

5. *Roman Missal*, 143.

Friday: Stir (Up) Power[6]

The verb *to stir* summarizes today's prayers and antiphons. In the Collect, we ask God to stir his power. Among its many meanings, *to stir* implies movement or goading into action; however, *to stir up* means to cause trouble or to agitate. So, the Collect presents us with a double entendre. We ask God to get into action and protect and rescue us from our human sinfulness so that God can save us. The Entrance Antiphon expresses the same idea—albeit in a gentle manner—stating that the LORD will descend from heaven with splendor, visit us with peace, and give us eternal life. The Prayer over the Offerings reminds God that we humans have no merits on our own and must rely on his protective mercy. Thus, we need God to teach us to judge wisely the things of the planet upon which we live in order that we may hold firm to heavenly things. The Communion Antiphon, a gloss on Paul's Letter to the Philippians, reminds us that we are waiting for Christ's return in glory, when he will stir (up) our mortal existence into glorified existence (Phil 3:20–21).

Saturday: Show Your Face[7]

The Entrance Antiphon for this last day of the first week of Advent employs words from Psalm 80: "Restore us, O God; let your face shine, that we may be saved. Stir up your might, and come to save us!" (Ps 80:3, 2b) The petition that God let his face shine upon people is echoed in the Collect, which requests that God bestow his grace of compassion on those who await the coming in glory of his only-begotten Son, Jesus Christ. Just as Christ set free the human race from its enslavement to sin—giving it true freedom—with his first coming in the lowliness of human flesh (Preface I of Advent),[8] when he comes again, he will enhance that freedom with eternal life by completing the design that the Father formed long ago (Preface I of Advent).[9] Thus, while we prepare for such a feast, we pray the Communion Antiphon from the CB (NT) book of Revelation in which Jesus says, "See, I am coming soon; my reward is with me, to repay according to everyone's work" (Rev. 22:12). When he comes, he will show us his face!

---

6. *Roman Missal*, 144.

7. *Roman Missal*, 145.

8. *Roman Missal*, 534–35.

9. *Roman Missal*, 534–35.

SECOND WEEK OF ADVENT

Sunday: Save the Nations[10]

The Entrance Antiphon for the Second Sunday of Advent comes from a gloss on two verses found in the HB (OT) prophet Isaiah. First, the people of Zion—those who live in Jerusalem—are told to weep no more because God, who graciously hears their cries, will answer them (Isa 30:19). Second, ". . . [T]he LORD will cause his majestic voice to be heard . . ." (Isa 30:30). The first point from Isaiah is echoed in the Communion Antiphon, a gloss on two verses from the OT (A) prophet Baruch. "Arise, O Jerusalem," begins Baruch, "stand upon the height" (Bar 5:5a). The second half of the antiphon comes from Baruch 4:36: "Look toward the east, O Jerusalem, and see the joy that is coming to you from God." In both antiphons, the LORD is coming to save the nations. That is why the Collect petitions God to keep all earthly events from hindering those who set out hastily to meet the Son, who is coming in glory. Thus, those of all nations can learn this wisdom and be admitted to his company; indeed, that will be a day of joy that comes from God.

Monday: Hear the Word[11]

"Hear the word of the LORD, O nations, and declare it in the coastlands far away" begins the Entrance Antiphon from the prophet Jeremiah (31:10a). The antiphon continues with a part of a verse from Isaiah: "Be strong, do not fear! Here is your God. He will come and save you" (Isa 35:4a, c). The Communion Antiphon, a gloss on a psalm verse and a verse from Isaiah, begins: "Remember me, O LORD, when you show favor to your people" (Ps 106:4a). The second half comes from King Hezekiah's prayer, reminding the LORD how he has walked before him in faithfulness with a whole heart (Isa 38:3a). Both antiphons are summarized in the Collect, which applies them to the first coming of Jesus and petitions God to let us come before him to celebrate the incarnation of his only-begotten Son, a great mystery. The Prayer over the Offerings reminds us that what we celebrate on earth gains for us the prize of eternal redemption. Likewise, the Prayer after Communion states that we walk among passing things now, while loving the things of heaven that endure.

10. *Roman Missal*, 146.
11. *Roman Missal*, 147.

Tuesday: Look Forward in Joy[12]

Salvation has come to the ends of the earth, states today's Collect. And because this is so, we ask God to enable us to look forward in joy to the celebration of the glorious nativity of Christ. The Entrance Antiphon, a gloss on two verses from the prophet Zechariah, announces the salvation that has come to the earth. ". . . [T]he LORD my God will come, and all the holy ones with him," declares Zechariah (14:5b). He adds, "And there shall be continuous day (it is known to the LORD), not day and not night, for at evening time there shall be light" (Zech 14:7). The first half of the Entrance Antiphon is echoed in the Communion Antiphon, taken from the Second Letter to Timothy. The writer declares, "From now on there is reserved for me the crown of righteousness, which the Lord, the righteous judge, will give me on that day, and not only to me but also to all who have longed for his appearing" (2 Tim 4:8). Thus, we find ourselves standing in between the first appearance of Jesus at his birth in Bethlehem and second appearance in glory. We celebrate his nativity while we wait for his parousia, his coming in glory.

Wednesday: Heavenly Physician[13]

Because of the many gospel stories about Jesus healing people of various diseases, in early Christianity he was often called the divine physician or the heavenly physician. Today's Collect asks God to remove our weariness as we long for the comforting presence of the divine physician, Jesus Christ. As we prepare the way to celebrate his first coming in the flesh, we hear the words of Paul in his First Letter to the Corinthians in the Entrance Antiphon which are focused on his second coming: ". . . [T]he Lord comes, who will bring to light the things now hidden in darkness and will disclose the purposes of the heart" (1 Cor 4:5a). The Communion Antiphon emphasizes both the Lord GOD's coming with might (Isa 40:10) and his healing of the eyes of the blind (Isa 35:5), giving light to those in darkness. These glosses on verses from Isaiah are applied to Jesus to emphasize his coming with healing power in the past and in the future. The Prayer over the Offerings asks God to accomplish the saving work he began with Jesus' first coming as, in the Prayer after Communion, we prepare to celebrate the coming feasts of his birth and epiphany.

12. *Roman Missal*, 148.
13. *Roman Missal*, 149.

Thursday: The Blessed Hope[14]

We live our lives waiting for Christ's return in glory. Such spirituality is expressed in today's Communion Antiphon, which comes from the Letter to Titus. The author explains to his readers that "in the present age" they are "to live lives that are self-controlled, upright, and godly, while [they] wait for the blessed hope and the manifestation of the glory of [their] great God and savior, Jesus Christ" (Titus 2:12–13). The same verse is found in the embolism following the Lord's Prayer in which we pray that we may be kept free from sin and safe from distress as we await the blessed hope and the coming of our Savior, Jesus Christ.[15] According to the Entrance Antiphon, a gloss on Psalm 119, the LORD, whose ways are truth, is near (Ps 119:151–152). And so we pray in the Collect that God will stir our hearts to make ready the paths for the coming of his only-begotten Son. Our blessed hope is to be found worthy to serve God with pure minds and to inherit this great promise in which we dare to hope (Preface I of Advent) when all is made manifest.[16]

Friday: With Lighted Lamps[17]

There is a theme of waiting for salvation with lighted lamps that permeates the Mass texts today. This theme echoes the unique parable found in Matthew's Gospel about the ten bridesmaids; five of them took no extra oil, and five of them took plenty of extra oil as they waited for the bridegroom to arrive (Matt 25:1–13). A lamp was a small (about 4 inches in diameter), flat, covered pitcher with a hole for a reed wick at one end, a handle at the other end, and a small hole in which olive oil was poured in the middle. Having another container of oil indicates watchfulness for Christ's return. The Entrance Antiphon declares this when it states that the Lord will come to visit his people and bestow eternal life on them. And the Communion Antiphon, a gloss from Paul's Letter to the Philippians, emphasizes this. ". . . [I]t is from [heaven] that we are expecting a Savior, the Lord Jesus Christ," writes the apostle. "He will transform the body of our humiliation that it may be conformed to the body of his glory . . ." (Phil 3:20–21). While standing with lighted lamps, we pray that God, out of his great mercy, will rescue us (Prayer over the Offerings).

14. *Roman Missal*, 150.

15. *Roman Missal*, 664–65.

16. *Roman Missal*, 534–35.

17. *Roman Missal*, 151.

Saturday: Dawning Glory[18]

Today's Collect begins by asking almighty God to let the splendor of his glory dawn in our hearts. The Entrance Antiphon petitions the LORD similarly: "Restore us, O God; let your face shine, that we may be saved. You who are enthroned upon the cherubim, shine forth" (Ps 80:3, 1b). Another way to write about God's dawning glory is to refer to his shining face. According to the Collect, in the presence of such light, the shadows of the night are scattered and we are seen as children of the light when Christ advents again. The Communion Antiphon, taken from the CB (NT) book of Revelation, portrays Jesus stating, "See, I am coming soon; my reward is with me, to repay according to everyone's work" (Rev 22:12). One work in which all of us are engaged is offering the sacrifice of the body and blood of Christ. The Prayer over the Offerings states that we do this unceasingly in order to complete the saving work that Jesus began in sacred mystery—his death and resurrection. According to the Prayer after Communion, the divine sustenance of the eucharistic elements both cleanses us of our faults and prepares us to celebrate the coming feasts.

THIRD WEEK OF ADVENT

Sunday: Rejoice[19]

Rejoicing in the Lord permeates today's Mass texts. The theme begins with the Entrance Antiphon, two verses taken from Paul's Letter to the Philippians: "Rejoice in the Lord always; again I will say, Rejoice. The Lord is near" (Phil 4:4, 5b). The Collect asks God to see how his people are faithfully awaiting the celebration of his Son's nativity. It also petitions God to enable those awaiting Christmas to achieve the joys of the great salvation Jesus brought and celebrate with glad rejoicing. The Communion Antiphon, a gloss from a verse from the prophet Isaiah, also exhorts rejoicing; the reader is told to declare ". . . to those who are of a fearful heart, 'Be strong, do not fear! Here is your God. He will come and save you'" (Isa 35:4). Rejoicing is also found in the third strophe of the Solemn Blessing for Advent, which indicates that we are rejoicing now with devotion at Jesus' first coming in the flesh with the hope of eternal life when he comes in glory (Blessings at the End of Mass and Prayers over the People, I. For Celebrations in the Different

18. *Roman Missal*, 152.
19. *Roman Missal*, 153.

Liturgical Times, 1. Advent).[20] Thus, the rejoicing is about God's entrance into the world to save people in the person of his only-begotten Son, whose coming in glory will find us rejoicing all the more.

Monday: Grace[21]

Grace is God's invisible gift of himself to people. In today's Collect, we ask God to visit us with the grace of Jesus Christ. This is expressed in two ways. First, we ask God, metaphorically, to turn his head and with his good ear to hear our cry. Second, we ask him, dualistically, to cast light on the darkness of our hearts. Hearing our prayer and shining light on us are ways God visits us with grace. These themes are echoed in the Entrance Antiphon, a gloss on a verse from the prophet Jeremiah and one from the prophet Isaiah. "Hear the word of the LORD, O nations, and declare it in the coastland far away" begins Jeremiah (31:10a). Then, Isaiah picks up, "Be strong, do not fear! Here is your God" (Isa 35:4ab). The Communion Antiphon, also a gloss on two biblical verses, petitions the LORD to show favor, that is, to grace, his people (Ps 106:4). Then, employing part of King Hezekiah's prayer, the prophet Isaiah records the request to walk before the Lord in faithfulness with a whole heart (Isa 38:3), that is, in grace. In other words, all is grace. Advent is our time to become aware that God bestows himself upon us constantly.

Tuesday: New Creation[22]

Today's Collect is a reflection on the new creation into which we have been made through God's only-begotten Son, Jesus. In his Second Letter to the Corinthians, Paul states, ". . . [I]f anyone is in Christ, there is a new creation: everything old has passed away; see, everything has become new!" (2 Cor 5:17) In his Letter to the Galatians, he declares that "a new creation is everything!" (Gal 6:15) This new creation, referred to in the Collect as the handiwork of God's mercy, is based on the Pauline comparison between the first Adam, who was a new creation but lost the newness through disobedience, and the second Adam, Christ Jesus, who was a new creation through obedience to God. Thus, the Collect petitions God to cleanse us from every

20. *Roman Missal*, 674.

21. *Roman Missal*, 154. If today is December 17, go to the reflection for December 17 following the Fourth Sunday of Advent reflection.

22. *Roman Missal*, 155. If today is December 17, go to the reflection for December 17 following the Fourth Sunday of Advent reflection.

type of stain of sin of our old way of life in preparation for Christ's return in glory. The Entrance Antiphon, a gloss on two verses from the prophet Zechariah, is focused on the LORD God's coming (Zech 14:5b), as is the Communion Antiphon, which echoes our longing for the Lord's—the just Judge's—appearance (2 Tim 4:8).

Wednesday: Healing[23]

Because the Entrance Antiphon, the Prayer over the Offerings, the Preface, the Communion Antiphon, and the Prayer After Communion have been employed in previous Advent Masses (Wednesday of the First Week of Advent and Wednesday of the Second Week of Advent), today's reflection is confined to the Collect. The prayer presumes the division between this life and the next life. In it we ask almighty God that the coming Solemnity of the Nativity may bestow healing on us now, in this present life, and bring us the reward of eternal life. Most people do not think about Christmas as a feast that heals, but, indeed, it does. When warring—minimally disagreeing—family members gather to share the feast of foods on December 25 or on another day around that time, healing can occur around the table. Children, who may feel alienated for any number of reasons, are gathered in and healed. Frictions with in-laws often disappear when grandparents bestow gifts upon grandchildren. The healing of any kind that we experience in this life at Christmastime gives us a taste and a feel for the peace that awaits us in eternal life.

Thursday: Glad[24]

Because the Entrance Antiphon, the Prayer over the Offerings, the Preface, the Communion Antiphon, and the Prayer After Communion have been employed in previous Advent Masses (Thursday of the First Week of Advent and Thursday of the Second Week of Advent), today's reflection is confined to the Collect. We invoke God by declaring that we are unworthy servants. Referring to ourselves as unworthy servants directly echoes a verse spoken by the Lukan Jesus to his apostles: ". . . [W]hen you have done all that you were ordered to do, say, 'We are worthless slaves; we have done only what

23. *Roman Missal*, 156. If today is December 17, go to the reflection for December 17 following the Fourth Sunday of Advent reflection.

24. *Roman Missal*, 157. If today is December 17, go to the reflection for December 17 following the Fourth Sunday of Advent reflection.

we ought to have done!'" (Luke 17:10) Because we are unworthy servants, we ask God to gladden us with the saving advent of his only-begotten Son. The advent of Jesus Christ is ambiguous, as it may refer to his first coming, two thousand years ago, and/or it may refer to his coming in glory. The Entrance Antiphon emphasizes the nearness of the LORD (Ps 119:151), and the Communion Antiphon emphasizes the waiting for the blessed hope and the manifestation of the glory of our great God and Savior, Jesus Christ (Titus 2:13).

Friday: Grace Before and After[25]

Because the Entrance Antiphon, the Prayer over the Offerings, the Preface, the Communion Antiphon, and the Prayer After Communion have been employed in previous Advent Masses (Friday of the First Week of Advent and Friday of the Second Week of Advent), today's reflection is confined to the Collect. This prayer begins by stating that God's grace surrounds us. It goes before us and it follows after us. Because God chooses freely to share himself, his life, with us, we discover that we are in God waiting to be filled more and more with his own life. We acknowledge that we are awaiting the coming of God's only-begotten Son with heartfelt desire; this waiting is echoed in the Entrance Antiphon with its statement that the Lord will come in splendor from heaven to visit us with eternal grace. Likewise, the Communion Antiphon reminds us that we are waiting for the Savior who will transform our mortality into immortality (Phil 3:20–21). Thus, while waiting for this to occur, we need God's help now and in the life to come, expressed in the Collect. In other words, we need ever more grace that sustains us now into eternity.

FOURTH WEEK OF ADVENT

Sunday: Bring Forth a Savior[26]

The Entrance Antiphon for the Fourth Sunday of Advent sets the theme for the rest of the Mass. The prophet Isaiah addresses the heavens, and he tells them to rain righteousness that the earth may open and salvation spring

---

25. *Roman Missal*, 158. If today is December 17, go to the reflection for December 17 following the Fourth Sunday of Advent reflection.

26. *Roman Missal*, 159.

up (Isa 45:8). The Collect declares that we have received the message of the (arch)angel Gabriel concerning the incarnation of Jesus, the springing up of salvation. The Prayer over the Offerings asks God to sanctify the bread and wine on the altar with the same Holy Spirit who filled the womb of the Blessed Virgin Mary with his power to conceive salvation, Jesus. Another verse from the prophet Isaiah forms the Communion Antiphon: "Look, the young woman is with child and shall bear a son, and shall name him Immanuel" (Isa 7:14b). All these words are summarized eloquently in Preface II of Advent, which reminds us that the prophets' oracles foretold the Savior's coming, while his mother, Mary, longed for him with the deepest love.[27] Now, as Advent comes quickly to an end and the feast of our salvation, the nativity, draws nearer (Prayer after Communion), we press forward to share in the glory of Christ's resurrection (Collect).

December 17: Humanity[28]

The days from December 17 to the 24 form an octave (eight days) of preparation for the Nativity of the Lord. Today's focus is on Jesus' humanity. In the Collect, we declare that God's Word took flesh in the ever-virgin womb of Mary, and we ask that just as he shared our human nature in order to redeem it, we may share in his divinity. In the Prayer over the Offerings, we ask that we may be nourished with the bread of heaven, and, in the Prayer after Communion, we ask God to inflame us with the Holy Spirit that when Christ comes in glory, he may find us shining like bright torches. Because Christmas is near, the Entrance Antiphon, a gloss from a verse of the prophet Isaiah, exhorts, "Sing for joy, O heavens, and exult, O earth . . . ! For the LORD has comforted his people . . ." (Isa 49:13). The Communion Antiphon, a gloss on a verse from the prophet Haggi, portrays the LORD declaring, ". . . I will shake all the nations, so that the treasure of all nations shall come, and I will fill this house with splendor . . ." (Hag 2:7). Thus, while the texts are focused on Jesus' first coming as a man, they also narrate his coming in eucharistic bread and wine, while we continue to wait for his return in glory.

---

27. *Roman Missal*, 536–37.

28. *Roman Missal*, 160. On the weekdays of Advent, December 17 to 24, the following reflections are used on the days to which they are assigned, with the exception of the Fourth Sunday of Advent, which has its own reflection above.

December 18: Healed Mortality[29]

The theme permeating today's Mass texts is the healing of our mortality that was accomplished by Jesus' birth, that is, his becoming human. The Entrance Antiphon, using John the Baptist's title for Jesus—Lamb of God (John 1:29, 36)—states that Christ the king is coming. According to the Order of Mass, the Lamb of God takes away the sins of the world.[30] The Collect asks God to set us free from our old slavery to sin by the newness of his only-begotten Son's nativity. The Prayer over the Offerings requests that we be made companions of Christ for all eternity, for by his death our own mortality was healed. This healed mortality, signified by Christ's resurrection, has received God's mercy, and now we honor the coming feasts of our redemption. The one named Emmanuel, states the Communion Antiphon, means God-with-us; it is a gloss on a verse from Matthew's Gospel (1:23), which is itself a gloss on a verse from the prophet Isaiah (7:14). Because we are members of the body of the Christ now, we share in the newness of him who is always with us.

December 19: Gifts[31]

Today's Mass texts present the divine gifts we have received. First, the Collect declares that it is through the child-bearing of the Blessed Virgin Mary that God has revealed the radiance of his glory to the world. Second, God has revealed to us the incarnation, which we prepare to celebrate with reverence. Third, in the Prayer over the Offerings, we state that God has sanctified the gifts of bread and wine with his power. Fourth, in the Prayer after Communion, we specifically name the eucharistic gifts of the body and blood of Christ, and we ask God to arouse in us the desire for his gifts yet to come. While naming God's gifts, we are, fifth, also preparing to welcome the nativity of our Savior, in the words of the Prayer after Communion, and honor it with pure minds. The Entrance Antiphon, a gloss on a verse from the Letter to the Hebrews, further emphasizes the Lord's coming; it states: "[I]n a very little while, the one who is coming will come and will not delay" (Heb 10:37). Likewise, the Communion Antiphon, a verse from Zechariah's song, declares, "By the tender mercy of our God, the dawn from on high will break upon us . . . to guide our feet into the way of peace" (Luke 1:78–79).

29. *Roman Missal*, 161.

30. *Roman Missal*, 667–68.

31. *Roman Missal*, 162.

December 20: Root of Jesse[32]

Jesse is the father of King David. Once the monarchy in Judah comes to an end with the Babylonian Captivity, the prophet Isaiah instills the hope that God will raise up a new king from David's line. Today's Entrance Antiphon contains Isaiah's words: "A shoot shall come out from the stump of Jesse, and a branch shall grow out of his roots" (Isa 11:1). "Then the glory of the LORD shall be revealed, and all people shall see it together, for the mouth of the LORD has spoken" (Isa 40:5). The author of Luke's Gospel declares that "all flesh shall see the salvation of God" (Luke 3:6) before he presents the angel telling Mary that she will conceive in her womb and bear a son, and she will name him Jesus (Luke 1:31) in the Communion Antiphon. He is the branch from Jesse's root. The Communion Antiphon is echoed in the Collect, which declares that God's Word was received by Mary through the message of the angel, and with her consent, she became the dwelling place of divinity with the power of the Holy Spirit. We pray that we may follow her example in doing God's will (Collect) and possess the gifts for which we have hoped in faith (Prayer over the Offerings), while enjoying divine protection and true peace (Prayer after Communion) under the reign of Jesse's shoot.

December 21: Watchful in Prayer[33]

Preface II of Advent declares what one aspect of God's gift of prayer is that we already rejoice at the mystery of Jesus' nativity in the hope that when he comes in glory, he may find us watchful in prayer and exulting in his praise.[34] The same idea is found in today's Collect, which states that we rejoice at the coming of God's only-begotten Son in our flesh now so that when he comes in glory, we may enjoy eternal life. By celebrating the eucharist, we step into the mystery of salvation, according to the Prayer over the Offerings, taking the gifts that God gives of bread and wine and receiving them back transformed into the body and blood of Christ. The Prayer after Communion refers to this as a divine mystery that provides protection for people and abundant health in mind and body. In the words of the Entrance Antiphon, a gloss on two verses from the prophet Isaiah, our watchfulness in prayer enables us to recognize Immanuel (Isa 7:14), that God is with us (Isa 8:10). The Communion Antiphon, consisting of Elizabeth's words to Mary, praises her for remaining

32. *Roman Missal*, 163.
33. *Roman Missal*, 164.
34. *Roman Missal*, 536–37.

watchful in prayer: ". . . [B]lessed is she who believed that there would be a fulfillment of what was spoken to her by the Lord" (Luke 1:45).

December 22: Opened Gates[35]

Today's Entrance Antiphon sets the theme for today's Mass texts. "Lift up your heads, O gates! And be lifted up, O ancient doors! That the King of glory may come in" (Ps 24:7). The opened gates are a portal allowing God to enter his Temple in Jerusalem. Another portal, according to the Collect, is the incarnation of the only-begotten Son of God in the womb of the Blessed Virgin Mary. Seeing the human race having fallen into death, God willed to redeem it by coming from the world above to the world below in the person of Jesus. The Prayer over the Offerings mentions the portal of God's grace that cleanses us through the very mysteries we serve, while the Prayer after Communion mentions the portal that will open when our Savior comes again. Our prayer is that we will carry worthy deeds with which to meet Christ and merit his company and rewards. When this last portal is opened, we will join Mary in declaring, "My soul magnifies the Lord, . . . for the Mighty One has done great things for me, and holy is his name" (Luke 1:46, 49).

December 23: Nativity Draws Near[36]

The theme running through today's Mass texts is the nearness of Christmas. The Collect reminds God that we see how near is the nativity of his Son according to the flesh. The Prayer over the Gifts asks that our oblation be our reconciliation with God that we may celebrate the nativity of our redeemer with minds made pure. And the Prayer after Communion asks God to grant us peace and to see us standing ready with lighted lamps for Jesus' coming. The Entrance Antiphon, a gloss on two HB (OT) verses, anticipates the nearness of Christmas by proclaiming that "a child has been born for us; . . . and he is named . . . Mighty God" (Isa 9:6), and "May all nations be blessed in him . . ." (Ps 72:17b). Christ's second coming is anticipated in the Communion Antiphon, a verse from the CB (NT) book of Revelation. In the letter to the church in Laodicea, Jesus states, "Listen! I am standing at the door, knocking; if you hear my voice and open the door, I will come in to you and eat with you, and you with me" (Rev 3:20). Our prayer is that God's mercy

35. *Roman Missal*, 165.
36. *Roman Missal*, 166.

will flow through his Son, born of the Virgin Mary, and establish his dwelling place among us (Collect)—both through our celebration of Christmas and his return in glory.

December 24, Morning Mass: Come Quickly[37]

Today's Collect is addressed to the Lord Jesus, whom we ask to come quickly and not to delay. Likewise, the Prayer over the Offerings asks God to cleanse us of our sins that we may be worthy to stand with pure hearts for the coming in glory of Christ. And the Prayer after Communion asks God to bestow upon us everlasting gladness as we prepare to celebrate in adoration his Son's nativity. While the three prayers are focused on the solace and relief we have in Jesus Christ's coming—both past and future—the antiphons are focused on his presence already. The Entrance Antiphon quotes Paul's Letter to the Galatians: ". . . [W]hen the fullness of time had come, God sent his Son, born of a woman . . ." (Gal 4:4). The Communion Antiphon quotes the first line of Zechariah's canticle in Luke's Gospel: "Blessed be the Lord God of Israel, for he has looked favorably on his people and redeemed them" (Luke 1:67). Thus, on Christmas Eve, we look forward to Christmas Day while looking back to Jesus' birth and asking him to come quickly in glory (Rev. 22:20).

37. *Roman Missal*, 167.

2

The Christmas Season

DECEMBER 25: THE NATIVITY OF THE LORD

Vigil: Glory[1]

After 4 p.m. on Christmas Eve, the first Mass of Christmas is celebrated. The theme running through the Mass texts is seeing the glory of the Lord. In the Entrance Antiphon, Moses and Aaron tell the Israelites that "in the morning [they] shall see the glory of the LORD" (Exod 16:7). The Communion Antiphon, a verse from the prophet Isaiah, states, ". . . [T]he glory of the LORD shall be revealed, and all people shall see it together . . ." (Isa 40:5). Thus, the glory of the LORD becomes the glory of the birth of our Lord Jesus Christ, whom, according to the Collect, we welcome joyfully as our redeemer. The Prayer over the Offerings declares that in the coming festivities God makes manifest the beginnings of our redemption. In the Prayer after Communion, we ask God to grant us new vigor through our celebration of the birth of his only-begotten Son, which gladdens us year by year as we await the fullness of our redemption—the coming in glory of Christ as judge of the world (Collect). Preface I of the Nativity of the Lord summarizes all this declaring that

1. *Roman Missal*, 171.

the Word made flesh is a new light of the Father's glory that now shines upon the eyes of our mind.[2]

Mass during the Night: Union[3]

The second Mass of Christmas is celebrated sometime during the night of December 24–25 before sunrise on December 25. The theme of the texts is best expressed in Preface II of the Nativity of the Lord.[4] While Jesus' divine nature is invisible, he has appeared visibly in human nature, bringing a unity to all creation. The Prayer over the Offerings asks God to accept the gifts of bread and wine which will be holy exchanged into the body and blood of Christ through which our human nature is united to divine nature. In the Prayer after Communion, we declare that we are gladdened through our celebration of the nativity, and we ask that our honorable way of living may make us worthy of union with Christ. Both of the two optional Entrance Antiphons emphasize the birth of the Son. The first is a verse from a Judean king coronation hymn which declares the new monarch to be the LORD's son, who is begotten on the day of his anointing (Ps 2:7). The second is an exhortation to rejoice for the Savior has been born. The Communion Antiphon continues the theme with a verse from John's Gospel: ". . . [T]he Word became flesh and lived among us, and we have seen his glory . . ." (John 1:14). The Collect echoes the glory theme by stating that on this sacred night God makes radiant with splendor the true light, Jesus.

Mass at Dawn: Light[5]

Light is the theme of the Mass texts for the third Mass of Christmas at dawn. The Entrance Antiphon consists of a melding together of three biblical verses. The first states, "The people who walked in darkness have seen a great light" (Isa 9:2a), and the second continues, ". . . [H]e is named Wonderful Counselor, Mighty God, Everlasting Father, Prince of Peace" (Isa 9:6c), and the third declares that "of his kingdom there will be no end" (Luke 1:33). The Collect declares that we are bathed in the radiant light of the incarnate Word—that is, the light of faith—and we ask God to let that

2. *Roman Missal*, 538–39.
3. *Roman Missal*, 172–73.
4. *Roman Missal*, 540–41.
5. *Roman Missal*, 174.

light shine through our minds and deeds. The Prayer over the Offerings reminds us that Jesus was born a man, but shone forth as God, and we ask that the earthly gifts may give us what is divine. Our request in the Prayer after Communion is for the fullness of faith as we celebrate the nativity of the Lord. In the Communion Antiphon, we make the light-filled words of the prophet Zechariah our own: "Rejoice greatly, O daughter Zion! Shout aloud, O daughter Jerusalem! Lo, your king comes to you; triumphant and victorious is he . . ." (Zech 9:9).

Mass during the Day: Restored Divinity[6]

The fourth or last Mass of Christmas during the day is centered on the dignity of human nature restored to its divinity, according to the Collect. Our prayer is that we may share in Christ's divinity just as he shared in our humanity. The Prayer over the Offerings continues this theme by acknowledging the reconciliation between humanity and divinity, manifested in the birth of Jesus, which makes us wholly pleasing in God's sight. The Prayer after Communion refers to our restored divinity as divine generation which bestows upon us immortality. Preface III of the Nativity of the Lord calls Jesus' birth the holy exchange that restores our life; human mortality is made eternal.[7] Thus, the Entrance Antiphon declares, ". . . [A] child has been born for us, a son given to us; authority rests upon his shoulders; and he is named Wonderful Counselor . . ." (Isa 9:6). In the words of the Communion Antiphon, "All the ends of the earth have seen the victory of our God" (Ps 98:3b). In the words of the third strophe of today's Solemn Blessing, through the incarnation, God has brought together the earthly and heavenly realm.[8]

Sunday between December 25 and January 1, Holy Family of Jesus, Mary, and Joseph: Family Life[9]

The theme of the Mass texts is found in the Collect, which asks God to help us imitate the virtues of family life and the bonds of charity that existed in

6. *Roman Missal*, 175.

7. *Roman Missal*, 542–43.

8. *Roman Missal*, 674–75.

9. *Roman Missal*, 176–77. December 26 is the Feast of St. Stephen; December 27 is the Feast of St. John; December 28 is the Feast of the Holy Innocents. Reflections on those feasts can be found in chapter 7. The Feast of the Holy Family of Jesus, Mary, and Joseph is celebrated on the Sunday following Christmas, but if there is no Sunday

the family of Joseph, Mary, and Jesus. In the Prayer over the Offerings, we ask God to help us establish our families firmly in his grace through the intercession of Mary, the Mother of God, and Joseph, her spouse. Likewise, in the Prayer after Communion, we ask God to help us imitate the example of the holy family in facing the trials of this world that we may one day enjoy their company hereafter. The Entrance Antiphon, a verse from Luke's Gospel, is chosen because it mentions the holy family as a unit: "[The shepherds] went with haste and found Mary and Joseph, and the child lying in the manger" (Luke 2:16). With a gloss on a verse from the OT (A) prophet Baruch, the Communion Antiphon applies personified Lady Wisdom to God, who "appeared on earth and lived with humankind" (Bar 3:37) in the person of Jesus, son of Mary, foster son of Joseph, and Son of God.

December 29: God Loves the World[10]

The Entrance Antiphon firmly establishes the theme of today's Mass texts: ". . . God so loved the world that he gave his only Son, so that everyone who believes in him may not perish but may have eternal life" (John 3:16). The Collect immediately picks up this theme by declaring that God dispersed the world's darkness with Jesus' light. As we continue our celebration of Christmas, we ask God to bestow upon us his serene countenance while we acclaim with praise the nativity of the Lord. The Prayer over the Offerings declares that God loves us by taking the bread and wine we offer him and turning them into the body and blood of Christ through whom we receive God's very self. The Prayer after Communion reminds us that the eucharistic elements sustain our lives—a demonstration of God's love. Another way to speak about God's love for the world is found in the Communion Antiphon, a verse from Zechariah's canticle in Luke's Gospel: "By the tender mercy of our God, the dawn from on high will break upon us" (Luke 1:78). Indeed, it has in the birth of the only-begotten Son of God.

December 30: Gentle Silence[11]

"For while gentle silence enveloped all things, and night in its swift course was now half gone, your all-powerful word leaped from heaven, from the

---

because Christmas falls on Sunday, this feast is celebrated on December 30.

10. *Roman Missal*, 178.

11. *Roman Missal*, 179.

royal throne . . ." (Wis 18:14–15), states the Entrance Antiphon. While the author of the OT (A) book of Wisdom is describing the tenth plague, the slaying of the firstborn, today's Mass texts apply the words to the birth of Jesus, found in the Christmas Carol *Silent Night*. Thus, in the Collect, we pray that the newness of the silent birth of Jesus in the flesh will set us free from all sin. Likewise, although seemingly vague, the Prayer over the Offerings asks God to accept bread and wine with favor that what we profess silently with devotion and faith may be granted to us. The Prayer after Communion refers to the gentle silence as God's way of touching us in the body and blood of Christ. Thus, we pray to be made worthy to receive this gift through the very gift itself. In other words, Christ, in the gifts of his body and blood, makes us silently worthy to receive them. The Communion Antiphon captures this idea in a verse from John's Gospel: "From his fullness we have all received, grace upon grace" (John 1:16). Grace is given in the gentle silence that envelopes the whole world.

December 31: Eternal Things[12]

Today's Mass texts are focused on eternal things. This is expressed in the Prayer after Communion, which declares that God guides and sustains his people in many ways; often they experience his solace as earthly things pass away, but they continue to strive with deeper trust for things eternal. In the Collect, we ask God to number us among the members of his Son, who, through his nativity, has given us the beginning of the fullness of human salvation—an eternal thing. Eternal things are identified as gifts of true prayer and peace, which God gives us, as we partake of the sacred mystery of the body and blood of Christ, states the Prayer over the Offerings. The Entrance Antiphon, the same as the Christmas Mass during the Day, names the eternal thing as the child who has been born to us (Isa 9:5). The Communion Antiphon identifies the eternal thing as life: "God sent his only Son into the world so that we might live through him" (1 John 4:9b). In the words of Preface II of the Nativity of the Lord, the one who was begotten before all ages began to exist in time;[13] that is an eternal thing!

---

12. *Roman Missal*, 180–81.

13. *Roman Missal*, 540–41.

Second Sunday after the Nativity: Through Christ[14]

The three prayers of the Mass—Collect, Prayer over the Offerings, and Prayer after Communion—have four parts. The first part is the address to God, who is almighty and ever-living or, simply, Lord our God. The second part is praise of God; he may be the splendor of faithful souls or he may show us the way of truth and promise us life in his heavenly kingdom. The third part of every prayer is the petition; we may ask God to fill the world with his glory and reveal the radiance of his light to all people, or we may ask him to sanctify our offerings as we continue to celebrate the nativity of his Son, or we may ask him to cleanse us of our offenses and fulfill our just desires. The fourth and last part of every prayer is through Christ our Lord. In the Collect, it is always through Jesus Christ, who lives with the Father in the unity of the Holy Spirit. While today's Entrance Antiphon is the same as that for December 30, the Communion Antiphon further enhances our prayer through Christ: ". . . [T]o all who received him, who believed in his name, he gave power to become children of God" (John 1:12). Thus, as God's children we address him, praise him, petition him, and remind him that we are brothers and sisters of his Son, through whom we present our prayer.

Sunday between January 2 and January 8, Epiphany of the Lord: Light[15]

Vigil

The theme uniting the Vigil Mass texts for the Epiphany of the Lord is that of appearing light. The Prayer over the Offerings specifically declares that we are honoring the appearing of God's only-begotten Son, the light of the nations. The Entrance Antiphon, a gloss on a verse from Baruch, exhorts: "Arise, O Jerusalem, stand upon the height; look toward the east, and see your children gathered from west and east at the word of the Holy One, rejoicing that God has remembered them" (Bar 5:5). The city looks east where the sun first appears heralding the light of a new day. The Communion Antiphon, a gloss on a verse from the book of Revelation, declares, ". . . [T]he city [of Jerusalem] has no need of sun or moon to shine on it, for the glory

---

14. *Roman Missal*, 184. In the United States, the second Sunday after the Nativity of the Lord (Christmas) is the Epiphany; in other countries, Epiphany is celebrated on January 6.

15. *Roman Missal*, 187–89.

of God is its light, and its lamp is the Lamb" (Rev 21:23). In the Collect, we ask God to shine his light upon us so that we can pass through this world's shadows in order to get to the brightness of our eternal home. Likewise in the Prayer after Communion, we ask God to let the star of his justice shine always bright in our minds, by which we proclaim that our true treasure is our faith. The second strophe of the Solemn Blessing for this day declares that Christ appeared in the world as a light shining in darkness.[16]

During the Day

Today's Collect sets the theme of the Mass texts. We declare that God has revealed his only-begotten Son to the nations by the guidance of a star, a story unique to Matthew's Gospel (Matt 2:1–12). The journey of the magi is also hinted in the Prayer over the Offerings, where we offer bread and wine—the sacrifice received, Jesus Christ—and not gold or frankincense or myrrh, the gifts presented by the magi. A gloss on a verse from Matthew's Gospel forms the Communion Antiphon: ". . . [W]e [magi] observed [the new-born king of the Jews'] star at its rising, and have come to pay him homage" (Matt 2:2b). In the ancient world, if one were not a Jew, then he or she was a Gentile; thus, the magi from the East represent the first of the nations to accept the light of faith. In the Collect, we pray that we who already believe may one day see God's sublime glory. And in the Prayer after Communion, we ask God to go before us with his heavenly light that we may perceive with clear sight the mystery of Jesus' manifestation to the nations. According to the Entrance Antiphon, a gloss on two verses from Malachi and First Chronicles, the LORD has come (Mal 3:1) and he rules over all people (1 Chr 29:12), both Jews and Gentiles.

Monday Before/After Epiphany: Consubstantial[17]

The word *consubstantial* that we find in the Creed means that Jesus was begotten, not made, of the same substance as the Father; he was true God and true human.[18] This sets the theme for today's Mass texts. In the Collect before Epiphany, we profess that God's only-begotten Son was born of the

16. *Roman Missal*, 676.

17. *Roman Missal*, 190–91. From January 2 to the Saturday before the Feast of the Baptism of the Lord, the following reflections are used on the weekdays to which they are assigned.

18. *Roman Missal*, 525–27.

Virgin Mary in a body like our own; he died, and God raised him to share heavenly glory. In the Collect for after the Epiphany, we declare that while the eternal Word adorned the face of the heavens, he also accepted our flesh and was born of the Virgin Mary. In the words of the Preface of the Epiphany of the Lord, he appeared in our mortal nature in order to make us new by the glory of his immortal nature.[19] Thus, the glorious exchange of bread and wine into his body and blood, as stated in the Prayer over the Offerings, not only mirrors epiphanic events, but enables us to offer what God has given to us and, in return, receive God's very self, which constantly sustains our life (Prayer after Communion). According to the Communion Antiphon, ". . . [W]e have seen his glory, the glory as of a father's only son, full of grace and truth" (John 1:14). Thus, this day is holy, and this Mass manifests the great light that has come down upon the earth (Entrance Antiphon).

Tuesday Before/After Epiphany: New Creation[20]

According to the Collect before the Epiphany, we have been taken into the new creation accomplished by the childbearing of the Blessed Virgin Mary. The flesh of the Son of God was not tainted with sin, as was the rest of the human race. Likewise, the Collect after the Epiphany refers to God's only-begotten Son, who appeared outwardly in our flesh in order to inwardly transform us into a new creation. The Prayer after Communion echoes this theme when we declare that God touches us through the eucharist, which makes us into a new creation and worthy to receive the gift of the body and blood of Christ. The Communion Antiphon, a gloss on two biblical verses, emphasizes "the great love with which [God] loved us" (Eph 2:4) demonstrated "by sending his own Son in the likeness of sinful flesh" (Rom 8:3). The Entrance Antiphon, a gloss on two verses from Psalm 118, declares Jesus to be "the one who [came] in the name of the LORD," the one who "has given us light" (Ps 118:26a, 27a), the light of the new creation.

Wednesday Before/After Epiphany: Great Light[21]

The theme of great light is first established in the Entrance Antiphon for today. Quoting the prophet Isaiah, we declare, "The people who walked in

19. *Roman Missal*, 544–45.
20. *Roman Missal*, 192–93.
21. *Roman Missal*, 194–95.

darkness have seen a great light; those who lived in a land of deep dark-ness—on them light has shined" (Isa 9:2). The Collect before Epiphany names Jesus the bringer of salvation, that is, coming with the newness of heavenly light; we pray that that same light may dawn afresh in us and renew us. In the Collect after Epiphany, we name God as the one who bestows light on all the nations, and we pray that such brilliant light will be poured into our hearts. The Collect after Epiphany also asks God to give us the gladness of lasting peace, a theme echoed in the Prayer over the Offerings in which we acknowledge that God gives us the gift of true prayer and peace. This is how, according to the Prayer after Communion, that God guides and sustains us as things in this world pass away. "[T]his life was revealed," according to the First Letter of John, "and we have seen it and testify to it, and declare to you the eternal life that was with the Father and was revealed to us" (1 John 1:2) (Communion Antiphon). The Johannine life that has become visible is the great light.

Thursday Before/After Epiphany: Savior[22]

The Entrance Antiphon sets the theme for today's Mass texts. It declares that the Word, who was God, humbled himself to be born as the Savior of the world. The Collect before the Epiphany continues the theme by declaring that Jesus' nativity began the work of redemption for people. The Collect after Epiphany asks God that we may acknowledge the full splendor of our redeemer. The Savior, the Redeemer, chooses to be present in bread and wine, a glorious exchange, according to the Prayer over the Gifts, in order to sustain our lives constantly, according to the Prayer after Communion. This last point is presented in the Communion Antiphon, a verse from John's Gospel: ". . . God so loved the world that he gave his only Son, so that ev-eryone who believes in him may not perish but may have eternal life" (John 3:16). This brings us back to the Entrance Antiphon, a gloss on a verse from John's Gospel and a verse from Paul's Letter to the Philippians. "In the begin-ning was the Word, and the Word was with God, and the Word was God," writes the Johannine author (1:1). He was "born in human likeness. And being found in human form, he humbled himself and became obedient to the point of death—even death on a cross," states Philippians (2:7–8). Thus, did he save the world.

22. *Roman Missal*, 196–97.

Friday Before/After Epiphany: Made Fit[23]

The Prayer after Communion contains the theme for today's Mass texts. After declaring that through the sacrament of the body and blood of Christ God touches us, we pray that we may be made fit to receive God's gift of the body and blood of Christ through the gift itself. The Entrance Antiphon, a gloss on a verse from Psalm 112, declares that those who fear the LORD "rise in the darkness as a light for the upright; they are gracious, merciful, and righteous" (Ps 112:4). The antiphon applies the graciousness, mercifulness, and righteousness to God, who makes people fit to receive his gifts. The Collect before Epiphany requests that God makes fit his people to acknowledge and hold fast to their Savior by shining the light of his glory upon them and setting their hearts on fire. The Collect after Epiphany asks God ever more fully to make us fit by revealing to our minds the meaning of the nativity of the Savior of the world. In the Prayer over the Offerings, we ask God to make us fit to receive the heavenly mysteries through our devotion and faith. All of this making fit is summarized in the Communion Antiphon: "God's love was revealed among us in this way: God sent his only Son into the world so that we might live through him" (1 John 4:9).

Saturday Before/After Epiphany: United with God[24]

The Collect for after the Epiphany sets the theme for the Mass texts for today. We ask God that by his grace we may be found to be in the likeness of his only-begotten Son, in whom our human nature is united to God. Likewise, in the Prayer over the Offerings, we ask God that we may be united in mind and heart through our partaking in the body and blood of Christ. God, the giver of true prayer, our guide and sustainer, consoles us as things pass away with the promise of things eternal, we declare in the Prayer after Communion. Just as Jesus shared our human form through the childbearing of the Blessed Virgin Mary, we pray in the Collect before Epiphany, that we may one day become his companions in his kingdom of grace. In his Letter to the Galatians—a gloss forming the Entrance Antiphon—Paul refers to this as "the fullness of time" when "God sent his Son, born of a woman . . . so that we might receive adoption as children" (Gal 4:4–5). Quoting John's Gospel, the Communion Antiphon emphasizes this: "From his fullness we have all

23. *Roman Missal*, 198–99.
24. *Roman Missal*, 200–01.

received, grace upon grace" (John 1:16). Thus, through heaped grace, we are united to God through Christ.

Baptism of the Lord, Sunday after Epiphany: Baptism[25]

The Baptism of the Lord is a mini-Pentecost; just like Pentecost ends the Easter Season, the Baptism of Jesus ends the Christmas Season. The Entrance Antiphon from Matthew's Gospel sets the stage and theme: ". . . [W]hen Jesus had been baptized, just as he came up from the water, suddenly the heavens were opened to him and he saw the Spirit of God descending like a dove and alighting on him. And a voice from heaven said, 'This is my Son, the Beloved, with whom I am well pleased'" (Matt 3:16–17). The first optional Collect emphasizes the descent of the Holy Spirit upon Christ at his baptism in the Jordan River. The Prayer over the Offerings refers to Jesus' baptism as the washing away of the sins of the world. Our prayer in the first optional Collect is that the ever-living God will find us, who have been reborn of water and the Holy Spirit, pleasing to him. In the second optional Collect, our prayer is that we may be inwardly transformed through Jesus, whom we recognize as outwardly just like ourselves, as, in the words of the Prayer after Communion, we listen to God's only-begotten Son and become God's children in name and in truth. In the Preface, we declare that the Spirit's descent in the likeness of a dove indicates that Jesus has been anointed and sent to deliver the gospel to all. Quoting John the Baptist's words in John's Gospel, the Communion Antiphon echoes this last thought: "I saw the Spirit descending from heaven like a dove, and it remained on him. . . . I myself have seen and have testified that this is the Son of God" (John 1:32, 34).

---

25. *Roman Missal*, 202–06.

3

The Lenten Season

ASH WEDNESDAY AND DAYS AFTER

Ash Wednesday: Dust[1]

The Entrance Antiphon from the OT (A) book of Wisdom on Ash Wednesday explains what the all-merciful God does: He overlooks people's sins so they may repent; he loves all things that exist; and he detests nothing of all he made (Wis 11:23–24). The introductory words to the rite of blessing and distributing of ashes emphasize penitence to which God responds with forgiveness. On this first day of Lent, we remember that we are dust, and one day we will return to the dust and ashes we are. In the Prayer over the Offerings, we petition God to help us turn away from harmful pleasures

---

1. *Roman Missal*, 209–12.

through works of penance and charity during Lent. Thus, our Lenten prayer, fasting, and almsgiving will be pleasing to God and a healing remedy for us (Prayer after Communion). The Collect uses the metaphor of service in Christian warfare battling spiritual evils with weapons of self-restraint; this latter idea is echoed in the Prayer over the People, which asks God to pour a spirit of compunction on the people gathered before him, and, returning to the theme in the Entrance Antiphon, in his mercy to give them the rewards promised to those who do penance.

Thursday after Ash Wednesday: Inspiration[2]

In today's Collect, we ask God to prompt our actions with his inspiration so that all we do may begin with God and be brought to completion in us by God. Such acknowledgement of the LORD's sovereignty may be considered foolishness for modern people, who just presume that they are in charge of their lives. However, if we take to heart the basic premise of the Collect, we recognize that it is God who pardons our offenses (Prayer over the Offerings) and is the source of our salvation (Prayer after Communion). This is why the Communion Antiphon states: "Create in me a clean heart, O God, and put a new and right spirit within me" (Ps 51:10). This is not something that we do ourselves; the LORD does it in us. Our responsibility is to cooperate with him. In the Entrance Antiphon, the psalmist explains: ". . . I call upon God, and the LORD will save me. He will redeem me unharmed from the battle that I wage, for many are arrayed against me" (Ps 55:16, 18). The advice the psalmist gives is this: "Cast your burden on the LORD, and he will sustain you; he will never permit the righteous to be moved" (Ps 55:22). In the words of the Prayer over the People, this is the way of eternal life.

Friday after Ash Wednesday: Discipline[3]

The theme presented in the Mass texts for today is observance of the disciplines of Lent along our pilgrim journey; it is found in the Prayer over the People. The Communion Antiphon, a verse from Psalm 25, echoes this theme: "Make me to know your ways, O LORD; teach me your paths" (Ps 25:4). In the Collect, we ask God to look graciously on the prayer, fasting, and almsgiving—works of discipline—that we have begun, and we ask that

2. *Roman Missal*, 213.

3. *Roman Missal*, 214.

he will strengthen us to accomplish these bodily observances sincerely. In the Prayer over the Offerings, we ask the Lord to accept our intentions and to strengthen our self-restraint. Prayer, fasting, and almsgiving—traditional Lenten observances—are described as remedies of God's compassion in the Prayer after Communion. The Entrance Antiphon adds to today's petitions: "Hear, O LORD, and be gracious to me! O LORD, be my helper!" (Ps 30:10) Then, in the words of the Prayer over the People, we will offer endless thanks to the God of mercy in whose presence we desire to live forever.

Saturday after Ash Wednesday: Forgiveness, Mercy, Protection[4]

There are three themes that permeate the Mass texts today. The first concerns our weakness and need for forgiveness. In the Collect, we ask the ever-living God to look with compassion on us in our weakness. In the Prayer over the Offerings, we seek to be cleansed of our sins in order to offer ourselves with minds well pleasing to God. The second theme concerns divine mercy. In the Entrance Antiphon, each of us declares: "Answer me, O LORD, for your steadfast love is good; according to your abundant mercy, turn to me" (Ps 69:16). The Communion Antiphon taken from Matthew's Gospel is a gloss on a verse from the prophet Hosea (6:6): "'I desire mercy, not sacrifice.' For I have come to call not the righteous but sinners" (Matt 9:13). And the third theme concerns divine protection. In the Collect, we ask God to ensure us of his protection, while in the Prayer over the People, we ask that no dangers may bring affliction to those who trust in God, their protector. The Prayer after Communion brings all themes together when it declares that what remains a mystery in this life is the means for eternal life.

FIRST WEEK OF LENT

First Sunday of Lent: Forty Days[5]

On the first Sunday of Lent, we recall how Jesus' forty-day fast established the pattern of our forty-day Lenten journey (Preface). In the Collect, we ask God to help us understand the riches hidden in Christ through our observance of Lent. Those riches will be found in celebrating the paschal mystery (Preface), the death and resurrection of Christ during the Easter Season. The Prayer

4. *Roman Missal*, 215.

5. *Roman Missal*, 216–19.

over the Offerings refers to Lent as a venerable and sacred time, while in the Prayer after Communion, we petition God to make us hunger for Christ and to strive to live by every word that comes from God's mouth. This prayer is meant to echo the Communion Antiphon: "One does not live by bread alone, but by every word that comes from the mouth of God" (Matt 4:4; Deut 8:3). Thus, in the Prayer over the People, we ask God to bless all people with enduring hope in tribulation, strengthened virtue in temptation, and assured eternal redemption. In other words, we ask God to put into effect the Entrance Antiphon: When people call to the LORD, he will answer them; he will be with them in trouble, he will rescue them and honor them. With long life he will satisfy them, and show them his salvation (Ps 91:15–16).

Monday of the First Week of Lent: Mercy[6]

Today's theme is found in the Entrance Antiphon: "As the eyes of servants look to the hand of their master, as the eyes of a maid to the hand of her mistress, so our eyes look to the LORD our God, until he has mercy upon us. Have mercy upon us, O LORD, have mercy upon us . . ." (Ps 123:2–3). We ask God not to give us what we deserve, but to instruct us with heavenly teaching (Collect) that our manner of life may demonstrate conciliation and pardon (Prayer over the Offerings). God's mercy, echoed in the Penitential Act of every Mass, gives us help in mind and body, referred to as heavenly healing in the Prayer after Communion. It also enables us to see what we must do and gives us the strength to do it (Prayer over the People). Just as God shows us the mercy we ardently desire and request, we are instructed to pass it on. The Communion Antiphon, two verses from Matthew's Gospel, presents the king declaring that whatever we do for one of the least of people, we do it for him (Matt 25:40). If we have shown to others the mercy God has shown to us, then one day we will hear, "Come, you that are blessed by my Father, inherit the kingdom prepared for you from the foundation of the world" (Matt 25:34) (Communion Antiphon).

Tuesday of the First Week of Lent: Moderation[7]

The basic idea contained in the Mass texts for today is summarized in the Prayer after Communion: Through the moderation of earthly desires, we

6. *Roman Missal*, 220.

7. *Roman Missal*, 221.

pray that we may learn to love heavenly things. The Collect asks God to see the bodily discipline we impose upon ourselves during Lent in order to increase our longing for him. In the Prayer over the Offerings, we ask the Creator to accept our gifts of bread and wine and transform the temporal sustenance into food for eternal life. We are able to call upon God to sustain us in our Lenten moderation because—in the words of the Entrance Antiphon—the Lord has been our dwelling place in all generations; from everlasting to everlasting he is God (Ps 90:1–2). We are confident that when we call upon God for help in maintaining our Lenten disciplines, he will answer us, remove our distress, be gracious to us, and hear our prayer (Ps 4:1) (Communion Antiphon). This gives us confidence to ask for God to be our consolation in grief, our power to endure in tribulation, and our protection in peril, in the Prayer over the People.

Wednesday of the First Week of Lent: Forgiveness[8]

The theme knitting together today's Mass texts is forgiveness of sins and redemption. In the Prayer over the People, we ask the Lord to cleanse us from all sins in order to remove any evil that may have dominion over or cause trials in our lives. In the Prayer over the Offerings, we ask that the bread and wine we present on the altar will become an eternal remedy for us. Similarly, in the Collect, we seek renewal in mind by our Lenten good works through our bodily restraints of self-denial. Unending life is what we seek through sacramental nourishment in the Prayer after Communion. None of this is possible, of course, without God's mercy and steadfast love which have existed from of old, as stated in the Entrance Antiphon (Ps 25:6). This brings us back to forgiveness of sins and redemption. We ask God not to let sin exult over us, but to redeem us from all our troubles (Ps 25:2, 22) (Entrance Antiphon). The Communion Antiphon reminds us of our joy in taking refuge in God, and it petitions: "Spread your protection over [us], so that [we] who love your name may exult in you" (Ps 5:11b).

Thursday of the First Week of Lent: Prayer[9]

The Entrance Antiphon sets the theme and the tone of today's Mass texts: "Give ear to my words, O LORD; give heed to my sighing. Listen to the sound

8. *Roman Missal*, 222.
9. *Roman Missal*, 223.

of my cry, my King and my God, for to you I pray" (Ps 5:1–2). The theme of prayer and the tone of supplication are enhanced by the Communion Antiphon: "For everyone who asks receives, and everyone who searches finds, and for everyone who knocks, the door will be opened" (Matt 7:8). Such assurance leads us in the Collect to ask God to give us a spirit of always pondering what is right and hastening to do it. In the Prayer over the Offerings, we approach the LORD in supplication—echoing the antiphons above—and in the Prayer over the People, we ask God to show his mercy to those who make supplication to him so that they may know what is right to ask in order to receive what they seek. We acknowledge that we cannot exist without God, but with our prayer for his help we can live according to his will (Collect) as he turns our hearts towards him (Prayer over the Offerings). In other words, we ask God to inspire us to pray for that which he knows we need.

Friday of the First Week of Lent: Reconciled[10]

We acknowledge that through God's power and kindness, he wills us to be reconciled to himself and to save us for eternal life in the Prayer over the Offerings. This is expressed in the Communion Antiphon, a part of a verse from the prophet Ezekiel: "As I live, says the Lord GOD, I have no pleasure in the death of the wicked, but that the wicked turn from their ways and live . . ." (Ezek 33:11). The Entrance Antiphon turns God's will that we be reconciled into a petition: O LORD, "Relive the trouble of my heart, and bring me out of my distress. Consider my affliction and my trouble, and forgive all my sins" (Ps 25:17–18). The Collect asks God to let our Lenten disciple bear fruit in us so that we may be even more conformed to the Easter observances for which we are preparing to celebrate in four weeks. Likewise, the Prayer over the People asks God to see how our outward Lenten observances of prayer, fasting, and almsgiving bring about inward change. The eucharist we celebrate today restores us to new life and takes us into the mystery of salvation (Prayer after Communion).

Saturday of the First Week of Lent: God's Will[11]

Knowing God's will is the theme permeating today's Mass texts. The Entrance Antiphon presents one way of knowing the divine will: keeping

10. *Roman Missal*, 224.

11. *Roman Missal*, 225.

Torah. The psalmist sings: "The law of the LORD is perfect, reviving the soul; the decrees of the LORD are sure, making wise the simple" (Ps 19:7). Another way to know the divine will is to pray that God turns our hearts to him which will result in works of charity and worship (Collect). Only God, according to the Prayer over the Offerings, can make us worthy of the gifts he bestows on us. A third way to know God's will is found in the Communion Antiphon: In the sermon on the mount, Jesus says, "Be perfect . . . as your heavenly Father is perfect" (Matt 5:48). Perfect does not mean without fault; perfect means that we show the same integrity and purity of heart that God does. In other words, we know the divine will by being whole in the same way that God is whole. God consoles us and imbues us with heavenly teaching in order to help us know his will (Prayer after Communion). The Prayer over the People asks God to bless us so that we never stray from his will and, therefore, always rejoice in his gifts.

SECOND WEEK OF LENT

Second Sunday of Lent: Listen[12]

The focus of the Mass texts for the Second Sunday of Lent is listening to God's beloved Son (Collect). The Communion Antiphon, a part of a verse from Matthew's Gospel's account of Jesus' transfiguration, expresses it best: God says, "This is my Son, the Beloved; with him I am well pleased; listen to him!" (Matt 17:5) We ask God to nourish us inwardly with his word, which will give us spiritual sight, and so we may rejoice to behold his glory (Collect), revealed on the holy mountain where his Son was transfigured. The Entrance Antiphon phrases the same idea this way: "Your face, LORD, do I seek. Do not hide your face from me" (Ps 27:8b–9a). The Prayer over the People seeks God's blessing to keep people faithful to the gospel in order to reach the glory displayed by Jesus in his transfiguration. Our hope, expressed in the Prayer after Communion, is that the glory we experience on earth will lead us to the glory of heaven. Thus, in the Prayer over the Offerings, we seek sanctification in preparation for the celebration of the paschal festivities—the suffering, death, and resurrection of Christ—which, according to the Preface, manifests how the passion of Jesus leads to the glory of Christ's resurrection.

12. *Roman Missal*, 226–29.

Monday of the Second Week of Lent: Eternal Things[13]

In the words of Preface II of Lent, we seek to be freed from disordered affections during Lent, dealing with things in this passing world while holding to the things that endure eternally.[14] Today's Collect emphasizes this when we acknowledge that God has taught us to chasten our bodies in order to heal our souls. Likewise, in the Prayer over the Offerings, we ask the Lord to free us from worldly attractions so that, in the words of the Prayer after Communion, we may become heirs of heavenly joy. Put simply: We are not here to stay. Lenten prayer, fasting, and almsgiving are designed to refocus us on what really matters, but without God's help we are unable to strengthen our own hearts. That is why in the Prayer over the People, we ask God to confirm our hearts and strengthen them with his grace. In the Entrance Antiphon, we ask the LORD to redeem us and to be gracious to us (Ps 26:11). Then, our supplication will be constant and our love will be sincere. In the words of the Communion Antiphon, we will be mercifully just as our Father is merciful (Luke 6:36).

Tuesday of the Second Week of Lent: From Mercy to Praise[15]

In today's Mass texts, there is a movement from seeking mercy from God to praising him. The Collect acknowledges that God guards the church in his unceasing mercy, keeps all her members from harm, and brings them salvation. The Entrance Antiphon petitions God's mercy: "Give light to my eyes, or I will sleep the sleep of death and my enemy will say, 'I have prevailed . . .'" (Ps 13:3–4). The Prayer over the Offerings seeks God's sanctifying mercy within us which includes being cleansed of any earthly faults. The Prayer after Communion seeks an increase in devoutness of life so that God's salvific work of conciliation may take place in us. Mercy gives way to praise. The Prayer over the People declares that the recognition of forgiveness erupts in rejoicing in God's blessing. The Communion Antiphon expresses the same idea this way: "I will give thanks to the LORD with my whole heart; I will tell of all your wonderful deeds. I will be glad and exult in you; I will sing praise to your name, O Most High" (Ps 9:1–2).

---

13. *Roman Missal*, 230.

14. *Roman Missal*, 548–49.

15. *Roman Missal*, 231.

Wednesday of the Second Week of Lent: Good Works[16]

The author of the Letter of James would be very pleased with today's Collect because it asks God to keep us schooled always in good works. In the Communion Antiphon, we remember Jesus' good work of coming "not to be served but to serve, and to give his life a ransom for many" (Matt 20:28). And in Preface III of Lent, we ask God to let our self-denial give him thanks by humbling our pride, feeding the poor, and imitating him in his kindness to all.[17] Then, in the words of the Prayer over the Offerings, the gifts we offer will help to undo the bonds of our sins and bring us to eternal salvation (Prayer after Communion). We ask for God's protection here and in the life to come. The Entrance Antiphon emphasizes this latter point in a petition: "Do not forsake me, O LORD; O my God, do not be far from me; make haste to help me, O Lord, my salvation" (Ps 38:21–22). And the Prayer over the People seeks an abundance of grace and protection from God along with health of mind and body, the fullness of charitable good works, and deeper devotion to God. Thus, the origin of our good works is the God who inspires them in us.

Thursday of the Second Week of Lent: Inward Change[18]

Today's theme in the Mass texts is best illustrated in the Prayer over the Offerings in which we ask God to let what our outward Lenten discipline declares bring about an inward change. Our prayer, fasting, and almsgiving are our visible Lenten disciplines that should change us from the outside in. In the Collect, we acknowledge that God delights in innocence and restores it, while the Prayer after Communion requests that the reception of the body and blood of Christ may be active in its effects within us and work ever more strongly within us. No change can come about unless God helps us with his grace, which becomes support, guidance, and protection (Prayer over the People). This latter idea is found in the Entrance Antiphon: "Search me, O God, and know my heart; test me and know my thoughts. See if there is any wicked way in me, and lead me in the way everlasting" (Ps 139:23–24). The Entrance Antiphon is echoed in the Communion Antiphon: "Happy are those whose way is blameless, who walk in the law of the LORD" (Ps 119:1).

16. *Roman Missal*, 232.

17. *Roman Missal*, 550–51.

18. *Roman Missal*, 233.

Friday of the Second Week of Lent: Holy Things to Come[19]

The basic theme that ties together today's Mass texts is attainment of holy things to come, as voiced in the Collect. We ask God to cleanse us through our Lenten practices and to lead us in sincerity of heart to the goal of everlasting life. The Prayer over the Offerings seeks God's grace as preparation to celebrate worthily and to be led to a devout manner of life. The Prayer after Communion seeks the Lord's help in setting our life's course in order to attain the redemption he has promised, and the Prayer over the People asks the Lord for health in order to be constant in good works so as to merit his protection. The Entrance Antiphon, then, becomes a plea for help to attain holy things: "In you, O LORD, I seek refuge; do not let me ever be put to shame; in your righteousness deliver me" (Ps 31:1). And the Communion Antiphon expresses how this is accomplished: ". . . God . . . sent his Son to be the atoning sacrifice for our sins" (1 John 4:10). The Son not only showed us how to live devoutly in God's presence, but he revealed the holy things to come for those who do so.

Saturday of the Second Week of Lent: Lost and Found[20]

The Communion Antiphon for today expresses the basic ideas found in the Mass texts. It comes from the unique narrative of the prodigal son in Luke's Gospel. The father tells his older son that they have "to celebrate and rejoice, because [his younger] brother . . . was dead and has come to life; he was lost and has been found" (Luke 15:32). The operative metaphor is that the old man's younger son was gone or lost, a type of death from the father's perspective, but he has returned or been found, a type of life from the father's point of view. Thus, in the Collect we ask God to guide us through our present life and its inevitable death to the light in which he dwells. The Prayer over the Gifts asks God to lead us onward to the gift of salvation. And the Prayer after Communion petitions the Lord to fill the inner depths of our hearts with his divine life that we may one day share in the fullness of grace. With God's ears of mercy open to our prayers, we desire that he will inspire us to ask what is pleasing to him and then to grant what we ask in the Prayer over the People. All of this is available to us because "[t]he LORD is gracious and merciful, slow to anger and abounding in steadfast love," states the Entrance Antiphon

---

19. *Roman Missal*, 234.
20. *Roman Missal*, 235.

(Ps 145:8). "The LORD is good to all, and his compassion is over all that he has made" (Ps 145:9).

THIRD WEEK OF LENT

Third Sunday of Lent: Mercy[21]

The Communion Antiphon states: "Even the sparrow finds a home, and the swallow a nest for herself, where she may lay her young, at your altars, O LORD of hosts, my King and my God. Happy are those who live in your house, ever singing your praise" (Ps 84:3–4). The image of birds making their nests on the upper ledges of the Temple gives us a picture of God's mercy. The Collect declares God to be the author of every mercy and all goodness; God lifts us up with his mercy. And the Prayer over the People seeks his mercy through the grace of loving him and our neighbor. Like birds nesting on Temple ledges in need of protection from the elements, we, too, are in need of protection from sin. The Lenten remedy is prayer, fasting, and almsgiving, as stated in the Collect, which we hope will bring pardon for our sins and spark forgiveness of our neighbor (Prayer over the Offerings). Our prayer is that what is brought about in us through Lent may one day come to true completion (Prayer after Communion). Then, like the birds' view from their nests, we, too, can say: "My eyes are ever toward the LORD, for he will pluck my feet out of the net" (Ps 25:15) (Entrance Antiphon).

Monday of the Third Week of Lent: Transformation[22]

Transformation is the theme woven through today's Mass texts. It is stated best in the Prayer over the Offerings, in which we ask God to transform the tokens of our service—bread and wine—into the sacrament of salvation. Likewise, in the Collect we ask God to transform the church through his government of grace; without him the church cannot stand secure. In the Prayer after Communion, we seek purification and unity that result from the transforming power of the eucharist. And in the Prayer over the People, we acknowledge that God's right hand protects, purifies, and gives instruction to his people so that they may be transformed from solace in this life to the good things to come in the next life. Thus, in the words of the Entrance Antiphon,

21. *Roman Missal*, 236–39.
22. *Roman Missal*, 240.

each of us should say: "My soul longs, indeed it faints for the courts of the LORD; my heart and my flesh sing for joy to the living God" (Ps 84:3). Likewise, in the Communion Antiphon, we exclaim, "Praise the LORD, all you nations! For great is his steadfast love toward us . . ." (Ps 117:1–2).

Tuesday of the Third Week of Lent: Help for Service[23]

The first of two themes permeating today's Mass texts is God's help. It is introduced in the Entrance Antiphon: "I call upon you, for you will answer me, O God; incline your ear to me, hear my words" (Ps 17:6). Then, in the Collect we ask God not to forsake us with his grace, which enables us to seek his help. In the Prayer over the Offerings, the help we seek is cleansing of our faults, and in the Prayer after Communion, we state that we need life, pardon, and protection, which is echoed in the Prayer over the People. The second theme is also announced in the Collect: dedication to God's holy service. In the Prayer over the Offerings, we ask that our oblation be pleasing to God's almighty power, and in the Prayer over the People, we ask that we be pleasing to God. With God's help, we can "walk blamelessly and do what is right," according to Psalm 15:2, the Communion Antiphon. In other words, our dedication to God's service is dependent upon his help. Then, we are guarded as "the apple of the eye," and we are hidden "in the shadow of [God's] wings," like a mother hen or mother bird gathers her brood under her for protection (Ps 17:8) (Entrance Antiphon).

Wednesday of the Third Week of Lent: Path of Life[24]

"You show me the path of life [, O LORD]. In your presence there is fullness of joy . . ." (Ps 16:11), we state in the Communion Antiphon. The theme of the path of life is echoed in the Entrance Antiphon: "Keep my steps steady according to you promise, and never let iniquity have dominion over me" (Ps 119:133). The path of life and the steady steps we take during Lent are referred to as a school of Lenten observance in the Collect. God's word nourishes us, and our holy restraint keeps us on the path of devotion to God. While traveling, we need God to defend us and to keep us from every danger (Prayer over the Offerings). The heavenly banquet we celebrate in the eucharist is our food for the journey, and it carries a promise from on high,

23. *Roman Missal*, 241.
24. *Roman Missal*, 242.

we state in the Prayer after Communion. Finally, while we walk the path of life, we need to conform to God's teachings, the resolve of which comes from God himself. While traveling, we are devoted to God and united in prayer (Collect). The result of keeping on the path to life is the bestowal of God's favor to be in his presence forever.

Thursday of the Third Week of Lent: Press Forward[25]

Today's Mass texts begin to turn our gaze toward the feast of salvation, referred to in the Collect as the celebration of the paschal mystery. In other words, we begin to look forward to Holy Week—Palm Sunday of the Passion of the Lord—and the Paschal Triduum—Holy Thursday, Good Friday, and Easter. In the words of the Collect, we press forward eagerly to the end of Lent. The Entrance Antiphon assures us of salvation, which, in the Prayer after Communion, we seek to possess in mystery and to demonstrate by the way we live. The Prayer over the Offerings reminds us of God's promise to reward us with his truth, which is defined in the Communion Antiphon as diligently keeping God's precepts and statutes (Ps 119:4–5). Our Lenten goal is to let God cleanse us from every taint of wickedness (Prayer over the Offerings), and with his loving kindness, in which we trust, enable us to seek what is right and do the good we desire to do. In the Prayer over the People, we acknowledge that we are totally dependent upon God's grace and mercy, that all we are is because of him.

Friday of the Third Week of Lent: Strengthening Grace[26]

We need God to pour his grace, himself, into us during Lent, we state in today's Collect. This grace will move us away from desires that keep us from being pleasing in God's sight, according to the Prayer over the Offerings, and enable us to obey God's teaching (Collect). Instead of grace, in the Prayer after Communion, we ask for God's strength to work in us, to pervade our minds and bodies that we may be brought to the fullness of redemption. As always, we implore God's mercy and trust his kindness in the hope that he will spread his gifts far and wide. We learn from the Entrance Antiphon that the LORD is great and does wondrous things; he alone is God (Ps 86:10). Our response it to love the LORD with all our

25. *Roman Missal*, 243.
26. *Roman Missal*, 244.

heart, and with all our understanding, and with our strength, and to love our neighbor as ourselves, according to the Communion Antiphon; such love is much more important than all whole burnt offerings and sacrifices (Mark 12:33). We pray that our love and our offerings will be salutary—of great value— for us in the Prayer over the Offerings.

Saturday of the Third Week of Lent: Blessings[27]

In the Prayer over the People, we ask God to bless us with his right hand— his power—that we may seek him with all our heart and merit the granting of what we ask. Seeking God is expressed in the Prayer over the Offerings, in which we ask to be made worthy to approach the mystery of bread and wine becoming the body and blood of Christ and hand them on to others. In the Prayer after Communion, we seek truly to revere the holy gifts of the body and blood of Christ with which God nourishes us. In the Entrance Antiphon, we seek never to forget the LORD's benefits, especially his forgiveness for our iniquities (Ps 103:2–3). Echoing the Entrance Antiphon, the Communion Antiphon becomes our petition: "God, be merciful to me, a sinner!" (Luke 18:13). We trust that our seeking will also enable us to rejoice in our annual Lenten observance with our heart set on the paschal mysteries—the suffering, death, and resurrection of Jesus Christ (Collect)—at the end of Lent. By granting what we ask, we are able to be gladdened by the effects of God's grace in our lives.

FOURTH WEEK OF LENT

Fourth Sunday of Lent: Rejoice[28]

The basic theme running through the Mass texts for the Fourth Sunday of Lent is rejoicing. The Entrance Antiphon establishes the theme: "Rejoice with Jerusalem, and be glad for her, all you who love her; rejoice with her in joy, all you who mourn over her—that you may nurse and be satisfied from her consoling breast" (Isa 66:10–11a). The operative metaphor in those verses is portrayal of the city as a mother nursing her children at her breasts. Just as God restored Jerusalem after her destruction by the Babylonians, so, through his Word, Jesus Christ, he has reconciled the human race to himself

---

27. *Roman Missal*, 245.

28. *Roman Missal*, 246–49.

(Collect). Our gifts of bread and wine remind us of the eternal remedy Jesus gave for the salvation of the whole world (Prayer over the Offerings). Our rejoicing is because God has enlightened our minds and illumined our hearts with his grace so that, in the words of the Prayer over the People, we no longer walk in the shadow of death. God sustains the weak and gives life by his unfailing light. Thus, with eager faith, we joyfully hasten toward the solemn celebrations of Holy Week to come (Collect).

Monday of the Fourth Week of Lent: Journey[29]

We are on a journey both throughout this life to eternity and our Lenten trip preparing us to celebrate the sacred mysteries beyond all telling, in the words of the Collect. Thus, we ask God to guide the church according to his eternal design (Collect). In the Prayer over the Offerings, we seek to be cleansed from our earthly ways, being renewed by growth in eternal life as we continue both journeys. In the Prayer after Communion, we ask that God's gifts make us new and lead us on the journey to eternal life. The same idea of renewal, which occurs on any journey, both within and without, is found in the Prayer over the People, in which we seek perseverance on both spiritual journeys. While on our way, we pray the words of the psalmist, found in the Entrance Antiphon: ". . . I trust in the LORD. I will exult and rejoice in your steadfast love . . ." (Ps 31:67), while remembering God's words to the prophet Ezekiel in the Communion Antiphon: "I will put my spirit within you, and make you follow my statutes, and be careful to observe my ordinances" (Ezek 36:27). As Spirit-filled pilgrims, we continue on the path to the imminent Paschal Triduum and the distant trail to life eternal.

Tuesday of the Fourth Week of Lent: Devotion[30]

Devotion is the theme running through today's Mass texts. Devotion is deep love and commitment, dedication and loyalty, enthusiasm and admiration, fervent religious and spiritual feeling. During Lent, in the words of the Collect, we engage in exercises of holy devotion—prayer, fasting, and almsgiving—in order to prepare ourselves to celebrate the paschal mystery of the death and resurrection of Jesus Christ and to praise God for his gift of salvation. Thus, the gifts of bread and wine we offer to God, which come

29. *Roman Missal*, 250.
30. *Roman Missal*, 251.

from him, effect healing in us that brings us to share in the immortality which Christ already shares (Prayer over the Offerings). The Prayer over the People asks our merciful God to keep us devoted to him that we may receive whatever kindness is for our good. In the Entrance Antiphon, we express our devotion, singing or saying a verse from the prophet Isaiah: "Ho, everyone who thirsts, come to the waters; and you that have no money, come, buy and eat!" (Isa 55:1a) Our devotion is based on God's deep love and commitment to us, as expressed in Psalm 23—the Communion Antiphon—which echoes Isaiah: "The LORD is my shepherd, I shall not want. He makes me lie down in green pastures; he leads me beside still waters" (Ps 23:1–2).

Wednesday of the Fourth Week of Lent: Answer[31]

The Entrance Antiphon is a prayer-plea to God for help. ". . . [A]s for me, my prayer is to you, O LORD. At an acceptable time, O God, in the abundance of your steadfast love, answer me" (Ps 69:13). It summarizes the theme in today's Mass texts. In the Collect, we seek God's mercy and pardon even as we admit our guilt. In the Prayer over the Offerings, we ask God in his mercy to wipe away all that is old in us while increasing the grace of salvation and newness of life in us. And in the Prayer after Communion, we pray that the gifts given to us by God will not bring his judgment to us who accept them. We are reminded in the Communion Antiphon that "God did not send the Son into the world to condemn the world, but in order that the world might be saved through him" (John 3:17). The Prayer over the People seeks God's help as a shield of loving-kindness—returning us to the abundance of steadfast love in Psalm 69—protecting us throughout our journey in this world to God, the highest good. The acceptable time—mentioned in Psalm 69 above—is the Season of Lent.

Thursday of the Fourth Week of Lent: Purification[32]

Today's Mass texts are focused on purification. The Collect invokes God's mercy to cause our Lenten penance to correct us and our good works to school us in keeping God's commands as we approach the paschal festivities in two weeks. In the Entrance Antiphon, we declare that "the hearts of

31. *Roman Missal*, 252.
32. *Roman Missal*, 253.

those who seek the Lord rejoice." Thus, we should "[s]eek the LORD and his strength;" we should "seek his presence continually" (Ps 105:3–4); it is he who purifies us. In the Prayer over the Gifts, we seek to be cleansed and protected from every evil. And in the Prayer after Communion, we ask that the body and blood of Christ we have received purify us and give us freedom from all blame; anyone possessing a guilty conscience should glory in the fullness of God's remedy. In the Prayer over the People, we ask God to keep us safe, to defend us, and to prepare us—purified from sin—to persevere in love. The Communion Antiphon reminds us that it is God who purifies us. The LORD, records Jeremiah, says, "I will put my law within them, and I will write in on their hearts; and I will be their God, and they shall be my people" (Jer 31:33).

Friday of the Fourth Week of Lent: Assistance[33]

The basic thread tying together today's Mass texts is the heavenly assistance we can count on from God. In the Collect, we acknowledge that God prepares fitting helps for all of us weak people. In fact, in the Prayer over the Gifts, we note that God not only cleanses us of our weaknesses, but he leads us to him, the very source of our help, with great purity. We pass from what was old to what is new, according to the Prayer after Communion, leaving behind former ways in order to be renewed by God in holiness, another way to pray about heavenly assistance. In the Prayer over the People, we ask God to protect us with his heavenly assistance as we profess our trust in his mercy. Our prayer of petition, then, is found in the Entrance Antiphon: "Save me, O God, by your name, and vindicate me by your might. Hear my prayer, O God; give ear to the words of my mouth" (Ps 54:1–2). We know that God has offered heavenly assistance through his Son, Jesus Christ. The Communion Antiphon declares that "[i]n him we have redemption through his blood, the forgiveness of our trespasses, according to the riches of his grace" (Eph 1:7).

Saturday of the Fourth Week of Lent: Abundant Grace[34]

According to today's Mass texts, we rely upon God's mercy to direct our hearts with his grace, without which we cannot find favor in God's sight

---

33. *Roman Missal*, 254.
34. *Roman Missal*, 255.

(Collect). A similar idea is expressed in the Prayer over the Gifts. We declare that the gifts we offer to God come from him; likewise, the turning of our defiant wills to him is due to the grace of his mercy. The gifts of the body and blood of his Son purify us and make us pleasing to him, according to the Prayer after Communion. It is due to the abundance of heavenly grace which God bestows upon us that we are able to draw near to the coming festivities of Holy Week and the Easter Season. Our reliance upon God's mercy is expressed in the Entrance Antiphon: "The cords of death encompassed me; the torrents of perdition assailed me . . . . In my distress I called upon the LORD; to my God I cried for help. From his temple he heard my voice . . ." (Ps 18:4, 6). Indeed, he has heard our pleas: We have been ransomed "with the precious blood of Christ, like that of a lamb without defect or blemish," states the Communion Antiphon (1 Pet 1:19).

FIFTH WEEK OF LENT

Fifth Sunday of Lent: Death and Life[35]

In some ways, the Fifth Sunday of Lent anticipates Palm Sunday of the Passion of the Lord next Sunday. In the Collect, we beseech God to help us walk eagerly in the same generosity that enabled Jesus to hand himself over to death because he loved the world. The Communion Antiphon, a verse spoken by Jesus in John's Gospel, continues the theme: "Very truly, I tell you, unless a grain of wheat falls into the earth and dies, it remains just a single grain; but if it dies, it bears much fruit" (John 12:24). In the Prayer after Communion, we pray that we may always be counted among the members of the body of Christ, bearing fruit. We long for the gift of God's mercy in the Prayer over the People, and ask God to grant what we ask of him at his prompting and consider it a generous gift received. The teachings of our Christian faith, acknowledged in the Prayer over the Offerings, enable us to pray for help in the Entrance Antiphon: "Vindicate me, O God, and defend my cause against an ungodly people; from those who are deceitful and unjust deliver me!" (Ps 43:1)

---

35. *Roman Missal*, 256–59.

Monday of the Fifth Week of Lent: Newness[36]

The purpose of penance—prayer, fasting, and almsgiving—during Lent is, in the words of the Collect, to pass from former ways of life to newness of life. Even the practice of penance is a gift of God's grace; it is a blessing. That is why we ask in the Prayer over the Offerings that we may bring a joyful purity of heart to God as the result of our Lenten penance. Likewise, in the Prayer after Communion, after acknowledging the blessings God bestows upon us in the sacraments, we ask that we may be cleansed of our faults through the reception of the body and blood of Christ, whom we follow to God. Once we are set free from sins, we live a holy way of life, as stated in the Prayer over the People. In the words of the Communion Antiphon, we recognize Jesus as "the light of the world. Whoever follows [him] will never walk in darkness but will have the light of life" (John 8:12). Thus, in the Entrance Antiphon we ask God to be gracious to us when people trample on us or when our foes oppress us all day long (Ps 56:1) and to hasten our steps toward him (Prayer after Communion).

Tuesday of the Fifth Week of Lent: God's Will[37]

The many aspects of doing God's will permeate today's Mass texts. The Entrance Antiphon reminds us to "[w]ait for the LORD; [to] be strong, and let [our] heart take courage; [to] wait for the LORD!" (Ps 27:14) Thus, in the Collect, we seek perseverance in obeying God's will so as to be signs of people dedicated to his service and attract others. In the Prayer over the Offerings, we offer the sacrifice of conciliation—a reference to the death and resurrection of Christ which restored our relationship with God—which moves God to compassion, pardon, and helping us do his will. The words of the Johannine Jesus in the Communion Antiphon echoes the death and resurrection of Christ: ". . . I, when I am lifted up from the earth, will draw all people to myself" (John 12:32).We are ever seeking what is divine, we state in the Prayer after Communion, which enables us to be worthy to approach and receive God's gifts. For those who do God's will, according to the Prayer over the People, God shows mercy to those who hope in him, and they receive the grace of consolation which makes them even better to do God's will.

36. *Roman Missal*, 260–61.
37. *Roman Missal*, 262.

Wednesday of the Fifth Week of Lent: Metaphors[38]

Today's Mass texts are a pastiche of metaphors. In the Entrance Antiphon, the LORD is referred to as the deliverer, who rescued the psalmist from his enemies, even exalting him above his adversaries (Ps 18:48). This act is referred to as compassion in the Collect; we ask God to enlighten our hearts and to stir a sense of devotion in us. The Prayer over the Offerings declares that the gifts of bread and wine we offer come from God, honor his name, and become remedies for our healing. The Father "has rescued us from the power of darkness," according to the Communion Antiphon, "and transferred us into the kingdom of his beloved Son, in whom we have redemption, the forgiveness of sins" (Col 1:13–14). The remedies mentioned in the Prayer over the Offerings are revisited in the Prayer after Communion, in which the body and blood of Christ is called heavenly medicine. It purges evil from us and strengthens us with God's protection. And the divine compassion mentioned in the Collect is revisited in the Prayer over the People, in which we ask God to endow us with confident hope in his compassion so that we may feel the effects of his mercy.

Thursday of the Fifth Week of Lent: Keeping Commands[39]

According to the Prayer over the People, we ask God to help us with his grace to reject what does not please him and to be filled with delight at keeping his commands. The Entrance Antiphon interprets his commands as adhering to the new covenant mediated by Christ "so that [we] who are called may receive the promised eternal inheritance, because a death has occurred that redeems [us] from the transgressions under the first covenant" (Heb 9:15). The Collect interprets keeping the commands by placing our hope in God's mercy and pleading that he help us persevere in a holy way of life in order to inherit his promise. The Prayer over the Offerings expands this understanding to include the salvation of the whole world. God nourishes us with his saving gifts, feeding us in this present age with the body and blood of his Son, so that we may share in eternal life in the next world, according to the Prayer after Communion. The Communion Antiphon summarizes all this in a question: "[God] who did not withhold his own Son, but gave him up for all of us, will he not with him also give us everything else?" (Rom 8:32)

38. *Roman Missal*, 263.
39. *Roman Missal*, 264–65.

Friday of the Fifth Week of Lent: Cross[40]

On this last Friday of Lent, we are presented with the cross. In the second optional collect, we remember the Blessed Virgin Mary in John's Gospel standing at the foot of the cross and contemplating the passion of Jesus, her Son. We ask that we may cling to God's only-begotten Son and receive the fullness of grace. The Prayer over the Offerings petitions the merciful God to make us worthy to gather around his altar and to be saved by constant participation in the eucharist, which celebrates the death and resurrection of Christ. It is the cross we share through the body and blood of Christ that drives from us anything that might harm us (Prayer after Communion). The Communion Antiphon reminds us: "[Christ] himself bore our sins in his body on the cross, so that, free from sins, we might live for righteousness; by his wounds [we] have been healed" (1 Pet 2:24); it also echoes the first optional Collect. Now that we have been healed, we seek the grace of God's protection so that we may serve him in peace of mind (Prayer over the People). Our prayer is found in the Entrance Antiphon: "Be gracious to me, O LORD, for I am in distress . . . . [D]eliver me from the hand of my enemies and persecutors. Do not let me be put to shame, O LORD, for I call on you . . ." (Ps 31:9, 15, 17).

Saturday of the Fifth Week of Lent: Needing Grace[41]

Grace is the act of God sharing himself with people. On this last Saturday of Lent, we ask God for the grace and the will to do what he commands. In the Prayer over the Offerings, we ask that the gifts offered as a result of our fasting will make us worthy of God's grace. We ask that we may be sharers in the divine nature of Christ in the Prayer after Communion; this is another way to petition God for grace. In the Prayer over the People, our prayer is for mercy; we ask God not to let us, who have been redeemed by the death of Jesus, be harmed by our sins or weighed down by our trials. This last sentiment is also found in the Collect, in which we state that we have been reborn in Christ and made a chosen race and a royal priesthood. Jesus was handed over, states the Communion Antiphon, "to gather into one the dispersed children of God" (John 11:52). Our prayer is found in the Entrance Antiphon: ". . . O LORD, do not be far away! O my help, come quickly to my aid!" (Ps 22:19) We make the psalmist's words our own,

40. *Roman Missal*, 266–67.
41. *Roman Missal*, 268–69.

saying, ". . . I am a worm, and not human; scorned by others, and despised by the people" (Ps 22:7); thus, we are in need of God's grace.

HOLY WEEK

Palm Sunday of the Passion of the Lord: Hosanna[42]

The title for this Sunday emphasizes its two main points. The first is Jesus' triumphal entry into Jerusalem, while we hold palm or other leafy branches. The Entrance Antiphon captures this first point: "Hosanna to the Son of David! Blessed is the one who comes in the name of the Lord! Hosanna in the highest heaven!" (Matt 21:9) According to the address given by the bishop or priest, Jesus enters Jerusalem to accomplish his paschal mystery—his passion and resurrection. So, we follow Jesus in triumphal exultation, and we arrive at the cross. The Collect states that Jesus becomes the example of humility; we pray that we may follow him through patient suffering (passion) to a share in his resurrection. The Prayer over the Gifts reminds us that reconciliation cannot be merited; it is due to the mercy of God. The Preface makes this clear when it states that Jesus' death washed away our sins, and his resurrection purchased our justification. In the Prayer after Communion, the cross is mentioned again because it brought us resurrection. We ask God to look upon his family in the Prayer over the People; Jesus did not hesitate to undergo the agony of the cross for all people.

Monday of Holy Week: Paschal Festivities[43]

We ask God to keep safe all of us who trust in God's mercy that we may celebrate the paschal festivities—Jesus' death and Christ's resurrection—both bodily and mindfully in the Prayer over the People. Likewise, in the Collect we ask God to revive us through our observance of the passion of God's only-begotten Son, Jesus Christ, because, otherwise, we fail in our weakness. According to Preface II of the Passion of the Lord, the days of Jesus' passion and Christ's resurrection are approaching.[44] The Prayer over the Offerings makes us aware that the sacred mysteries we celebrate in the eucharist are gifts of God's mercy which cancel judgment and enable us to bear fruit for

---

42. *Roman Missal*, 273–86.

43. *Roman Missal*, 287.

44. *Roman Missal* 556–57.

eternal life. The Prayer after Communion asks God to continue his ever-watchful love and to keep us safe even as we share the remedy of the body and blood of Christ for eternal salvation. Thus, in the Entrance Antiphon, we pray that the LORD will rise up and defend us (Ps 35:1–2). That sentiment is echoed in the Communion Antiphon: "Do not hide your face from me in the day of my distress. Incline your ear to me; answer me speedily in the day when I call" (Ps 102:2).

Tuesday of Holy Week: Passion[45]

Today's Mass texts are focused on celebrating the Lord's passion—suffering, death, and resurrection—in order to grow in holiness. In the Collect, we ask God to help us celebrate the mysteries of the Lord's passion. In the Prayer over the Offerings, we ask God to look favorably on all who partake of the gifts, which will become the body and blood of Christ, so they may share in their fullness. We ask God to make us partakers of eternal life in the Prayer after Communion. And in the Prayer over the People, our petition is for mercy that cleanses us from former ways in order to embrace new holiness. The Communion Antiphon also reminds us of the Lord's passion: "[God] who did not withhold his own Son, but gave him up for all of us, will he not with him also give us everything else?" (Rom 8:32) Thus, in the Entrance Antiphon, we join the psalmist in addressing the LORD and saying, "Do not give me up to the will of my adversaries, for false witnesses have risen against me, and they are breathing out violence" (Ps 27:12). We pray in confidence knowing that the death of Jesus leads to the resurrection of Christ.

Wednesday of Holy Week: Tree of Life[46]

This last full day of Lent is focused on the cross and the new life that emerged from that tree. The Entrance Antiphon, a pastiche of parts of verses from Paul's Letter to the Philippians, states that Christ Jesus "humbled himself and become obedient to the point of death—even death on a cross" (Phil 2:8). The Collect declares that God willed his Son to submit to the yoke of the cross, while the Prayer over the Offerings refers to the celebration of Jesus' passion in mystery. In the Prayer after Communion, we are reminded that Jesus' death in time, called a ransom in the Communion Antiphon

45. *Roman Missal*, 288.
46. *Roman Missal*, 289.

(Matt 20:28), is what we celebrate in the eucharist. The new life that comes from the cross is also found throughout today's Mass texts. The Entrance Antiphon declares that "at the name of Jesus every knee should bend, in heaven and on earth and under the earth, and every tongue should confess that Jesus Christ is Lord, to the glory of God the Father" (Phil 2:10–11). In the Collect, we petition God to give us the grace of the resurrection, while in the Prayer over the Gifts, we seek to experience the grace of Jesus' passion. We seek assurance of perpetual life in the Prayer after Communion. And in the last Lenten Prayer over the People, we ask God to enable us to share unceasingly in the paschal mysteries—the cross and resurrection—as we are led by our Lenten works to newness of life.

4

The Sacred Paschal Triduum

HOLY THURSDAY OF THE LORD'S SUPPER:
SACRED MEAL[1]

Wherever the memorial of the sacrifice of the cross is celebrated, the work of redemption is accomplished, states the Prayer over the Offerings. The Evening Mass of the Lord's Supper on Holy Thursday is focused on the celebration of the eucharist today as the sacrifice of the cross two thousand years ago. The Entrance Antiphon, a gloss from a verse in Paul's Letter to the Galatians, makes this clear: "May I never boast of anything except the cross of our Lord Jesus Christ, by which the world has been crucified to me, and I to the world" (Gal 6:14). The eucharist celebrates the cross, salvation, life, and resurrection. The Collect refers to the sacred supper, a sacrifice

---

1. *Roman Missal*, 298–313.

entrusted to the church for all eternity, as a banquet of love. The Preface identifies Jesus as the eternal priest who instituted the eucharistic pattern on the cross by offering himself to God and commanding us to do the same. The Communion Antiphon presents Paul's understanding of what Jesus did on the night before he died on the cross: ". . . [W]hen he had given thanks, he broke [the loaf of bread] and said, 'This is my body that is for you. Do this in remembrance of me.' In the same way he took the cup also, after supper, saying, 'This cup is the new covenant in my blood. Do this, as often as you drink it, in remembrance of me'" (1 Cor 11:24–25). Our prayer is that the celebration of the cross at the supper in this present time will bring us to the eternal banquet in eternity.

GOOD FRIDAY OF THE PASSION OF THE LORD: PASCHAL MYSTERY[2]

Today's liturgical texts explore the meaning of the paschal mystery. The first Prayer option explains that by shedding his blood Christ established the paschal mystery. The second Prayer option explains that Jesus abolished death for earthly people, and that through the sanctification of grace, he established new life for heavenly people. While the cross is being shown for veneration, we are told to behold the wood on which hung the salvation of the world; the cross is where the paschal mystery began. Thus, on this Good Friday, we pray that the church will persevere steadfastly in confessing God's name; we pray for the pope, for the local ministers—bishop, priests, and deacons—and all the faithful. We pray for catechumens, for Christian unity, for the Jews, for those who do not believe in Christ or God, for those in public office, and for those suffering any kind of tribulation—disease, hunger, imprisonment—and for the safe return of travelers. In the Prayer after Communion, we are reminded again that it was through his death and resurrection that Christ established the paschal mystery. And in the Prayer over the People, we seek God's abundant blessing for those who have honored the death of Jesus in the hope of sharing in his resurrection. We also petition God for pardon, comfort, an increase of faith, and assuredness of everlasting redemption.

2. *Roman Missal*, 314–38.

HOLY SATURDAY EASTER VIGIL
IN THE HOLY NIGHT: FIRE AND WATER[3]

Once darkness has descended on Holy Saturday evening, with the lighting of a blazing fire we declare that Christ has passed over from death to life. The words used to instruct those gathered around the fire use light to explain the paschal mystery. Jesus died in darkness, but Christ arose in light. We ask God to inflame us with heavenly desires in the prayer of blessing for the fire. Once the Paschal Candle—representing the risen Christ—is lit from the fire, we declare that it is the light of Christ rising in glory, dispelling the darkness of the night. In the Easter Proclamation, we note that the glorious light of the Paschal Candle floods the earth like lightning streaking from one end of the sky to the other, like the pillar of fire that lit the way for Israel through the Red Sea. Standing in the awesome glory of the light, we declare that the night is as bright as day. Even though the flame is shared, it is never dimmed; it overcomes the darkness and sheds light on all of us. In the Prayer after the Seventh Reading, we call upon God as eternal light and ask him to let the whole world know and see that what was cast down is raised up anew. The Collect echoes this idea, declaring that God made the night radiant with the glory of Christ's resurrection. Alleluia! Alleluia!

or

This is the night when Israel passed from slavery in Egypt to freedom by treading dry-shod through the Red Sea, states the Easter Proclamation. These are the waters of rebirth, according to the first option of the Prayer after the Third Reading. The Red Sea prefigures the baptismal font, according to the second option of the Prayer after the Third Reading. Likewise, the nation delivered from slavery prefigures the Christian people, who have been reborn by sharing the Spirit. In the waters of baptism, we are washed clean, according to the Prayer after the Sixth Reading. The minister's words before blessing water refer to the baptismal font as the place of rebirth, as does the prayer after the Litany of Saints. From the beginning of creation, states the Blessing of Baptismal Water, the Spirit has hovered over the waters, while the great flood foreshadowed regeneration. Jesus' own baptism in the Jordan River was his anointing with the Holy Spirit. The water that flowed from the Johannine Jesus' side represents the beginning of baptism. Thus, the minister asks God to fill the water with the Holy Spirit so that all who are washed clean in it will rise to new life as newborn children through water and the Spirit. Alleluia! Alleluia!

---

3. *Roman Missal*, 342–86.

EASTER SUNDAY OF THE RESURRECTION
OF THE LORD: RESURRECTION[4]

The Collect sets the theme for today's Mass texts. Through the resurrection of Jesus from the dead, God has conquered death. "I have risen," states Christ in the first option for the Entrance Antiphon, and "I am still with you. . . . [O LORD, you] lay your hand upon me. Such knowledge is too wonderful for me" (Ps 139: 18, 5–6). The second option for the Entrance Antiphon is a pastiche of verses from Luke's Gospel and the book of Revelation. "The Lord has risen indeed . . . ," the eleven are saying (Luke 24:34). ". . . [T]o him be glory and dominion forever and ever. Amen" (Rev 1:6). Alleluia is added to almost every line of both Entrance Antiphons and to the Communion Antiphon to express the paschal gladness by which the church is reborn and nourished (Prayer over the Offerings). Likewise, the Prayer after Communion mentions the paschal mysteries, which renew the church and bring her members to the glory of the resurrection. The Communion Antiphon summarizes the major points of Easter Sunday: ". . . [O]ur paschal lamb, Christ, has been sacrificed. Therefore, let us celebrate the festival . . . with the unleavened bread of sincerity and truth" (1 Cor 5:7b–8). Alleluia! Alleluia!

---

4. *Roman Missal*, 387–88.

5

The Easter Season

FIRST WEEK OF EASTER

Monday within the Octave of Easter: Risen[1]

The joyful celebration of the resurrection of Jesus Christ which was begun yesterday—Easter Sunday—flows now through fifty days of the Easter Season. The first option for the Entrance Antiphon, addressed to the newly baptized, declares: ". . . [T]he LORD [has brought you into] a land flowing with milk and honey . . . that the teaching of the LORD may be on your lips" (Exod 13:5, 9). The second option for the Entrance Antiphon declares that the Lord has risen from the dead; thus, we continue to exult and rejoice. In the Collect, we rejoice for those who were baptized during the Easter Vigil or

---

1. *Roman Missal*, 389.

on Easter Sunday, and we pray that all the baptized will hold fast to the faith. Likewise in the Prayer over the Offerings, we pray for renewed confession of God's name and the newly baptized. The newly baptized are referred to as those set on the way of salvation in the Prayer after Communion; we ask God to make them worthy of his gifts. The Communion Antiphon returns us to the resurrection; it states, "We know that Christ, being raised from the dead, will never die again; death no longer has dominion over him" (Rom 6:9). Alleluia!

Tuesday within the Octave of Easter: Paschal Remedies[2]

The theme permeating today's Mass texts is paschal remedies found in the Collect. Paschal refers to Easter, and remedies refer to the treatment for sin given by Jesus' death and resurrection. The Collect calls this a heavenly gift, which gladdens us now on earth with the hope of heavenly rejoicing. The same sentiment is found in the Prayer over the Offerings; we petition God to provide his protective care so that the remedies we have received will lead us to eternal gifts. Eternal happiness awaits those who have been baptized, according to the Prayer after Communion. The Entrance Antiphon, a gloss on two verses from the OT (A) book of Sirach mentions that Lady Wisdom gives "the water of wisdom to drink" (Sir 15:3); this water makes the drinkers strong and will raise them to eternal life. The paschal remedies have been accomplished by Jesus Christ. In the Communion Antiphon, the author of the Letter to the Colossians summarizes it this way: ". . . [I]f you have been raised with Christ, seek the things that are above, where Christ is, seated at the right hand of God. Set your minds on things that are above, not on things that are on earth" (Col 3:1–2). Alleluia!

Wednesday within the Octave of Easter: Transformation[3]

The theme permeating today's Mass texts is transformation. The Collect establishes the theme by declaring that God gladdens us every year with the Lord's resurrection so that we, who celebrate it, may be transformed like him into eternal joy. The Entrance Antiphon features the transforming words said to the sheep on the Son of Man's right hand, as told by the Matthean Jesus in a parable: "Come, you that are blessed by my Father, inherit the

---

2. *Roman Missal*, 390.

3. *Roman Missal*, 391.

kingdom prepared for you from the foundation of the world" (Matt 25:34). The Prayer over the Offerings seeks God's transformation of salvation of mind and body in us. We ask to be cleansed of all old ways and transformed into a new creation in the Prayer after Communion. And the Communion Antiphon, taken from the Lukan narrative of the two disciples on their way from Jerusalem to Emmaus, explains how Jesus "had been made known to them in the breaking of the bread" (Luke 24:35); the two disciples were transformed by their encounter in word and then in breaking bread with the risen Christ. Our prayer is that we, too, recognize the risen Lord in his word and sacrament. Alleluia!

Thursday within the Octave of Easter: Reborn[4]

The focus of today's Mass texts is on the newly baptized from the Easter Vigil and Easter Sunday—both adults and children. In the Collect, we pray for all who have been reborn in the baptismal font that they will be united in faith and in deed. We offer our gifts of bread and wine for those reborn in hope of God's increased help (Prayer over the Offerings). The Communion Antiphon continues the theme, stating that the newly baptized "are a chosen race, a royal priesthood, a holy nation, God's own people in order that [they] may proclaim the mighty acts of him who called [them] out of darkness into his marvelous light" (1 Pet 2:9). The voices of newly baptized infants are heard in the Entrance Antiphon: ". . . [T]he righteous . . . sang hymns, O Lord, to your holy name, and praised with one accord your defending hand; for wisdom opened the mouths of those who were mute, and made the tongues of infants speak clearly" (Wis 10:20–21). In the Prayer after Communion, we ask God to hear all of us and bring us help in this life to ensure us of eternal gladness. Alleluia!

Friday within the Octave of Easter: Paschal Mystery[5]

Today's Mass texts are focused on the paschal mystery: the death of Jesus and the resurrection of Christ. The Collect declares that God gave the paschal mystery to us in order to reconcile the human race. In the Prayer over the Offerings, we ask God to perfect within us the exchange that takes place in the paschal offerings. And in the Prayer after Communion, we name the

4. *Roman Missal*, 392.
5. *Roman Missal*, 393.

passion (suffering and death) of Jesus as our means of redemption, and we rejoice in his resurrection. The new passover of Jesus from death to life is paralleled in the Entrance Antiphon—which recounts the first passover—when the Israelites passed over from death to life before crossing the Red Sea: "[God] led [the Israelites] in safety, so that they were not afraid; but the sea overwhelmed their enemies" (Ps 78:53). The Communion Antiphon serves as a reminder of celebrating the paschal mystery in the eucharist: "Jesus said to [his disciples], 'Come and have breakfast.' Jesus . . . took the bread and gave it to them, and he did the same with the fish" (John 21:12a, 13). Our prayer is that God will so dispose our minds to what we celebrate in faith that it may be expressed in our deeds (Collect). Alleluia!

Saturday within the Octave of Easter: Baptism[6]

The theme of baptism is woven through today's Mass texts. In the Collect, we acknowledge that it is by the abundance of God's grace that he gives increase to the number of people who believe in him. Then, we ask him to look with divine favor and to clothe with immortality those he has chosen for baptism. The Prayer over the Offerings contains the reference to baptism in the phrase *paschal mysteries*, which celebrates the death and resurrection of Christ and every person baptized. This is made clear in the Communion Antiphon: "As many of you as were baptized into Christ have clothed yourselves with Christ" (Gal 3:27). The theme is also found in the Prayer after Communion in which we ask God to look with kindness on those he was pleased to renew by eternal mysteries and to grant them the incorruptible glory of the resurrection. The Entrance Antiphon, a vague reference to the exodus through the Red Sea, further emphasizes baptism: "[The LORD] brought his people out with joy, his chosen ones with singing" (Ps 105:43). By dying, Jesus destroyed our death, we pray in the Preface I of Easter, and by rising, he restored our life.[7] Baptism begins the process of being reborn into resurrected life. Alleluia!

---

6. *Roman Missal*, 394.
7. *Roman Missal*, 558–59.

SECOND WEEK OF EASTER

Second Sunday of Easter: Paschal Feast[8]

In the Prayer after Communion, we pray that our reception of the paschal sacrament—the body and blood of the risen Christ—may have an effect that continues in our minds and hearts. The effect that we want to continue is found in the Collect, which begins by naming God's mercy in giving us the yearly celebration of the paschal feast. Then, the prayer presents the elements of the paschal feast: the font in which we have been washed, the Spirit in whom we have been reborn, and the blood in whom we have been redeemed. That is why the first choice of an Entrance Antiphon states, "Like newborn infants, long for the pure, spiritual milk, so that by it you may grow into salvation" (1 Pet 2:2). The Prayer over the Offerings, which contains an optional line—about those brought to new birth through baptism—asks God to accept the gifts of bread and wine so that we may be renewed in confession of God's name. The point about confessing God's name is illustrated in the Communion Antiphon. Jesus tells Thomas, "Put your finger here and see my hands. Reach out your hand and put it in my side. Do not doubt but believe" (John 20:27). Alleluia! Alleluia!

Monday of the Second Week of Easter: Renewal[9]

Renewal means to begin something again. Renewal is the theme of today's Mass texts. The Entrance Antiphon speaks of the renewal of life that took place in the dead body of Jesus in the tomb: "We know that Christ, being raised from the dead, will never die again; death no longer has dominion over him" (Rom 6:9). In the Collect, we declare that God has renewed us with paschal remedies, causing us to transcend our earthly image and to be transformed into the heavenly image of the risen Christ. Renewal is found in the Prayer over the Offerings, in which we exult that the gifts of bread and wine we bring bear fruit eternally while causing us great gladness right now. The Prayer after Communion returns to the theme of renewal having taken place through eternal mysteries which bring about the incorruptible glory of the resurrection. Renewal is possible because, in the words of the Communion Antiphon, "Jesus came [on the evening of the resurrection]

8. *Roman Missal*, 395–96.
9. *Roman Missal*, 397.

and stood among [his disciples] and said, 'Peace be with you'" (John 20:19). And with that greeting he renewed their faith in him.

Tuesday of the Second Week of Easter: Rejoice[10]

Rejoicing and gladness permeate today's Mass texts. The Entrance Antiphon establishes it: "Let us rejoice and exult and give [God] the glory . . . . For the Lord our God the Almighty reigns" (Rev 19:7a, 6b). In the Collect, we ask God to enable us to proclaim the power of the risen Lord, while, in the Prayer over the Offerings, we seek delight in the paschal mysteries that God's ongoing renewal in us may be the cause of our joy. We ask God to hear our prayer for help in this life and ensure our eternal gladness in the Prayer after Communion. Our rejoicing and gladness spark us to look forward to possess the fullness of God's gift in our own resurrection (Collect), as we already share it in the holy exchange of bread and wine into the body and blood of Christ which redeems us now (Prayer after Communion). Our rejoicing and gladness is best understood from Christ's instructions to his disciples: "Thus it is written, that the Messiah is to suffer and to rise from the dead on the third day. Was it not necessary that the Messiah should suffer these things and then enter into his glory?" (Luke 24:46, 26) We rejoice and are glad because we know the power of Jesus' suffering as our own.

Wednesday of the Second Week of Easter: Dignity[11]

According to today's Mass texts, we have already been restored to our original dignity by the death and resurrection of Christ; yet, we do not posses it totally or fully. Our yearly remembrance of Christ's resurrection, according to the Collect, is to celebrate in faith what we hope to possess one day in unending love by rising again (Collect). The Prayer over the Offerings refers to this as a wonderful exchange—both of bread and wine and death for life— which enables us to partake in the Godhead now, as we continue to grow in truth and demonstrate it with a worthy way of life. God imbues us with heavenly mysteries now, states the Prayer after Communion, so that we pass over every day to new life in God's presence. The Communion Antiphon reminds us that Jesus chose us out of the world and appointed us to go and bear fruit that will last (John 15:16, 19). Thus, the best response we can give

10. *Roman Missal*, 398.

11. *Roman Missal*, 399.

to God's initiative is found in the Entrance Antiphon: ". . . I will extol you, O LORD, among the nations . . . . I will tell of your name to my brothers and sisters . . ." (Pss 18:49; 22:22).

Thursday of the Second Week of Easter: Presence[12]

Today's Mass texts are about the effects of divine presence. The Entrance Antiphon begins this theme by recalling the LORD's presence with his people during the Exodus: "O God, when you went out before you people, when you marched through the wilderness, the earth quaked, the heavens poured down rain . . . at the presence of God, the God of Israel" (Ps 68:7–8). The Collect presents the effects of the paschal sacrifice of Jesus Christ for the salvation of the world: Serving as high priest, Christ now intercedes on our behalf with God. Because he was like us in body, he brings us reconciliation with God; because he was like God in divinity, he frees us from sin. The effect of God's purifying graciousness, according to the Prayer over the Offerings, is that our prayers rise to God with the gifts of bread and wine, and he conforms both us and them to the mysteries of his love. We are restored to eternal life by the resurrection of Christ, according to the Prayer after Communion, so we ask God to increase the fruits of his paschal sacrament while filling our hearts with the strength of the saving food of the body and blood of his Son. Finally, the effect of the resurrection, according to the Communion Antiphon, is Christ's presence with us always until the end of the age (Matt 28:20).

Friday of the Second Week of Easter: Praise[13]

On this second Friday of the Easter Season, we proclaim God's praise. The Entrance Antiphon states that we praise God for redemption accomplished by the Lamb: ". . . [Y]ou were slaughtered and by your blood you ransomed for God saints from every tribe and language and people and nation; you have made them to be a kingdom and priests serving our God . . ." (Rev 5:9b–10). In the Collect, we praise God for disposing our hearts to offer him worthy prayer. In the Prayer over the Offerings, we praise God in accepting our gifts and for keeping us in his protective care so that we never lose what we have received from him. In the Prayer after Communion, we praise God

12. *Roman Missal*, 400.

13. *Roman Missal*, 401.

for having redeemed us through the passion of his Son and enabled us to rejoice in his Son's resurrection. Our praise in the Communion Antiphon is an acclamation from Paul's Letter to the Romans: "[Jesus our Lord] was handed over to death for our trespasses and was raised for our justification" (Rom 4:25). We praise God for enabling us to extol him by dutifully proclaiming his praise (Collect).

Saturday of the Second Week of Easter: Chosen[14]

Today's Entrance Antiphon establishes the theme of today's Mass texts: ". . . [Y]ou are a chosen race, a royal priesthood, a holy nation, God's own people, in order that you may proclaim the mighty acts of him who called you out of darkness into his marvelous light" (1 Pet 2:9). In the first optional Collect, we declare that through the paschal mystery, God has cancelled the sentence of death—calling us out of darkness—through the resurrection of Christ—into his marvelous light. In the second optional Collect, we declare that through the paschal mysteries, God has opened the gates of his mercy, and we pray that he will keep us on the path of life. In the Prayer over the Offerings, we ask God to sanctify our gifts and ourselves so that we, his chosen race, his royal priesthood, his holy nation, his own people, become an eternal offering to him. By receiving the body and blood of Christ, we share in the paschal mystery of Jesus' death and Christ's resurrection, we state in the Prayer after Communion. Our prayer is that our gifts offered and received will cause growth in charity in us. Our glimpse of marvelous light now is but a foretaste of what awaits us. The Communion Antiphon quotes the Johannine Jesus' desire: "Father, I desire that those also, whom you have given me, may be with me where I am, to see my glory, which you have given me because you loved me before the foundation of the world" (John 17:24).

THIRD WEEK OF EASTER

Third Sunday of Easter: Joy[15]

The theme for the Third Sunday of Easter is established in the Entrance Antiphon: "Make a joyful noise to God, all the earth; sing the glory of his name; give to him glorious praise" (Ps 66:1–2). Joy continues in the Collect. We

---

14. *Roman Missal*, 402.

15. *Roman Missal*, 403–4.

ask God to let us exult forever in our renewed youthfulness of spirit. Then, we ask that as we rejoice now in the glory of our adoption, so one day may we rejoice on the day of resurrection. The Prayer over the Offerings refers to us as an exultant church to which God gives the cause for great gladness—resurrection—which will one day result in perpetual happiness. Two of the three Communion Antiphons—there is a choice for each cycle of Scripture texts—are focused on recognizing Jesus in the breaking of bread which results in great joy (Luke 24:35; John 21:12–13). Anyone of the five possible Easter Prefaces contains the joy of praising God even more gloriously during the Easter Season as we celebrate the sacrifice of Christ, our Passover.[16] We declare that we, every land, and every people are overcome with paschal joy resulting in shouts of praise even as we await the glory of our own resurrection (Prayer after Communion).

Monday of the Third Week of Easter: Transformation[17]

Transformation permeates today's Mass texts. The Entrance Antiphon, which identifies Jesus as the good shepherd, declares that the one who willingly laid down his life for his flock of sheep has been raised—transformed. In the Collect, we acknowledge our own transformation that has occurred because we put away our old selves in order to live like Christ, who has healed us with his paschal remedies—death and resurrection—which conform our new selves to Christ's nature. The Prayer over the Offerings explains the transformation that occurs when bread and wine are offered to God; he changes them into the body and blood of his Son. Likewise, our prayers rising to God transform us by God's mighty love. Our transformation results in peace, not peace that the world gives—as stated in the Communion Antiphon—but the peace that the risen Christ gives (John 14:27). Through the eucharist, we are transformed, that is, restored from earthly life to eternal life; our prayer is that God will increase the fruits of the eucharistic passover and strengthen us with its food throughout our lifetime of transformation into the nature of Christ.

16. *Roman Missal*, 558–67.
17. *Roman Missal*, 405.

Tuesday of the Third Week of Easter: Open Gates[18]

The operative metaphor in today's Collect is opening the gates. In the ancient world of walled cities, an open gate was a liability, especially at night. An enemy could sneak into the city and cause lasting harm. So, at a certain time in the evening, all the gates to the outside world were locked and bared, much like forts in the days of the Wild West. Today's Collect declares that God has made his heavenly kingdom vulnerable by opening wide its gates to all who have been reborn of water and the Spirit. Thus, we pray that God will increase grace in us so that with all sin removed, we may not be lacking in anything that he has promised. So, as we stand before the heavenly gates, we sing the Entrance Antiphon: "Praise our God, all you his servants, and all who fear him, small and great. Now have come the salvation and the power and the kingdom of our God and the authority of his Messiah . . ." (Rev 19:5; 12:10a). The Prayer over the Offering and the Prayer after Communion are the same as for the Third Sunday of Easter. However, the Communion Antiphon echoes the means of crossing through the gates into the heavenly city: ". . . [I]f we have died with Christ, we believe that we will also live with him" (Rom 6:8).

Wednesday of the third Week of Easter: Universal Renewal[19]

Because the Prayer over the Offerings and the Prayer after Communion for today are the same as those for Tuesday of the Second Week of Easter, we will focus on today's Collect and antiphons. The Collect asks God to be present to his family; because God is present everywhere and at all time, the prayer is asking God to raise our awareness of his presence. We ask him to ensure that those he has endowed with the grace of faith will share eternally in the resurrection of Christ. Preface IV of Easter captures this idea when it declares that the old order has been destroyed, the whole universe has been renewed, and integrity of life has been restored through Christ's resurrection.[20] The Communion Antiphon declares that Christ has redeemed us with his blood, and he has been raised, bathing us in his light. Our response to this great deed of God's Son is found in the Entrance Antiphon: "My mouth is filled with your praise [, O LORD], and with your glory all day long. My lips will shout for joy when I sing praises to you . . ." (Ps 71:8, 23).

18. *Roman Missal*, 406.

19. *Roman Missal*, 407.

20. *Roman Missal*, 564–65.

Thursday of the Third Week of Easter: Compassion[21]

Compassion is the theme in today's Collect. The Prayer over the Offerings and the Prayer after Communion for today are the same as for Wednesday of the Second Week of Easter; thus, our focus is on the Collect and the antiphons. We ask God to let us feel his compassion in the Collect. It is during the Easter Season that God's sympathy for us becomes visible in the suffering and death of his Son, Jesus Christ. During the Easter Season, we are made more aware of God's gift of compassion, as we remember the death and resurrection of his Son. We ask that we, who have been freed from darkness, may hold firmly to the truth. This sentiment is reinforced in the Communion Antiphon: ". . . [Christ] died for all, so that those who live might live no longer for themselves, but for him who died and was raised for them" (2 Cor 5:15). Our response to God's compassion is provided in the Entrance Antiphon: "I will sing to the LORD, for he has triumphed gloriously . . . . The LORD is my strength and my might, and he has become my salvation" (Exod 15:1b, 2a). God's triumph, strength, and might are demonstrations of his compassion.

Friday of the Third Week of Easter: From Death to Life[22]

There is a movement from death to life that grounds today's Mass texts. The theme is established by the Entrance Antiphon: "Worthy is the Lamb that was slaughtered to receive power and wealth and wisdom and might and honor and glory and blessing!" (Rev 5:12) Likewise, the Communion Antiphon declares that the crucified One is risen from the dead, and he has redeemed us. According to the Collect, through the eucharist we come to know the grace that flows from the Lord's resurrection. In the Prayer over the Offerings, we seek God's sanctification and acceptance of our gifts, which represent the death and resurrection of his Son. Then, after sharing the body and blood of the crucified and risen Christ, in the Prayer after Communion, we state that we have done what Jesus commanded us to do in his memory and pray that it will bring us growth in charity. The Collect reminds us that it is the love of the Holy Spirit that brings us to new life on the other side of death. Our spiritual sacrifices here and now, according to the Prayer over the Offerings, represent death, but by eternally offering ourselves to God, we receive newness of life, just like Jesus did.

21. *Roman Missal*, 408.
22. *Roman Missal*, 409.

Saturday of the Third Week of Easter: Baptism[23]

Because today's Prayer over the Offerings and Prayer after Communion are the same as Friday of the Second Week of Easter, we will focus on the Collect and the antiphons. That focus is baptism. The Entrance Antiphon establishes it: "[W]hen you were buried with [Christ] in baptism, you were also raised with him through faith in the power of God, who raised him from the dead" (Col 2:12). The Collect picks up the focus by mentioning the font of baptism in which God has made new those who believe in him. We ask God to keep safe all who have been reborn in baptism with his Son by defeating every onslaught of error and preserving faithfully the grace of God's blessing bestowed in baptism. We ask God to keep us from losing what we have received in baptism. We are able to accomplish this through unity among God's chosen people. The Communion Antiphon, a prayer of Jesus, expresses this: "I ask . . . that they may all be one. As you, Father, are in me and I am in you, may they also be in us, so that the world may believe that you sent me" (John 17:20–21).

FOURTH WEEK OF EASTER

Fourth Sunday of Easter: Shepherd and Sheep[24]

The Communion Antiphon for today establishes the major theme of the Mass texts: shepherd and sheep. It proclaims that the good shepherd, Jesus, who laid down his life and willingly died for his sheep, has been raised. The Collect refers to us as a humble flock; we desire to follow our brave shepherd, Jesus Christ, to the joys of heaven. In the Prayer after Communion, we petition God, the kind shepherd, to look upon the flock—the sheep he has redeemed with the blood of his Son—and to settle it in eternal pastures. The Communion Antiphon and prayers contain obvious echoes of Psalm 23; even though the Prayer over the Offerings is repeated from Saturday within the Octave of Easter, Tuesday of Week Two of Easter, and Wednesday of Week Three of Easter, its reference to paschal mysteries reminds us of the passover lamb to which Jesus is often compared. The Entrance Antiphon paints a broader pastoral picture, declaring, ". . . [T]he earth is full of the steadfast love of the LORD. By the word of the LORD the heavens were made . . ." (Ps 33:5–6).

23. *Roman Missal*, 410.
24. *Roman Missal*, 411.

Monday of the Fourth Week of Easter: Paschal Mysteries[25]

Today's Prayer over the Offerings is the same for Monday of the Second Week of Easter, the Third Sunday of Easter, and Tuesday of the Third Week of Easter, and the Prayer after Communion is the same as Saturday within the Octave of Easter, Monday of the Second Week of Easter, Sunday of the Third Week of Easter, and Tuesday of the Third Week of Easter. Thus, our focus is on the antiphons and the Collect. The Collect refers to God as the light of the blessed, who has given us the gift of the paschal mysteries on earth. The Entrance Antiphon specifies what the paschal mysteries are: "We know that Christ, being raised from the dead, will never die again; death no longer has dominion over him" (Rom 6:9). Jesus died, and God raised him from the dead—those are the paschal mysteries. The Communion Antiphon specifies the resurrection: "When it was evening on that day, the first day of the week, and the doors of the house where the disciples had met were locked for fear of the Jews, Jesus came and stood among them and said, 'Peace be with you'" (John 20:19). Our prayer in the Collect is that we may rejoice for ages unending in the full measure of God's grace demonstrated in the resurrection of his Son.

Tuesday of the Fourth Week of Easter: Glorious Rejoicing[26]

Today's Prayer over the Offerings is the same for Saturday within the Octave of Easter, Tuesday of the Second Week of Easter, Wednesday of the Third Week of Easter, and the Fourth Sunday of Easter, and the Prayer after Communion is the same as Thursday within the Octave of Easter, Tuesday of the Second Week of Easter, and Wednesday of the Third Week of Easter. Thus, our focus is on the antiphons and the Collect. The Entrance Antiphon establishes the theme of rejoicing. "Let us rejoice and exult and give [the Lord our God] the glory. For the Lord our God the Almighty reigns" (Rev 19:7a, 6b). The Collect continues the theme of rejoicing with its statement about celebrating the Lord's resurrection. Our prayer is that God will grant our desire to merit the joy of our redemption. The Communion Antiphon, two pieced-together verses from Luke's Gospel, reminds us "that the Messiah [was] to suffer and to rise from the dead on the third day . . . and then enter into his glory" (Luke 24:46, 26). Christ's resurrected glory is what keeps us rejoicing throughout the Season of Easter.

25. *Roman Missal*, 412.
26. *Roman Missal*, 413.

Wednesday of the Third Week of Easter: Descriptions of God[27]

Today's Prayer over the Offerings and Prayer after Communion are the same for Wednesday of the Second Week of Easter and Thursday of the Third Week of Easter. Thus, our focus is on the antiphons and the Collect. Three descriptions of God are given in the Collect. First, God is declared to be the life of the faithful; those who trust God are given his grace, his very life. Second, God is described as the glory of the humble; those who submit to God's love enjoy his guiding presence in which they exult. And third, God is the blessedness of the just; those who do what is right are declared to be blissful for doing the right thing. The Communion Antiphon, words of Jesus from John's Gospel, further explains these three descriptions: "You did not choose me but I chose you [out of the world]. And I appointed you to go and bear fruit, fruit that will last . . ." (John 15:16, 19). In the Collect, we ask God to listen to our prayers that we may thirst for what he promises and have our fill of his plenty. Then, in the words of the Entrance Antiphon, we can declare: ". . . I will extol you, O LORD, among the nations . . . . I will tell of your name to my brothers and sisters . . ." (Pss 18:49; 22:22).

Thursday of the Fourth Week of Easter: Earthquake and Rain[28]

Today's Prayer over the Offerings and Prayer after Communion are the same for Thursday of the Second Week of Easter and Monday of the Third Week of Easter. Thus, our focus is on the antiphons and the Collect. Today's Entrance Antiphon recalls two aspects of a theophany—a manifestation of God's presence: an earthquake and rain. "O God, when you went out before you people, when you marched through the wilderness, the earth quaked, the heavens poured down rain . . . at the presence of God, the God of Israel" (Ps 68:7–8). The Collect considers God's restoration of human nature to a greater dignity than it had when he first created it to be another theophany or manifestation of his presence. His enduring presence is emphasized in the Communion Antiphon, the last line of Jesus in Matthew's Gospel: ". . . Remember, I am with you always, to the end of the age" (Matt 28:20). While standing in God's presence, in the Collect, we ask him to remember his loving kindness, especially toward all those who have been baptized, and

27. *Roman Missal*, 414.
28. *Roman Missal*, 415.

to preserve in them the gifts of grace and blessing, that is, awareness of his enduring presence.

Friday of the Fourth Week of Easter: Redemption[29]

Today's Prayer over the Offerings is the same for Tuesday within the Octave of Easter, Friday of the Second Week of Easter, and Saturday of the Third Week of Easter, and the Prayer after Communion is the same for Friday within the Octave of Easter, Friday of the Second Week of Easter, and Saturday of the Third Week of Easter. Thus, our focus is on the antiphons and the Collect which express the theme of redemption. The Entrance Antiphon establishes that theme by presenting a portion of the song of the four living creatures and the twenty-four elders to the Lamb: ". . . [B]y your blood you ransomed for God saints from every tribe and language and people and nation; you have made them to be a kingdom of priests serving our God . . ." (Rev 5:9b–10). The Collect addresses God as the author of freedom and salvation who has redeemed people through the shedding of his Son's blood. The Communion Antiphon refers to redemption as a handing over: "[Jesus our Lord] was handed over to death for our trespasses and was raised for our justification" (Rom 4:25). Our prayer, then, is that God will grant us life, protect us, and enable us to rejoice in redemption unharmed forever (Collect).

Saturday of the Fourth Week of Easter: Eternal Life[30]

Today's Prayer over the Offerings and Prayer after Communion are the same for Saturday of the Second Week of Easter and Friday of the Third Week of Easter. Thus, our focus is on the antiphons and the Collect which present us the result of Easter: eternal life. In the Collect, we ask God to show benevolence to us and to let our observance of Easter benefit us for eternal life. The death and resurrection of Jesus is referred to as the heavenly remedy given to us in our celebration of Easter for fifty days. Eternal life is the Johannine Jesus' prayer in the Communion Antiphon: "Father, I desire that those also, whom you have given me, may be with me where I am, to see my glory, which you have given me . . ." (John 17:24). Likewise, the Entrance Antiphon reminds us that we "are a chosen race, a royal priesthood, a holy nation, God's own people, in order that [we] may proclaim the mighty acts of him who called

29. *Roman Missal*, 416.
30. *Roman Missal*, 417.

[us] out of darkness into his marvelous light" (1 Pet 2:9). Our summons into God's marvelous light is our call to begin to enjoy eternal life now.

FIFTH WEEK OF EASTER

Fifth Sunday of Easter: Bearing Fruit[31]

The Mass texts for the Fifth Sunday of Easter are focused on bearing fruit. The Communion Antiphon establishes this theme by employing words of the Johannine Jesus: "I am the true vine, and my Father is the vinegrower. I am the vine, you are the branches. Those who abide in me and I in them bear much fruit . . ." (John 15:1, 5). The bearing-fruit theme is expressed in the Collect as God always being in the process of accomplishing the paschal mystery within us. The paschal mystery is the death and resurrection of Jesus that first takes place, as the Collect makes clear, in baptism's death and resurrection. Those who are made new in this way are placed under God's protective care so that they can bear much fruit and come to the joy of eternal life. Thus, in the Entrance Antiphon, we state: "O sing to the Lord a new song, for he has done marvelous things. . . . [H]e has revealed his vindication in the sight of the nations" (Ps 98:1a, 2). The Prayer over the Offerings and the Prayer after Communion are the same as Wednesday of the Second Week of Easter, Thursday of the Third Week of Easter, and Wednesday of the Fourth Week of Easter.

Monday of the Fifth Week of Easter: Right Hand[32]

We seek God's everlasting help in today's Collect, which refers to his right hand. In biblical understanding, the right hand is the place of power. So, the Collect asks God to encompass us with his right hand in order to defend us from all evil with the resurrection of Jesus Christ, God's Son. In other words, God's power was demonstrated by raising Christ from the dead. So protected with God's right hand (power), states the Collect, we make our way in this life using God's heavenly gifts. The Entrance Antiphon expresses a similar idea by referring to Christ as the good shepherd who laid down his life for the sheep and willingly died for the whole flock. The Communion Antiphon, some of the Johannine Jesus' words to his disciples before his

31. *Roman Missal*, 418.
32. *Roman Missal*, 419.

death, expresses his gift of peace to them: "Peace I leave with you; my peace I give to you. I do not give to you as the world gives" (John 14:27ab). The Prayer over the Offerings and the Prayer after Communion are the same as Thursday of the Second Week of Easter, Monday of the Third Week of Easter, and Thursday of the Fourth Week of Easter.

Tuesday of the Fifth Week of Easter: Death Destroyed, Life Restored[33]

The theme of today's Mass texts is best expressed in Preface I of Easter. By dying, Christ our passover has destroyed our death, and by rising, he restored our life.[34] The Collect expresses this by declaring that God restored us to eternal life by raising Christ from the dead. And the Communion Antiphon expresses the theme of restoration this way: ". . . [I]f we have died with Christ, we believe that we will also live with him" (Rom 6:8). Our prayer is that God will give us constancy in faith and hope so that we do not doubt the promise of eternal life he has made to us. With such faith and hope, we echo parts of songs from the CB (NT) book of Revelation in the Entrance Antiphon: "Praise our God, all you his servants, and all who fear him, small and great. Now have come the salvation and the power and the kingdom of our God and the authority of his Messiah . . . (Rev 19:5; 12:10a). The Prayer over the Offerings is the same as Monday of the Second Week of Easter, the Third Sunday of Easter, Tuesday of the Third Week of Easter, and Monday of the Fourth Week of Easter. The Prayer after Communion is the same as Saturday of the First Week of Easter, Monday of the Second Week of Easter, the Third Sunday of Easter, Tuesday of the Third Week of Easter, and Monday of the Fourth Week of Easter.

Wednesday of the Fifth Week of Easter: Restorer of Innocence[35]

Today's Collect addresses God as a restorer and a lover of innocence. As a restorer, God returns us to our original created condition through the death and resurrection of his Son, Jesus Christ. As a lover of innocence, God removes our sin, creating us anew. This last point is highlighted by the Communion Antiphon, which declares the Lord risen and shining his light on all

33. *Roman Missal*, 420.
34. *Roman Missal*, 558–59.
35. *Roman Missal*, 421.

whom he has redeemed—restored to innocence—by his blood shed on the cross. Our prayer is that God direct our hearts to himself so that those who have been restored and created anew—set free from darkness—may never stray from the light of truth. We praise God in the words of the Entrance Antiphon: "My mouth is filled with your praise, and with you glory all day long. My lips will shout for joy when I sing praises to you . . ." (Ps 71:8, 23). The Prayer over the Offerings is the same as Saturday within the Octave of Easter, Tuesday of the Second Week of Easter, Wednesday of the Third Week of Easter, the Fourth Sunday of Easter, and Tuesday of the Fourth Week of Easter. The Prayer after Communion is the same as Thursday within the Octave of Easter, Tuesday of the Second Week of Easter, Wednesday of the Third Week of Easter, and Tuesday of the Fourth Week of Easter.

Thursday of the Fifth Week of Easter: Glorious Triumph[36]

The Entrance Antiphon captures the spirit of today's Mass texts: "I will sing to the LORD, for he has triumphed gloriously . . . . The LORD is my strength and my might, and he has become my salvation" (Exod 15:1b, 2a). God's gloriously triumph of the escape of the Israelites from the Egyptian pharaoh and his army is applied to the triumph of Christ over death. The Communion Antiphon states, ". . . [Christ] died for all, so that those who live might live no longer for themselves, but for him who died and was raised for them" (2 Cor 5:15). In the Collect, we name God's glorious triumph as grace which makes sinners just and turns the pitiable into the blessed. Thus, we ask God to stand by his works and gifts and those he has justified by faith so they do not lack perseverance but remain confident that they will triumph gloriously with Christ. The Prayer over the Offerings and the Prayer after Communion are the same as Wednesday of the Second Week of Easter, Thursday of the Third Week of Easter, Wednesday of the Fourth Week of Easter, and the Fifth Sunday of Easter.

Friday of the Fifth Week of Easter: Conformed[37]

According to today's Collect, we have been conformed to the paschal mysteries. This means that through baptism into death and resurrection, we have died and been raised with Christ; we have been shaped into his pattern of

---

36. *Roman Missal*, 422.

37. *Roman Missal*, 423.

death and life. His death and resurrection are the paschal or passover mysteries. The Entrance Antiphon emphasizes this: "Worthy is the Lamb that was slaughtered to receive power and wealth and wisdom and might and honor and glory and blessing!" (Rev 5:12) Likewise, the Communion Antiphon emphasizes the same paschal mysteries in declaring that the crucified One is risen from the dead, and he redeemed us. Thus, duly conformed to the paschal mysteries, we pray that the joy of our celebration of Christ's death and resurrection may both protect and save us with its perpetual power. The Prayer over the Offerings and the Prayer after Communion are the same as Saturday of the Second Week of Easter, Friday of the Third Week of Easter, and Saturday of the Fourth Week of Easter.

Saturday of the Fifth Week of Easter: Baptismal Death and Resurrection[38]

Baptism is the theme expressed in today's Collect. It is through the regenerating power of baptism that God confers heavenly life on us. This is so because baptism is a death and resurrection like Christ's. The Entrance Antiphon makes this clear: "[W]hen you were buried with [Christ] in baptism, you were also raised with him through faith in the power of God, who raised him from the dead" (Col 2:12). The Collect states that through baptism God renders us capable of immortality by justifying us. Our prayer is that he will guide us to the fullness of glory. That fullness is expressed by the Johannine Jesus' prayer in the Communion Antiphon for those who will believe in Jesus through the word of his disciples. Jesus prays that "they may all be one. As you Father, are in me and I am in you, may they also be in us, so that the world may believe that you have sent me" (John 17:21). The Prayer over the Offerings is the same as Tuesday within the Octave of Easter, Friday of the Second Week of Easter, Saturday of the Third Week of Easter, and Friday of the Fourth Week of Easter. The Prayer after Communion is the same as Friday within the Octave of Easter, Friday of the Second Week of Easter, Saturday of the Third Week of Easter, and Friday of the Fourth Week of Easter.

38. *Roman Missal*, 424.

SIXTH WEEK OF EASTER

Sixth Sunday of Easter: Days of Joy[39]

As early as the Sixth Sunday of Easter, with two weeks of the Easter Season remaining, there is already attention being given to Pentecost. The Communion Antiphon contains these words of the Johannine Jesus: "If you love me, you will keep my commandments. And I will ask the Father, and he will give you another Advocate, to be with you forever" (John 14:15–16). However, even with this reference to the Advocate (Paraclete), the primary focus is on our heartfelt celebration and devotion given to these Easter days of joy, as stated in the Collect. The Entrance Antiphon exhorts: ". . . [D]eclare this with a shout of joy, proclaim it, send it forth to the end of the earth; say, 'The LORD has redeemed his servant Jacob!'" (Isa 48:20) Our prayer in the Collect is that what we are reliving in remembrance—the death and resurrection of Christ—we may demonstrate in all we do. The Prayer over the Offerings and the Prayer after Communion are the same as Thursday of the Second Week of Easter, Monday of the Third Week of Easter, Thursday of the Fourth Week of Easter, and Monday of the Fifth Week of Easter.

Monday of the Sixth Week of Easter: Paschal Fruit[40]

The Prayer over the Offerings is the same as Monday of the Second Week of Easter, the Third Sunday of Easter, Tuesday of the Third Week of Easter, Monday of the Fourth Week of Easter, and Tuesday of the Fifth Week of Easter, and the Prayer after Communion is the same as Saturday within the Octave of Easter, Tuesday of the Second Week of Easter, Wednesday of the Third Week of Easter, the Fourth Sunday of Easter, Tuesday of the Fourth Week of Easter, and Wednesday of the Fifth Week of Easter. Thus, only the antiphons and Collect will be presented here. The Collect asks our merciful God to enable us to experience the fruit produced by the paschal observances. In other words, we petition God to grant us to live in the death and resurrection of Christ. The Entrance Antiphon explores this further: "We know that Christ, being raised from the dead, will never die again; death no longer has dominion over him" (Rom 6:9). Now we, who have died and been raised in the waters of baptism, will never die again. Another fruit of marking Easter is the peace that results from knowing that death no longer has power over

---

39. *Roman Missal*, 425.
40. *Roman Missal*, 426.

us. The Communion Antiphon states, ". . . Jesus came and stood among [his disciples] and said, 'Peace be with you'" (John 20:19).

Tuesday of the Sixth Week of Easter: Sharing in Resurrection[41]

The Prayer over the Offerings is the same as Saturday within the Octave of Easter, Tuesday of the Second Week of Easter, Wednesday of the Third Week of Easter, the Fourth Sunday of Easter, Tuesday of the Fourth Week of Easter, and Wednesday of the Fifth Week of Easter, and the Prayer after Communion is the same as Thursday within the Octave of Easter, Tuesday of the Second Week of Easter, Wednesday of the Third Week of Easter, Tuesday of the Fourth Week of Easter, and Wednesday of the Fifth Week of Easter. The Collect very simply petitions God to give us a share in the resurrection of Christ, who, in the Communion Antiphon states "that the Messiah is to suffer and to rise from the dead on the third day . . . and then enter into his glory" (Luke 24:46, 26). Our petition is that we may in truth experience the new and eternal life that Jesus now shares with the Father and the Spirit after we, too, are raised from the dead. Thus, in the Entrance Antiphon, we join the great multitude singing, "For the Lord our God the Almighty reigns, Let us rejoice and exult and give him the glory . . ." (Rev 19:6b–7a).

Wednesday of the Sixth Week of Easter: Return in Glory[42]

Today's Collect contains a hint of Advent! We ask God to make us worthy to rejoice at Christ's coming with all the saints. The first two weeks of the Advent Season are focused on Christ's return in glory. Today, according to the Collect, we celebrate in mystery the solemnities of Christ's resurrection. Those solemnities are preceded by remembering his suffering and death, and they are followed by his ascension and gift of the Holy Spirit (Pentecost). Adding in Christ's coming with all the saints points us toward the beginning of the next liturgical year, while reminding us of the angels' promise of his return (Acts 1:11). Another hint of Advent and Jesus coming with the saints is found in the Communion Antiphon, words of Jesus to his disciples: "You did not choose me but I chose you . . . out of the world. And I appointed you to go and bear fruit, fruit that will last" (John 15:16, 19). Because our true home is not here, but with the Lord, in the Entrance Antiphon, we sing: ". . .

41. *Roman Missal*, 427.
42. *Roman Missal*, 428.

I will extol you, O LORD, among the nations, and sing praises to your name. I will tell of your name to my brothers and sisters . . ." (Pss 18:49; 22:23). The Prayer over the Offerings and the Prayer after Communion are the same as Wednesday of the Second Week of Easter, Thursday of the Third Week of Easter, Wednesday of the Fourth Week of Easter, the Fifth Sunday of Easter, and Thursday of the Fifth Week of Easter.

Solemnity of the Ascension of the Lord: Ascension and Presence[43]

Vigil

In a biblical, three-storied universe, the Jesus who came from the heavens above and was incarnate of the Virgin Mary on the earth returns to the heavens from which he came. As the Collect states, he ascended as his apostles looked on. The Entrance Antiphon emphasizes his ascension: "Sing to God, O kingdoms of the earth; sing praises to the Lord. Ascribe power to God, whose . . . power is in the skies" (Ps 68:32, 34). Preface I of the Ascension of the Lord explains that he ascended not to distance himself from us but to show us where we will follow him.[44] The Collect reminds us that he continues to live with us now—because God is everywhere—and, because we are united to him; already we live with him in glory. The Prayer over the Offerings refers to him as our high priest, who is seated at God's right hand and intercedes for us with the Father. The Communion Antiphon emphasizes his royal position: ". . . [W]hen Christ had offered for all time a single sacrifice for sins, 'he sat down at the right hand of God'" (Heb 10:12; cf. Ps 110:1). He enables us to approach the royal throne of grace to obtain God's mercy. In the Prayer after Communion, we ask God to kindle a longing for our heavenly homeland in our hearts as we press onward, following in Christ's footsteps from earth to the heavens, which he has entered before us.

During the Day

The theme of today's Mass texts is ascension-presence. The ascension is expressed in the Entrance Antiphon's words of two men in white robes to Jesus' disciples: "Men of Galilee, why do you stand looking up toward heaven. This

---

43. *Roman Missal*, 431–33. In some countries, Ascension is moved to the following Sunday.

44. *Roman Missal*, 568–69.

Jesus, who has been taken up from you into heaven, will come in the same way as you saw him go into heaven" (Acts 1:11). Ascension is also expressed by both optional collects. The first asks God to gladden us and make us rejoice in thanksgiving for Christ's ascension; where he has gone before in glory we hope to follow. The second asks God to let our spirits dwell with him in the heavens. In the Prayer over the Offerings, we honor the ascension and seek through the holy exchange of bread and wine into the body and blood of Christ an experience of ascending to heavenly realms. Our petition in the Prayer after Communion is that our hope to share in Christ's ascension may draw us onward throughout our lives to where we will be united with God. The presence theme for today is expressed in the Matthean Jesus' last words to his disciples: ". . . [R]emember, I am with you always, to the end of the age" (Matt 28:20). Preface II of the Ascension of the Lord expresses the presence theme by stating that through his ascension, Christ has made us sharers in his divinity.[45]

Thursday of the Sixth Week of Easter: Redeeming Presence[46]

In today's Collect, we are reminded that God, who is in charge of everything he created, made us sharers in redemption. Our petition is that we may never cease to be thankful for the resurrection of Christ which accomplished our redemption. The Entrance Antiphon summarizes God's redeeming work among us this way: "O God, when you went out before your people, when you marched through the wilderness, the earth quaked, the heavens poured down rain at the presence of God, the God of . . . Israel" (Ps 68:7–8). The psalm describes the theophany of the divine presence in the same way as the resurrection of Christ from the dead is a theophany of the divine presence. The Communion Antiphon reminds us that the divine presence is with us always, even to the end of the age (Matt 28:20). The Prayer over the Offerings and the Prayer after Communion are the same as Thursday of the Second Week of Easter, Monday of the Third Week of Easter, Thursday of the Fourth Week of Easter, Monday of the Fifth Week of Easter, and the Sixth Sunday of Easter.

45. *Roman Missal*, 570–71.

46. *Roman Missal*, 434. This reflection is used when Ascension is moved to the following Sunday.

Friday of the Sixth Week of Easter: Eternal Redemption[47]

Both of today's Collects establish the theme of today's Mass texts: eternal redemption. In the first, to be used where the ascension has already been celebrated, God is acknowledged as restoring us to eternal life in the resurrection of Christ. The Entrance Antiphon emphasizes this theme: ". . . [Y]ou [, the Lamb,] were slaughtered and by your blood you ransomed for God saints from every tribe and language and people and nation; you have made them to be a kingdom and priests serving our God . . ." (Rev 5:9–10). In the second Collect, to be used where the ascension will be celebrated on the following Sunday, we ask God to accomplish through the truth of the gospel the eternal redemption it proclaims. The Communion Antiphon puts a Pauline spin on the meaning of eternal redemption: "[Jesus our Lord] was handed over to death for our trespasses and was raised for our justification" (Rom 4:25). Our prayer is that when the one seated at God's right hand comes again, he will clothe with immortality all the baptized (Collect). The Prayer over the Offerings is the same as Tuesday within the Octave of Easter, Friday of the Second Week of Easter, Saturday of the Third Week of Easter, Friday of the Fourth Week of Easter, and Saturday of the Fifth Week of Easter. The Prayer after Communion is the same as Friday within the Octave of Easter, Friday of the Second Week of Easter, Saturday of the Third Week of Easter, Friday of the Fourth Week of Easter, and Saturday of the Fifth Week of Easter.

Saturday of the Sixth Week of Easter: Mighty Acts[48]

The Entrance Antiphon exhorts us to "proclaim the mighty acts of him who called [us] out of darkness into his marvelous light" (1 Pet 2:9). In the Collect, to be used after the ascension has been celebrated, we hear about the mighty act of the promised gift of the Holy Spirit—manifest as fire and light—and we ask God to bestow spiritual gifts upon us, like Jesus gave manifold gifts of heavenly teaching to his disciples. In the Collect, to be used before the ascension is celebrated, the mighty act of God is identified as the shaping of our minds by the practice of good works as we hold fast to the paschal mystery: the death and resurrection of Jesus. The Communion Antiphon, words of the Johannine Jesus to his disciples, expresses his desire that God work another mighty act of darkness to light: "Father, I desire that those

47. *Roman Missal*, 435–36.
48. *Roman Missal*, 437.

also, whom you have given me, may be with me where I am, to see my glory, which you have given me . . ." (John 17:24). The Prayer over the Offerings and the Prayer after Communion are the same as Saturday of the Second Week of Easter, Friday of the Third Week of Easter, Saturday of the Fourth Week of Easter, and Friday of the Fifth Week of Easter.

SEVENTH WEEK OF EASTER

Seventh Sunday of Easter: God's Face[49]

The theme permeating today's Mass texts is seeking God's face. It is introduced in the Entrance Antiphon: "Hear, O LORD, when I cry aloud, be gracious to me and answer me! 'Come,' my heart says, 'seek his face!' Your face, LORD, do I seek. Do not hide your face from me" (Ps 27:7–9a). The Collect reminds us that the Savior of the human race, Jesus Christ, already sees the glory of God's face even as he continues to live among us. The Prayer over the Offerings asks God to let our prayers and gifts come before his face in order that we may one day pass over to the glory of heaven, where we will see his face. In the Communion Antiphon, we repeat a prayer of Jesus for unity that all may be one as he and the Father are one (John 17:22); thus, just as Jesus sees God's face, those united with him can also gaze upon the divine presence. We ask that what has already come to pass in Christ—seeing God's face—will be accomplished for the whole church in the Prayer after Communion. We need God to give us confidence and to hear our supplication that our celebration of the paschal mystery enables us one day to behold God's face.

Monday of the Seventh Week of Easter: Power of Spirit[50]

The shift from celebrating the resurrection of the Lord to concluding the Easter Season with Pentecost on Sunday now takes place. The Entrance Antiphon, concluding words of Jesus to his apostles before his ascension in the Acts of the Apostles, makes this clear: ". . . [Y]ou will receive power when the Holy Spirit has come upon you; and you will be my witnesses . . . to the ends of the earth" (Acts 1:8). The Collect asks God to send the power of the Holy Spirit to us so that we can know his will and express it in the way we

---

49. *Roman Missal*, 438. This reflection is used when Ascension is celebrated on the previous Thursday.

50. *Roman Missal*, 439.

live. In the Prayer over the Offerings, the Holy Spirit is referred to as the force of grace from on high. "I will not leave you orphaned; I am coming to you," states the Johannine Jesus in the Communion Antiphon. ". . . I will see you again, and your hearts will rejoice . . ." (John 14:18; 16:22). In Johannine language, the act of Jesus seeing his disciples again is his gift to them of the Advocate (Paraclete), the Holy Spirit, on Easter Sunday evening. The Prayer after Communion is the same as Wednesday of the Second Week of Easter, Thursday of the Third Week of Easter, Wednesday of the Fourth Week of Easter, the Fifth Sunday of Easter, Thursday of the Fifth Week of Easter, and Wednesday of the Sixth Week of Easter.

Tuesday of the Seventh Week of Easter: Spirit Coming Near[51]

The Prayer over the Gifts is the same as the Seventh Sunday of Easter, and the Prayer after Communion is the same as Saturday of the Second Week of Easter, Friday of the Third Week of Easter, Saturday of the Fourth Week of Easter, Friday of the Fifth Week of Easter, and Saturday of the Sixth Week of Easter. Our focus, then, is on the Collect and the antiphons, all of which continue to point us to Pentecost Sunday. This is expressed best in the Collect, which refers to the Holy Spirit coming near. Our prayer is that he will dwell graciously within us and make a perfect temple of his glory in us. The Holy Spirit is the topic of the Communion Antiphon, words of the Johannine Jesus: ". . . [T]he Advocate, the Holy Spirit, whom the Father will send in my name, will teach you everything, and remind you of all that I have said to you" (John 14:26). The Entrance Antiphon, from the book of Revelation, ties Pentecost back into Easter. John of Patmos's vision of the Son of Man says to him, ". . . I am the first and the last, and the living one. I was dead, and see, I am alive forever and ever" (Rev. 1:17b–18b).

Wednesday of the Seventh Week of Easter: Gift of Spirit[52]

The theme of the gift of the Holy Spirit continues in today's Mass texts. In the Collect, we ask God to help us, who have been gathered together by the Holy Spirit, to be devoted to him with all our heart and to be united in the purity of our intent to do his will. In the Prayer over the Offerings, our prayer is that God will complete the sanctifying work by which he is pleased to redeem us.

---

51. *Roman Missal*, 440.
52. *Roman Missal*, 441.

That sanctifying work is the gift of the Holy Spirit. Stated another way, the Prayer after Communion asks God to increase his grace—his Spirit with his cleansing power—within us and to make us ready to receive the gift of the Holy Spirit. The Communion Antiphon consists of words of the Johannine Jesus to his disciples about the role of the Spirit: "When the Advocate comes, whom I will send to you from the Father, the Spirit of truth who comes from the Father, he will testify on my behalf. You also are to testify . . ." (John 15:26–27). As we prepare to celebrate the coming of the Advocate, the Holy Spirit, we join in the Entrance Antiphon, "Clap your hands, all you peoples; shout to God with loud songs of joy" (Ps 47:1).

Thursday of the Seventh Week of Easter: Spiritual Gifts[53]

Today's Mass texts continue to prepare us to celebrate Pentecost. The Collect asks God to let the Spirit imbue us with spiritual gifts so that we may be pleasing to him and conformed to his will. Likewise, the Prayer after Communion seeks enlightenment from the instruction we receive from the mysteries—the body and blood of Christ under the forms of bread and wine—in which we participate. We also seek restoration that we may merit the gifts of the Spirit for which we prayed in the Collect. The Communion Antiphon also emphasizes preparation for Pentecost. The Johannine Jesus tells his disciples, ". . . I tell you the truth: it is to your advantage that I go away, for if I do not go away, the Advocate will not come to you; but if I go, I will send him to you" (John 16:7). While the Entrance Antiphon does not mention the Spirit, it does speak about grace, the act of God sharing himself with people, which can be understood to be Spirit: "Let us therefore approach the throne of grace with boldness, so that we may receive mercy and find grace to help in time of need" (Heb 4:16). The Prayer over the Offerings is the same as Saturday of the Second Week of Easter, Friday of the Third Week of Easter, Saturday of the Fourth Week of Easter, Friday of the Fifth Week of Easter, and Saturday of the Sixth Week of Easter.

Friday of the Seventh Week of Easter: Eternal Gates[54]

The operative metaphor that works through today's Mass texts is opening the gates of a city enclosed by a wall. Walled cities were a common sight in

---

53. *Roman Missal*, 442.

54. *Roman Missal*, 443.

the biblical world; outsiders were kept out by the wall; only insiders could enter the city through a gate. About the only remnant of that today is a so-called gated community. The Collect establishes the metaphor when God is named as unlocking the gates of eternity through the glorification of Christ and the light of the Holy Spirit. Once Adam and Eve left the garden of paradise, the gates were locked; now Christ has opened them. The light of the Holy Spirit is picked up in the Prayer over the Offerings, in which we ask God to make our gifts acceptable by the coming of the Holy Spirit and to cleanse our consciences. The Communion Antiphon reminds us, "When the Spirit of truth comes, he will guide you into all the truth" (John 16:13). The everlasting life, which is given to us in the banquet of the body and blood of Christ, is nothing other than the unlocked gates through which we pass after being nourished and cleansed. Our cleansing took place, according to the Entrance Antiphon, through Christ's blood: Christ "loves us and freed us from our sins by his blood, and made us to be a kingdom, priests serving his God and Father . . ." (Rev 1:5b–6). With the blood of Jesus, God unlocked for us eternity's gates.

Saturday of the Seventh Week of Easter: Waiting in Prayer[55]

This second to last day of the Easter Season finds us waiting in prayer for the gift of the Holy Spirit. The Entrance Antiphon reminds us of this: "All [Jesus' disciples] were constantly devoting themselves to prayer, together with certain women, including Mary the mother of Jesus, as well as his brothers" before Pentecost (Acts 1:14). The Prayer over the Offerings asks God to let the Holy Spirit come near to prepare our minds for eucharist and Pentecost because it is the Spirit who remits our sins and makes us acceptable in God's sight. In the Communion Antiphon, the Johannine Jesus declares to his disciples and to us, "[The Spirit of truth] will glorify me, because he will take what is mine and declare it to you" (John 16:14). The Collect reminds us that we have spent forty-nine days celebrating the paschal festivities, and so we pray that we can hold fast to them in the way we live our lives. Likewise, the Prayer after Communion reminds us that we have come from things of the past, leaving behind our former selves, to the new mysteries of the present which renew us in holiness and in mind.

---

55. *Roman Missal*, 444.

SOLEMNITY OF PENTECOST: GIFT OF THE HOLY SPIRIT[56]

Vigil

On the Vigil of Pentecost, in the address to the people, the bishop or priest invites all to ask God to bring to perfection his work in the world. In the Prayer after the First Reading, we declare that one of God's works is to form holy people into one by the unity of the Father, Son, and Holy Spirit. In the Prayer after the Second Reading, another of God's works is fire and lightning on Mount Sinai (Horeb); the fire and light are the Spirit, and we pray to be aflame with the Spirit. In the Prayer after Communion, again we ask that we be aflame with the Spirit through our reception of the body and blood of Christ. In the first optional Prayer after the Third Reading, we hear about God's work of restoring the fallen and preserving what he has restored. In the Prayer after the Fourth Reading, we ask God to fulfill his promise to make us witnesses before the world by the coming of the Holy Spirit. The final work of God is found in the Prayer over the Gifts; we ask God to pour out the blessing of the Spirit on the gifts of bread and wine. In times past, God did mighty works for his people. This evening we pray that the Holy Spirit, whom the Father has sent to us, will bring all his work in our world to perfection through us. Alleluia! Alleluia!

or

Another theme permeating the Vigil of Pentecost is baptism. This is expressed best in the first option of the Prayer after the Third Reading in which we pray that all people may be renewed by the sanctification of God's name and washed clean by the water of baptism. In the second option of the Prayer after the Third Reading, we declare that all whom God has brought to rebirth by his word may have the Holy Spirit poured out on them. And in the third option for the Prayer after the Third Reading, we exult because God has renewed our youthfulness of spirit, and we rejoice because he has restored our glory of adoption, which has taken place through baptism. Likewise in the second option of the Collect, we pray that the bright rays of the Spirit may shed his light on those who have been born again by grace in baptism. The Communion Antiphon are words of the Johannine Jesus: "On the last day of the festival, the great day, while Jesus was standing there, he cried out, 'Let anyone who is thirsty come to me, and let the one who believes in me drink'" (John 7:37–38a). All these references to baptism, when a person

---

56. *Roman Missal*, 447–57.

first receives the Spirit, are summed up in today's Preface. It declares that God bestowed the Holy Spirit on those he made his adopted children, and he brought the church to birth through the same Spirit, who is given to all people through baptism. Alleluia! Alleluia!

or

A third theme permeating the Mass texts for the Vigil of Pentecost is established in the Entrance Antiphon. Paul writes to the Romans: ". . . God's love has been poured into our hearts through the Holy Spirit that has been given to us" (Rom 5:5). The first option for the Collect explains that for fifty days we have been celebrating God's love in the paschal mystery—the death and resurrection of Christ. Our prayer is that out of the scattered nations on the earth one great chorus confessing God's love may arise; from many tongues God's love and grace can gather people into one. The Preface also emphasizes that Pentecost brings the paschal mystery to completion with the gift of the Spirit, who unites all people in love to Christ and demonstrates their unity—even though they speak many languages—in their profession of one faith. The Prayer over the Offerings asks God to imbue the church with love through the blessed gift of the Spirit that the truth of salvation may shine as love in us for the whole world to see. Alleluia! Alleluia!

During the Day

The first choice of the Entrance Antiphon on Pentecost Sunday declares, ". . . [T]he spirit of the Lord has filled the world, and that which holds all things together knows what is said" (Wis 1:7). This permeating Spirit is also emphasized in the Communion Antiphon: "All of [those gathered together in one place] were filled with the Holy Spirit and began to speak . . . about God's deeds of power" (Acts 2:4, 11). In the Collect, we petition God to sanctify the whole church by pouring out the gifts of the Spirit across the face of the earth, just like the windy Spirit of God once swept over the face of the waters (Gen 1:2). Likewise, just as divine grace was at work when the gospel was first proclaimed, as so narrated in the Acts of the Apostles, we ask God to fill again the hearts of all believers with the same Spirit. In the Prayer over the Gifts, we ask that the Spirit will reveal more abundantly to us the hidden mystery of the sacrifice we offer—the body and blood of Christ. The unity that results from eating the body and drinking the blood of Christ leads us to the profession of one faith, states the Preface. It is God who bestows spiritual gifts upon the church, states the Prayer after Communion, and so we pray that the grace we receive and the gift of the Spirit poured out on us will always retain its force so that the Spirit-infused food we share at the Lord's altar-table will gain for us abundant eternal redemption. Alleluia! Alleluia!

Monday after Pentecost, Memorial of the Blessed Virgin Mary, Mother of the Church: Mother[57]

The operative metaphor throughout the Mass texts is mother, a female parent. The unique scene in John's Gospel gives rise to this memorial and part of it serves as the second optional Communion Antiphon: Jesus on the cross said to the disciple [whom he loved], 'Here is your mother' (John 19:26–27). The Collect interprets the scene as Jesus appointing Mary as the mother of the church. The Preface interprets the scene as Mary taking to herself—as sons and daughters—all those who have been born to eternal life through the death and resurrection of Christ. Like the disciples who "were constantly devoting themselves to prayer, together with . . . Mary the mother of Jesus" (Acts 1:14) (Entrance Antiphon)—making her a pattern of the church at prayer (Preface)—in the Collect, we pray for the members of the church and their holiness to be a sign drawing other children to her; in the Prayer over the Offerings, we pray to be set on fire with the Virgin's charity and be united in the work of redemption; in the Prayer after Communion we seek the Mother's help in teaching and proclaiming the gospel. The Preface also mentions Mary's motherly activities as conceiving Jesus in her womb, giving birth to her Creator, nurturing him, and watching over the church with a mother's love. The first optional Communion Antiphon, presenting Mary as an intercessor, consists of two verses of the unique Johannine account of the wedding at Cana attended by Jesus' mother (John 2:1, 11).

FIRST SUNDAY AFTER PENTECOST, SOLEMNITY OF THE MOST HOLY TRINITY: THREE IN ONE[58]

Today's celebration is focused on one God as an eternal trinity and undivided unity (Prayer after Communion). In the Collect, we declare that God the Father sent the Word of truth and the Spirit of sanctification into the world and thus revealed the trinity of eternal glory and powerful unity. The

57. *Roman Missal*, 1345–49.
58. *Roman Missal* 495–98.

Preface expands this idea by declaring that the Father, the Son, and the Holy Spirit are one God, not like a single person, but in one substance. All three persons of the trinity are equal, eternal, and to be adored even as they possess a unity of substance. In the Prayer over the Offerings, we invoke the sanctifying power of the one God on our gifts of bread and wine and ask that they may be seen as an eternal offering to him. In the Prayer after Communion, we seek health of body and soul from the gifts of the body and blood of Christ we have received. In the Communion Antiphon, we are reminded that "because [we] are children, God has sent the Spirit of his Son into our hearts, crying, 'Abba! Father!'" (Gal 4:6) Thus, the Entrance Antiphon becomes a hymn of praise blessing God the Father, the only-begotten Son, and the Holy Spirit for the merciful love shown to us.

SUNDAY AFTER THE MOST HOLY TRINITY, SOLEMNITY OF THE MOST HOLY BODY AND BLOOD OF CHRIST: DIVINE NOURISHMENT[59]

On the second Sunday after Pentecost, we celebrate Corpus Christi. This day in honor of the eucharist is focused on Mass as a memorial of the passion and resurrection of Jesus Christ. The Preface refers to the Last Supper, when Jesus established the saving memorial of the cross, offering himself to the Father as the unblemished Lamb, a perfect sacrifice. The Collect asks Christ that as we reverence his presence—body and blood—under the forms of bread and wine that we may experience the fruits of redemption, which, according to the Prayer after Communion, foreshadow now the delights of the divine life to come in eternity. The Preface, too, states that with God's grace we hope to pass over to new life with Christ. In the Prayer over the Offerings, we acknowledge that bread and wine represent unity and peace. Many grains of wheat are ground to become one loaf of bread, and many grapes are squeezed to become one cup of wine. The Entrance Antiphon states that the LORD would feed his people "with the finest of the wheat, and with honey from the rock [he] would satisfy" them (Ps 81:16). The Preface refers to this as nourishment which makes us holy and unites us in one bond of charity. The Communion Antiphon, words of the Johannine Jesus, summarizes the Mass texts for today: "Those who eat my flesh and drink my blood abide in me, and I in them" (John 6:56).

59. *Roman Missal*, 499–501.

FRIDAY AFTER THE SECOND SUNDAY AFTER PENTECOST: SOLEMNITY OF THE MOST SACRED HEART OF JESUS: OPEN HEART[60]

The theme of today's Mass texts is found in the Preface, which states that the wonderful love of the Johannine Jesus was demonstrated by the blood and water flowing from his pierced side. The second optional Communion Antiphon narrates this uniquely Johannine event: ". . . [O]ne of the soldiers pierced his side with a spear, and at once blood and water came out" (John 19:34). His open heart functions as a wellspring of grace and draws us to drink from this spring of salvation (Preface). This is emphasized in the first optional Communion Antiphon; the Johannine Jesus declares: "Let anyone who is thirsty come to me, and let the one who believes in me drink. As the scripture has said, 'Out of the believer's heart shall flow rivers of living water.'" (John 7:37–38). In the first optional Collect, we declare that we glory in the heart of Jesus, while recalling the wonders of his love for us, and we pray that we may receive grace from his heart, a font of heavenly gifts. "The counsel of the LORD stands forever, the thoughts of his heart to all generations" (Ps 33:11), states the Entrance Antiphon, ". . . to deliver their soul from death, and to keep them alive in famine" (Ps 33:19). In the second optional Collect, we declare that the wounded heart of Jesus is the means for God's bestowal of mercy and the manifestation of his love, and we pray that our devotion may be found worthy. The Prayer over the Offerings echoes the second Collect; we pray that God will look upon the surpassing charity in the heart of Jesus and accept our gifts as expiation for our sins. The Prayer after Communion refers to the eucharist as a sacrament of charity which makes our hearts fervent with the fire of holy love and enables us to see Christ in our neighbor.

---

60. *Roman Missal*, 502–04.

6

Season of Ordinary Time

PART I

First Week in Ordinary Time: All Depends on God[1]

This week's Mass texts remind us that everything depends upon God. The Collect asks God to hear our prayers and to grant that we see what needs to be done and give us the strength to do it. Likewise, in the Prayer over the Offerings, we seek favor in God's sight with our offerings and bread and wine, but only God can use them to restore us to holiness. In the Prayer after Communion, we ask God to let us, who have been renewed with the body and blood of Christ, serve him with lives pleasing to him. The first option for the Communion Antiphon declares that with the LORD "is the

1. *Roman Missal*, 461.

fountain of life; in [his] light we see light" (Ps 36:9). Thus, it is made clear from whom comes the light. Similarly, the second option for the Communion Antiphon quotes the Johannine Jesus: "I came that they may have life, and have it abundantly" (John 10:10b). The Entrance Antiphon reminds us that in a biblical culture God sits upon a lofty throne, adored by angels, who sing to the name of the One whose empire is eternal. In other words, everything depends upon God.

Second Sunday (Week) in Ordinary Time: Worship God[2]

The theme of this Sunday's Mass texts is worship of God. The Entrance Antiphon establishes this theme: "All the earth worships you [, God,]; they sing praises to you, [they] sing praises to your name" (Ps 66:4). The Collect reminds us that God governs all things in heaven and on earth and deserves our worship, and the Prayer over the Offerings reminds us that God makes us worthy to participate in the eucharistic mysteries. In the Prayer after Communion, we state that the God we worship nourishes us with the heavenly bread that makes us one in mind and heart. Thus, the first option for the Communion Antiphon states, "You [, LORD,] prepare a table before me . . .; my cup overflows" (Ps 23:5). Because, in the words of the second option for the Communion Antiphon, "we have known and believe the love that God has for us" (1 John 4:16a), we ask the God we worship to hear our pleading and bestow peace upon us (Collect), to continue to accomplish the work of our redemption when the memorial of Jesus' sacrifice is celebrated (Prayer over the Offerings), and to pour the Spirit of love on us (Prayer after Communion).

Third Sunday (Week) in Ordinary Time: Grace Gives Life[3]

The Prayer after Communion establishes the theme of this Sunday's Mass texts. The prayer declares that God gives us the grace which brings us to new life. That is why we petition the ever-living God in the Collect to direct our actions with grace according to his will that we may abound in good works in the name of Jesus Christ. That is why we ask God to sanctify our offerings of bread and wine with grace that they may enable our salvation in the Prayer over the Gifts. That is why we seek always to glory in

2. *Roman Missal*, 462.
3. *Roman Missal*, 463.

God's gift of grace in the Prayer after Communion. All we can do is "[l]ook to [the LORD], and be radiant; so [our] faces shall never be ashamed" (Ps 34:5) in the first option for the Communion Antiphon. In the second option for the Communion Antiphon, the Johannine Jesus declares, "I am the light of the world. Whoever follows me will never walk in darkness but will have the light of life" (John 8:12); light is another way to write about grace. Because God lavishes his grace, himself, upon us, we join in the Entrance Antiphon: "O sing to the LORD a new song; sing to the LORD, all the earth. Honor and majesty are before him; strength and beauty are in his sanctuary" (Ps 96:1, 6).

Fourth Sunday (Week) in Ordinary Time: Salvation[4]

Today's Entrance Antiphon establishes the theme of the Mass texts. "Save us, O LORD our God, and gather us from among the nations, that we may give thanks to your holy name and glory in your praise" (Ps 106:47). The theme of salvation is found in the Prayer over the Offerings, in which we ask God to accept bread and wine and transform them into the sacrament of our salvation. Likewise, the theme of salvation is found in the first option for the Communion Antiphon: "Let your face shine upon your servant; save me in your steadfast love. Do not let me be put to shame, O LORD, for I call on you . . ." (Ps 31:16–17a). In the Prayer after Communion, we ask God, who has nourished us with the saving gifts of the body and blood of his Son, to help us to eternal salvation, while the true faith continues to increase. Because only God can save us, in the Collect we ask him to grant that we may honor him with our mind and to love others in truth. For the second option of the Communion Antiphon we join the Matthean Jesus in acknowledging that the poor in spirit are blessed, and theirs is salvation in God's kingdom, along with the meek, who will inherit the land (Matt 5:3–4).

Fifth Week (Sunday) in Ordinary Time: Creator God[5]

God is our creator. That is the theme of today's Mass texts. The Entrance Antiphon establishes the theme: "O come, let us worship and bow down, let us kneel before the LORD, our Maker! For he is our God . . ." (Ps 95:6–7). The Collect refers to us as God's family in need of being kept safe with our

4. *Roman Missal*, 464.

5. *Roman Missal*, 465.

Creator's unfailing care. The Prayer over the Offerings also refers to God as the Creator, who gives us gifts to sustain us. In the first optional Communion Antiphon, we thank our Creator "for his steadfast love, for his wonderful works to humankind. For he satisfied the thirsty, and the hungry he fills with good things" (Ps 107:8–9). In the second optional Communion Antiphon, we join the Matthean Jesus in declaring that those who hunger and thirst for righteousness will receive their fill from their Creator (Matt 5:5–6). It is the desire of our Maker, according to the Prayer after Communion, that we partake of the one bread of the body of Christ and that we drink from the one cup of the blood of Christ so that, united as one, we may bear fruit for the salvation of the world. We ask our Creator in the Collect to shower us with his heavenly grace, which defends us and protects us.

Sixth Sunday (Week) in Ordinary Time: Stronghold[6]

The theme permeating today's Mass texts is that God is our stronghold; he provides a defensive place to keep us save. The Entrance Antiphon states this most clearly: "You [, O LORD,] are indeed my rock and my fortress; for your name's sake lead me and guide me, . . . for you are my refuge" (Ps 31:3–4). The Collect explains that as our stronghold, God abides in hearts that are just and true, fashioning us by his grace into a dwelling place pleasing to him. In the Prayer over the Offerings, we ask our Stronghold to cleanse and renew us with our offerings that they may become the source of eternal reward for all who do his will. We should long for the heavenly food—the body and blood of Christ—by which we truly live, according to the Prayer after Communion, because it is a gift from God our Stronghold. The Communion Antiphon echoes this last point, recalling the food God gave his people in the desert: ". . . [T]hey ate and were well filled, for [the LORD] gave them what they craved. . . . [T]hey . . . satisfied their craving . . ." (Ps 78:29–30). The stronghold character of God is also found in the second option for the Communion Antiphon; the narrator of John's Gospel declares, ". . . God so loved the world that he gave his only Son, so that everyone who believes in him may not perish but may have eternal life" (John 3:16).

---

6. *Roman Missal*, 466.

Seventh Sunday (Week) in Ordinary Time: Rejoice in Salvation[7]

Salvation is the theme of today's Mass texts. It is introduced in the Entrance Antiphon. ". . . I trusted in your steadfast love," we sing with the psalmist; "my heart shall rejoice in your salvation. I will sing to the LORD, because he has dealt bountifully with me" (Ps 13:5–6). In the Collect, we pray that God will save us, who have pondered spiritual things and who in both word and deed please him. In the Prayer over the Offerings, we ask that our offering of bread and wine—what is due to God—will profit us for salvation. And in the Prayer after Communion, we pray that we experience the effects of the salvation pledged to us in the eucharist. Our response to salvation is found in both of the possible Communion Antiphons. In the first option, we say to God, ". . . I will tell of all your wonderful deeds. I will be glad and exult in you; I will sing praise to your name, O Most High" (Ps 9:1–2). In the second option, our response is the same as the Johannine Martha to Jesus: ". . . Lord, I believe that you are the Messiah, the Son of God, the one coming into the world" (John 11:27).

PART II

Eighth Sunday (Week) in Ordinary Time: What God has Done[8]

Today's Mass texts provide answers to a single question: What has God done for us? The first answer is found in the Entrance Antiphon: ". . . [T]he LORD was my support. He brought me out into a broad place; he delivered me, because he delighted in me" (Ps 18:18–19). The second answer is found in the Collect, in which we ask God to direct the course of the world with peace so that the church may rejoice and be untroubled. In the Prayer over the Offerings, the third answer to the question is given: God provides the gifts we offer and sees them as signs of our desire to serve him; thus, we ask that what he gives us and what we return may result in his mercy. The fourth answer to the question is found in the second optional Communion Antiphon: Jesus declares, ". . . [R]emember, I am with you always, to the end of the age" (Matt 28:20). And the fifth answer to the question is found in the Prayer after Communion; God nourishes us with the body and blood of his Son.

7. *Roman Missal*, 467.
8. *Roman Missal*, 468.

The food we enjoy now will, with God's mercy, enable us to share in eternal life. Because of all God does for us, we join the psalmist in the first optional Communion Antiphon, and say, "I will sing to the LORD, because he has dealt bountifully with me" (Ps 13:6).

Ninth Sunday (Week) in Ordinary Time: Mercy[9]

The theme of mercy found in today's Mass texts is introduced in the Entrance Antiphon: "Turn to me and be gracious to me [, O LORD], for I am lonely and afflicted. Consider my affliction and my trouble, and forgive all my sins" (Ps 25:16, 18). In the Collect, we declare that God's providence never fails; thus, we need his mercy to keep away from us anything that might harm us and to grant us only that which works for our good. In the Prayer over the Offerings, we trust in God's compassion and the purifying action of his grace, seeking to be cleansed by the offerings we place upon his altar. In both of the optional Communion Antiphons, we express our trust in God's mercy. In the first, we state, "I call upon you, for you will answer me, O God; incline your ear to me, hear my words" (Ps 17:6). In the second, we repeat words of the Markan Jesus: ". . . I tell you, whatever you ask for in prayer, believe that you have received it, and it will be yours" (Mark 11:24). In the Prayer after Communion, we ask God to show mercy by governing with the Spirit all those who share the body and blood of Christ, so that what they profess in words and works may merit entrance into the kingdom of God.

Tenth Sunday (Week) in Ordinary Time: Who God is[10]

Today's Mass texts answer the question: Who is God? The first answer is given in the Entrance Antiphon. God is light, salvation, and stronghold: "The LORD is my light and my salvation; whom shall I fear? The LORD is the stronghold of my life; of whom shall I be afraid? When evildoers assail me . . . they shall stumble and fall" (Ps 27:1–2). The Collect answers the question by declaring that God is the source for all good things. In the Prayer over the Offerings, God is identified as the kindly One, who looks upon our service and accepts our offerings. The first option for the Communion Antiphon declares, "The LORD is my rock, my fortress, and my deliverer, my God, my rock in whom I take refuge, my shield, and the

9. *Roman Missal*, 469.
10. *Roman Missal*, 470.

horn of my salvation, my stronghold" (Ps 18:2). The second option for the Communion Antiphon states, "God is love, and those who abide in love abide in God, and God abides in them" (1 John 4:16b). God is described as One who does healing work in the Prayer after Communion; he frees us from evil and leads us to do what is right. This last idea echoes the Collect, in which we ask God to prompt us to do what is right and then to guide us to do it. Thus, God is our moral guide.

Eleventh Sunday (Week) in Ordinary Time: Hear[11]

On the Eleventh Sunday in Ordinary Time, the Mass texts repeat our plea that God hear us. The Entrance Antiphon introduces the theme: "Hear, O LORD, when I cry aloud, be gracious to me and answer me! Do not cast me off, do not forsake me, O God of my salvation!" (Ps 27:7, 9c). After declaring God to be the strength of those who hope in him, we ask him to hear our pleas because without his grace we can do nothing; we cannot even follow his commands or please him with our resolve and our deeds. In the Prayer over the Offerings, we pray that the sustenance of the gifts of bread and wine, which become the body and blood of Christ, will not fail us in body or in spirit because God provides for the twofold needs of human nature: physical and spiritual food. Asking God to hear us is repeated in the first of the two Communion Antiphons: "One thing I asked of the LORD, that will I seek after: to live in the house of the Lord all the days of my life" (Ps 27:4ab). In the second option for the Communion Antiphon, we, like Jesus, ask God to hear our prayer: "Holy Father, protect them in your name that you have given me, so that they may be one, as we are one" (John 17:11b). The unity for which Jesus prayed is the same unity for which we pray in the Prayer after Communion. By eating the body and drinking the blood of Christ, we display the union of all with God.

Twelfth Sunday (Week) in Ordinary Time: God Provides[12]

Today's Mass texts are best summarized by stating that God provides. The first option for the Communion Antiphon states this theme best: "The eyes of all look to you [, O LORD], and you give them their food in due season" (Ps 145:15). In the Collect, we ask God to provide reverence and love of his

11. *Roman Missal*, 471.
12. *Roman Missal*, 472.

name from us and always to guide us, who are established on the foundation of his love. In the Prayer over the Offerings, we ask God to provide cleansing by the sacrifice of conciliation and praise we offer and to make us an offering pleasing to him. In the Prayer after Communion, we ask God to provide mercy to us, who are renewed and nourished by the body and blood of Christ and to make our reception of them the pledge of our redemption. The Entrance Antiphon strengthens our trust in God providing for our needs. "The LORD is the strength of his people; he is the saving refuge of his anointed," sings the psalmist, who then petitions God, "O save your people, and bless your heritage; be their shepherd and carry them forever" (Ps 28:8–9). The second option of a Communion Antiphon echoes the psalmist's prayer that God be his shepherd. The Johannine Jesus declares, "I am the good shepherd. And I lay down my life for the sheep" (John 10:11a, 15b).

Thirteenth Sunday (Week) in Ordinary Time: Song of Joy[13]

Today's Entrance Antiphon expresses the basic theme running through the Mass texts: exulting in joy before God. The psalmist sings, "Clap your hands, all you peoples; shout to God with loud songs of joy" (Ps 47:1). The first optional Communion Antiphon continues the exulting: "Bless the LORD, O my soul, and all that is within me, bless his holy name" (Ps 103:1). In the Collect, we express our joy because God has adopted us with his grace and made us children of light. We rejoice in the Prayer over the Offerings because God graciously accomplishes the effects of his mysteries. And we are glad in the Prayer after Communion because God fills us with life through the sacrifice we offer and receive: the body and blood of Christ. While we exult in joy before the LORD, we also petition him to keep us in the light of truth so that no darkness of error ever engulf us (Collect), that our deeds of service make us worthy of his gifts (Prayer over the Offerings), and that we be bound in charity, bearing fruit that lasts eternally. In the second optional Communion Antiphon, we remember that the Johannine Jesus prayed that we be united as one in charity: "I ask not only on behalf of these [disciples], but also on behalf of those who will believe in me through their word, that they may all be one. As you, Father, are in me and I am in you, may they also be in us, so that the world may believe that you have sent me" (John 17:20–21). As one, we exult in joy before God.

13. *Roman Missal*, 473.

Fourteenth Sunday (Week) in Ordinary Time: Unbounded Praise[14]

Our praise of God should reach from one end of the earth to the other, according to today's Mass texts. The Entrance Antiphon expresses this solidly: "We ponder your steadfast love, O God, in the midst of your temple. Your name, O God, like your praise, reaches to the ends of the earth" (Ps 48:9–10a). In the Collect, we praise God with holy joy from one end of earth to the other for having raised a fallen world through the abasement of his Son, Jesus Christ. In the Prayer over the Offerings, we praise God for purifying us and bringing us closer to eternal life day by day. In the Prayer after Communion, we praise God for replenishing us with the gifts of the body and blood of Christ which together form the prize of salvation, our rescue from slavery to sin (Collect). Our petitions include seeking eternal gladness from God (Collect) and never ceasing to praise him (Prayer after Communion). In the first optional Communion Antiphon we are invited to "taste and see that the LORD is good; happy are those who take refuge in him" (Ps 34:8). The last sentiment of Psalm 34 is echoed by the Matthean Jesus in the second optional Communion Antiphon: "Come to me, all you that are weary and are carrying heavy burdens, and I will give you rest" (Matt 11:28).

Fifteenth Sunday (Week) in Ordinary Time: Beholding Glory[15]

According to today's Mass texts, we seek the vision of God's glory. That theme is expressed in the Entrance Antiphon: "As for me, I shall behold your face in righteousness; when I awake I shall be satisfied, beholding your likeness" (Ps 17:15). In the Collect, we acknowledge that God shines the light of his glory on those who stray from the truth so that they may return to the correct path. In the Prayer over the Offerings, we ask God to bring greater holiness and glory in us who consume the body and blood of Christ. This is echoed in the Prayer after Communion, in which we ask God that, through our reception of the body and blood of Christ, the glorious and saving effects of our participation in the mystery may grow. The second optional Communion Antiphon, words of the Johannine Jesus, also echoes this last sentiment: "Those who eat my flesh and drink my blood abide in me, and I in them" (John 6:56). By abiding in Jesus, who abides in God, we are immersed

14. *Roman Missal*, 474.
15. *Roman Missal*, 475.

in the LORD's glory. It is like "the sparrow [who] finds a home, and the swallow a nest for herself, where she may lay her young, at [God's] altars, [the] LORD of hosts, [the] King and . . . God" (Ps 84:3), states the first optional Communion Antiphon. "Happy are those who live in your house, ever singing your praise" (Ps 84:4). Those who come to the Jerusalem Temple get a glimpse of the vision of God's glory, one which the sparrow and swallow enjoy every day! Our prayer is that we who bear the name Christian may reject everything contrary to the name of Christ and do only what honors it (Collect).

Sixteenth Sunday (Week) in Ordinary Time: Sacrifice[16]

The theme of sacrifice permeates today's Mass texts. In the Entrance Antiphon, we hear the words of the psalmist: "With a freewill offering I will sacrifice to you; I will give thanks to your name, O LORD, for it is good" (Ps 54:6). In the Prayer over the Offerings, we name the one perfect sacrifice of Jesus as bringing to completion all the offerings prescribed in the HB (OT), and we ask God to accept our sacrifice of bread and wine, just as he once accepted the gifts of Abel, son of Adam and Eve. The first option of a Communion Antiphon directly refers to "the LORD [who] is gracious and merciful" and how he has gained renown because of his wonderful deeds (Ps 111:4). Then, indirectly it mentions God's sacrifice: "He provides food for those who fear him; he is ever mindful of his covenant" (Ps 111:5). The result of our sacrifice of bread and wine is found in the Prayer after Communion. We ask God to lead all who have received the body and blood of Christ from their old ways of life to the new way of life shown to us by Jesus. A secondary theme of God coming to our help is also found in the Entrance Antiphon (Ps 54:4); in the Collect in which we ask God to increase the grace of hope, faith, and charity in us; and in the second option of a Communion Antiphon in which Jesus states that he waits at the door to be invited in and to share the sacrificial meal of those who live in the house (Rev 3:20).

Seventeenth Sunday (Week) in Ordinary Time: Foundation[17]

We find the theme of today's Mass texts in the Collect. We declare that God is our firm foundation, who bestows holiness, mercy, and all good things upon

16. *Roman Missal*, 476.
17. *Roman Missal*, 477.

us abundantly. It is out of the abundance of God's gifts to us that we make our offerings, states the Prayer over the Offerings. But the foundation for our gifts is the working of God's grace. According to the Prayer after Communion, once we have consumed the body and blood of Christ—the foundational and perpetual memorial of the death and resurrection of Christ given by Jesus to us in love—we pray that they will profit us for salvation. God, of course, is the foundation of all, as stated in the Entrance Antiphon: ". . . God [is] in his holy habitation. . . . God [is] in his sanctuary, the God of Israel; he gives power and strength to his people" (Ps 68:5, 35). He protects all who hope in him, serving as their ruler and guide through things that pass away while enabling them to hold fast to things that endure (Collect). Meanwhile, he sanctifies our present way of life through the liturgy and leads us to eternal gladness (Prayer over the Offerings). Our response to God being the foundation of our lives is found in the first option for the Communion Antiphon: "Bless the LORD, O my soul, and do not forget all his benefits" (Ps 103:2). According to the Matthean Jesus, in the second option for a Communion Antiphon, we will be counted among the merciful, who receive mercy, and among the pure in heart, who will see God, the foundation of our lives (Matt 5:7–8).

Eighteenth Sunday (Week) in Ordinary Time: God's Care[18]

Those whom God renews with the gifts of the body and blood of Christ receive his never-failing care, which makes them worthy of eternal salvation, according to the Prayer after Communion. God's care for people is expressed by the psalmist's plea in the Entrance Antiphon: "Be pleased, O God, to deliver me. O LORD, make haste to help me! You are my help and my deliverer; O LORD, do not delay!" (Ps 70:1, 5b) Likewise, in the Collect, we ask God to draw near to his people, to hear their prayers, and to answer all who glory in him as their creator and guide; he shows his never-failing care by restoring what he created and keeping safe all he has restored. In the Prayer over the Offerings, we declare that God shows his care for us by accepting our gifts and making us an eternal offering to him. The gifts we offer not only come from God's care, but once we offer them, they are returned to us as heavenly delights that give us God's protection. The first optional Communion Antiphon makes this clear: ". . . [Y]ou [, O Lord,] gave your people food of angels, and without their toil you supplied them from heaven with bread ready to eat, providing every pleasure and suited to every taste" (Wis 16:20). The Johannine Jesus shows his Godly, never-ending care for his followers, stating, in

18. *Roman Missal*, 478.

the second optional Communion Antiphon, "I am the bread of life. Whoever comes to me will never be hungry, and whoever believes in me will never be thirsty" (John 6:35).

Nineteenth Sunday (Week) in Ordinary Time: Covenants[19]

In the HB (OT), God makes covenants with his people. A covenant is a solemn agreement between a greater party (God) and a lesser party (people). God promises to take care of his people, and they promise to worship only him. In today's Entrance Antiphon, the psalmist tells God, "Have regard for your covenant," O LORD; "do not forget the life of your poor forever. Rise up, O God, plead your cause . . . . Do not forget the clamor of your foes, the uproar of your adversaries that goes up continually" (Ps 74:20, 19, 22–23). The Prayer over the Offerings explains that in the new covenant God gives us bread and wine to be offered to him, who transforms them into the body and blood of his Son, Jesus Christ, and then gives them back to us in the eucharistic meal. In the Prayer after Communion, we ask that the covenant meal in which we have participated will save us and confirm us in the light of God's truth. Both options for the Communion Antiphon emphasize sharing the body (bread) in the covenant meal. The first exhorts: "Praise the LORD, O Jerusalem! . . . [H]e fills you with the finest of wheat" (Ps 147:12, 14). The second comes from the Johannine Jesus, who declares, ". . . [T]he bread that I will give for the life of the world is my flesh" (John 6:51b). In the new covenant, according to the Collect, we have been taught to call God our Father by the Holy Spirit because he has adopted us as his sons and daughters. Our prayer is that we may keep the covenant and so enter into the inheritance God has promised.

Twentieth Sunday (Week) in Ordinary Time: Seeing and Loving[20]

Seeing and loving are the themes holding together today's Mass texts. "Behold our shield, O God; look on the face of your anointed" (Ps 84:9), begins the Entrance Antiphon. After asking God to look on the face of the king, the psalmist declares, "For a day in your courts is better than a thousand elsewhere" (Ps 84:10a). In the Collect, we declare that God prepares good

19. *Roman Missal*, 479.
20. *Roman Missal*, 480.

things that no eye can see for those who love him. The Prayer over the Offerings reminds us that what we see—bread and wine—undergoes a marvelous exchange into the body and blood of Christ. We offer to God what he has given to us, and we pray that we may merit to receive God's very self and to be considered coheirs of Christ in heaven (Prayer after Communion). Seeing is expressed in the Prayer after Communion in two ways: We are made partakers of Christ through the eucharist, and, thus, we are conformed to his image now on earth. In the Collect, we ask God to fill our hearts with the warmth of his love so that we may love him in all things and above all things and receive his promise of eternal life. The first optional Communion Antiphon states, ". . . [W]ith the LORD there is steadfast love, and with him is great power to redeem" (Ps 130:7). The love of the Johannine Jesus is demonstrated in the second optional Communion Antiphon: "I am the living bread that came down from heaven. Whoever eats of this bread will live forever . . ." (John 6:51).

Twenty-First Sunday (Week) in Ordinary Time: Unity[21]

According to today's Mass texts, it is God who brings about unity in the world. The Collect makes this theme clear when it addresses God as the one who causes the minds of believers to unite in a single purpose. The Prayer over the Offerings identifies God as he who gained for himself a people by adoption through the sacrificial death of Jesus Christ, and so we pray for the gifts of unity and peace. In the Prayer after Communion, we pray that God will complete his healing work and perfect and sustain us that we, united, may please him in all things. Our prayer is that we may love what God commands and desire what he promises while keeping ourselves fixed where true gladness is found (Collect). According to the first optional Communion Antiphon, unity is found in God's creation: ". . . [T]he earth is satisfied with the fruit of your work [, O LORD]. You . . . bring forth food from the earth, and wine to gladden the human heart . . ." (Ps 104:13–15). In the second optional Communion Antiphon, the Johannine Jesus puts unity this way: "Those who eat my flesh and drink my blood have eternal life, and I will raise them up on the last day" (John 6:54). Since it is God who brings about unity in the world, our individual prayer is found in the Entrance Antiphon: "Incline your ear, O LORD, and answer me . . . . [S]ave your servant who trusts in you . . . . [B]e gracious to me, O Lord, for to you do I cry all day long" (Ps 86:1–3).

21. *Roman Missal*, 481.

Twenty-Second Sunday (Week) in Ordinary Time: Mercy's Other Names[22]

God's mercy—referred to as graciousness, steadfast love, blessing, and good-ness—unites today's Mass texts. The theme is introduced in the Entrance Antiphon: "[B]e gracious to me, O Lord, for to you do I cry all day long. For you, O Lord, are good and forgiving, abounding in steadfast love to all who call on you" (Ps 86:3, 5). After identifying God as the giver of all good gifts, we ask the merciful One to put the love of his name in our hearts and to deepen our reverence for him. In the Prayer over the Offerings, we seek the blessing of salvation from our offerings of bread and wine. The first optional Communion Antiphon declares, "O how abundant is your goodness [, O LORD,] that you have laid up for those who fear you" (Ps 31:19a). God's mercy is displayed in his watchful care of us and in nurturing in us what is good (Collect). We pray that what we celebrate in mystery—bread and wine becoming the body and blood of Christ—God may accomplish in his merci-ful power in us (Prayer over the Offerings). We ask our merciful God that the food of charity—the body and blood of Christ—will confirm our hearts and stir us to serve him in our neighbor (Prayer after Communion). Two ways to serve the neighbor are found in the second optional Communion Antiphon, two verses from the Matthean Jesus' sermon on the mount: mak-ing peace and accepting persecution for the sake of doing what is right. The former results in us being named children of God, while the latter results in us being admitted to the kingdom of heaven (Matt 5:9-10).

Twenty-Third Sunday (Week) of Ordinary Time: Dependent on God[23]

"You are righteous, O LORD, and your judgments are right," begins today's Entrance Antiphon. "Deal with your servant according to your steadfast love ..." (Ps 119:137, 124). Because all of us depend on God for everything, in the Collect we are reminded that we are redeemed and receive adoption from God. In the Prayer over the Offerings, we acknowledge that God gives us the gifts of true prayer and peace. In the Prayer after Communion, we state that we depend on God for nourishment and life. In the words of the first optional Communion Antiphon, we are like "a deer [that] longs for flowing streams, so [our] soul longs for . . . God. [Our] soul thirsts for God, for the

22. *Roman Missal*, 482.

23. *Roman Missal*, 483.

living God" (Ps 42:1–2a). Depending on God, we seek true freedom and an everlasting inheritance (Collect); we seek to give proper homage to God and to be united in mind and heart (Prayer over the Offerings); we seek an eternal share in Christ's life from his word, his body, and his blood (Prayer after Communion). After all, in the second optional Communion Antiphon, the Johannine Jesus reminds us that he is "the light of the world," and "whoever follows [him] will never walk in darkness but will have the light of life" (John 8:12).

Twenty-Fourth Sunday (Week) in Ordinary Time: Mercy, Creator, Reciprocity[24]

First, there is a theme of mercy in today's Mass texts. In the Collect, we ask God to look on us that we may feel his mercy. In the Prayer over the Offerings, we ask God to accept our offerings of bread and wine and look upon them with his kind mercy. In the first optional Communion Antiphon we declare: "How precious is your steadfast love, O God! All people may take refuge in the shadow of your wings" (Ps 36:7). God's steadfast love is his mercy, which is like the outstretched wings of any mother bird providing protection for her chicks. Second, there is a theme that God is the creator and ruler of all things (Collect). The Entrance Antiphon states this as a prayer: "Reward those who wait for you [, O God,] and let your prophets be found trustworthy. Hear, O Lord, the prayer of your servants, according to your goodwill toward your people . . ." (Sir 36:21–22). It is also worthy of note that this section from the OT (A) book of Sirach begins, "Have mercy upon us, O God of all" (Sir 36:1). With God as our creator and ruler, we pray that we may serve him with all our heart (Collect) and that he will hear our prayers and accept our offerings (Prayer over the Offerings). Third, there is a theme of reciprocity; this is expressed in the Prayer over the Offerings, in which we declare that what each person offers to honor God's name serves the salvation of all. In the Prayer after Communion, we find the same reciprocity. We ask that the sharing of the body and blood of Christ will take possession of our minds and bodies so that God's will may prevail in us and not our own desires. This is accomplished, according to the second optional Communion Antiphon, by sharing in the blood of Christ through drinking from the cup of blessing and sharing in the body of Christ through the eating of a piece of the broken bread (1 Cor 10:16).

24. *Roman Missal*, 484.

Twenty-Fifth Sunday (Week) in Ordinary Time: Cry to God[25]

Today's Entrance Antiphon records God declaring that he is the salvation of all people. When they cry to him in distress, he hears them. So, in the Collect, we cry to God, asking that we may merit eternal life by keeping his commandments to love him and our neighbor. The first optional Communion Antiphon echoes the Collect, stating, "[LORD, y]ou have commanded your precepts be kept diligently. O that my ways may be steadfast in keeping your statutes!" (Ps 119:4–5) In the Prayer over the Offerings, we cry to God, asking that he receive with favor our offerings so that our devotion and faith may be rewarded through the mysteries we celebrate. In the Prayer after Communion, we cry to God to raise up all who are renewed with the body and blood of Christ that they may share eternal redemption in the mystery of bread (body) and wine (blood) and manifest it by the way they live. In the second optional Communion Antiphon, we join the Johannine Jesus, who echoes God's words (Ezek 34:11–16), in crying out: "I am the good shepherd. I know my own and my own know me" (John 10:14).

Twenty-Sixth Sunday (Week) in Ordinary Time: Just Judge[26]

Today's Entrance Antiphon, a pastiche of five verses from the book of Daniel, establishes the theme for today's Mass texts. It emphasizes how our sinfulness is justly judged by God, who displays his glory by forgiving us out of his abundant mercy: "You have executed true judgments [, O Lord God,] in all you have brought upon us . . . . For we have sinned and . . . not obeyed your commandments . . . . [B]ring glory to your name, O Lord, [and] deal with us in . . . your abundant mercy" (Sg Three 1:5, 6, 7, 20, 19 [Dan 3:31, 29, 30, 43, 42]). The Collect echoes the Entrance Antiphon when it addresses God as the one who shows his almighty power by pardoning and showing mercy. The Prayer over the Offerings addresses him as the merciful God, who accepts our offerings. And in the first optional Communion Antiphon, using the words of the psalmist, we seek God's mercy, saying, "Remember your word to your servant, in which you have made me hope. This is my comfort in my distress, that your promise gives me life" (Ps 119:49–50). Because God is merciful, we seek his abundant grace as we hasten to attain his promise of eternal life (Collect). Similarly, in the Prayer over the Offerings, we seek to

25. *Roman Missal*, 485.
26. *Roman Missal*, 486.

drink from the wellspring of his blessing. And in the Prayer after Communion, we seek restoration in mind and body—that is, to be coheirs in Christ's glory—from the suffering and death we endure. As the First Letter of John makes clear in the second optional Communion Antiphon, "We know love by this, that [the Son of God] laid down his life for us—and we ought to lay down our lives for one another" (1 John 3:16). In other words, Jesus' death and resurrection display God's mercy.

Twenty-Seventh Sunday (Week) in Ordinary Time: God's Will[27]

The Mass texts for today are focused on God accomplishing his will. The Entrance Antiphon is taken from the prayer of Mordecai in the book of Esther: "O Lord, Lord, you rule as king over all things, for the universe is in your power and there is no one who can oppose you when it is your will . . . , for you have made heaven and earth and every wonderful thing under heaven. You are Lord of all, and there is no one who can resist you, the Lord" (Add Esth 13:9–11 [Esth C:2–4]). This theme is echoed in the Collect, which declares that God, in his abundant kindness, surpasses our merits and grants our desires when we pray to him. He pours his mercy on us in order to pardon us and to give us what we do not even dare to ask. Because he accepts the sacrifice which he himself instituted—the body and blood of Christ, his Son—we trust that he will complete the sanctifying work, which redeems us, in us (Prayer over the Offerings). In the first option for the Communion Antiphon, we are reminded, "The LORD is good to those who wait for him, to the soul that seeks him" (Lam 3:25). Not only is God's will accomplished in the Eucharist, but we are refreshed by, nourished by, and transformed into what we consume: the body and blood of Christ. "Because there is one bread, we who are many are one body, for we all partake of the one bread" (1 Cor 10:17), states the second option for the Communion Antiphon.

Twenty-Eighth Sunday (Week) in Ordinary Time: Grace Before and After[28]

Grace is the subject of today's Mass texts. Grace, the act of God sharing himself with people, is a free, unearned gift. The Collect asks God to send his

27. *Roman Missal*, 487.

28. *Roman Missal*, 488.

grace to go before us and to follow after us so that we may do good works. In the Entrance Antiphon, the psalmist asks, "If you, O LORD, should mark iniquities, Lord, who could stand?" (Ps130:3) The answer is that no one could without God's grace. The psalmist adds, "But there is forgiveness with you, so that you may be revered" (Ps 130:4). In other words, God forgives with his grace so that we may turn and adore him. In the Prayer over the Offerings, we ask God to accept both our prayers and offerings, which are signs of our devotedness, and to bestow the grace we need one day to enter the glory of heaven. The second option for the Communion Antiphon echoes this statement: ". . . [W]hen [the Son] is revealed, we will be like him, for we will see him as he is" in glory (1 John 3:2b). Similarly, in the Prayer after Communion, we seek God's grace that enables us to share in the divine nature of his Son, Jesus Christ, which comes as nourishment from his body and blood. While "[t]he young lions suffer want and hunger," in the first option for the Communion Antiphon, "those who seek the LORD lack no good thing" (Ps 34:10); at all times his grace goes before and follows after.

Twenty-Ninth Sunday (Week) in Ordinary Time: Divine Shaping[29]

Not only does God sustain us, according to today's Mass texts, but God shapes us. The psalmist is confident that God hears his call. In the Entrance Antiphon, we state: "I call upon you, for you will answer me, O God; incline your ear to me, hear my words" (Ps 17:6). The psalmist's confidence turns into a plea: "Guard me as the apple of the eye; hide me in the shadow of your wings" (Ps 17:8). In the Collect, we ask God to shape us by conforming our will to his so that we can serve him in heartfelt sincerity. In the Prayer over the Offerings, we ask God to give us a sincere respect for the gifts he gives us; we also ask that we may be cleansed of our sins by the purifying action of his grace. The first optional Communion Antiphon returns to the theme of God sustaining us: "Truly the eye of the LORD is on those who fear him, on those who hope in his steadfast love, to deliver their soul from death, and to keep them alive in famine" (Ps 33:18–19). The second optional Communion Antiphon is focused on the sustaining power of the Markan Jesus: ". . . [T]he Son of Man came . . . to give his life a ransom for many" (Mark 10:45). The Prayer after Communion returns us to God's shaping power. We ask that we benefit from participation in the eucharist, and that the help God gives us in the present serves as a preparation for eternal life.

29. *Roman Missal*, 489.

Thirtieth Sunday (Week) in Ordinary Time: Seek the LORD[30]

Seeking God is the theme of today's Mass texts. The Entrance Antiphon expresses it most eloquently: ". . . [L]et the hearts of those who seek the LORD rejoice. Seek the LORD and his strength; seek his presence continually" (Ps 105:3–4). In the Collect, we seek an increase of faith, hope, and charity from God, who makes us love what he commands so that we can merit what he promises. In the Prayer over the Offerings, we seek that our offerings and service give God glory. In the first optional Communion Antiphon, we want to "shout for joy . . . in the name of our God . . ." because we seek his help, and he gives it to us (Ps 20:5). In the second optional Communion Antiphon, we seek to "live in love, as Christ loved us and gave himself up for us, a fragrant offering and sacrifice to God" (Eph 5:2). In the Prayer after Communion, we seek one day to possess in truth what we now celebrate in signs. We also seek the perfection that exists within the sacrament of the body and blood of Christ which is presented to us under the signs of bread and wine.

Thirty-First Sunday (Week) in Ordinary Time: Hasten[31]

The theme of hastening is found in today's Mass texts. The verb *to hasten* means *to make something happen more quickly.* The theme is introduced in the Entrance Antiphon: "Do not forsake me, O LORD; O my God, do not be far from me; make haste to help me, O Lord, my salvation" (Ps 38:21–22). In the Collect, we ask God to help us hasten without stumbling to receive what he has promised; it is only by his gift that we are even able to give him right and praiseworthy service. In the Prayer over the Offerings, our prayer is that God will hasten to receive our sacrificial offerings and to pour out his mercy on us. We hasten on "the path of life" which leads to God's "presence [where] there is fullness of joy" (Ps 16:11), in the first option for a Communion Antiphon. The Johannine Jesus urges us to hasten to eat of him in order to live: "Just as the living Father sent me, and I live because of the Father, so whoever eats me will live because of me" (John 6:57). Just like we asked God to hasten to help us in the Entrance Antiphon, in the Prayer after Communion, we ask him to hasten to increase his power in us; thus, renewed by the sacrament of the body and blood of his Son, we will be prepared by his gifts to us to receive the eternal life they promise.

30. *Roman Missal,* 490.
31. *Roman Missal,* 491.

Thirty-Second Sunday (Week) in Ordinary Time: Prayer Before God[32]

While praying may be obvious to those celebrating the eucharist, today's Mass texts raise our awareness to the fact that we are at prayer before God. The Entrance Antiphon makes this very clear: ". . . [L]et my prayer come before you [, O LORD]; incline your ear to my cry" (Ps 88:2). In the Collect, we pray that the almighty and merciful God will keep all adversity away from us; thus, unhindered in mind and body we can pursue in freedom the things that God treasures. In the Prayer over the Offerings, we pray that God's favor will fall on the gifts of bread and wine, which we use to remember the death and resurrection of Jesus, and see our offerings as an act of loving devotion. A favorite prayer for many people is found in the first optional Communion Antiphon: "The LORD is my shepherd, I shall not want. He makes me lie down in green pastures; he leads me beside still waters" (Ps 23:1–2). In Luke's Gospel, Cleopas and his unnamed companion tell Jesus' disciples "how [the risen Christ] had been made known to them in the [blessing prayer and the] breaking of the bread" (Luke 24:35), in the second optional Communion Antiphon. It is a prayer of thanks that we voice in the Prayer after Communion; we thank God for the nourishment he gives us even while we pray that the Spirit will be poured forth on us to secure the grace of integrity within us.

Thirty-Third Sunday (Week) in Ordinary Time: Assurances[33]

"For surely I know the plans I have for you, says the LORD, plans for your welfare and not for harm, to give you a future with hope" (Jer 29:11) begins the first of three verses forming today's Entrance Antiphon. Jeremiah addresses the Jewish captives in Babylon, stating, "Then when you call upon me and come and pray to me, I will hear you. . . . I will bring you back to the place from which I sent you into exile" (Jer 29:12, 14). God's promise to the Jews and the trust it evokes is echoed in today's Collect, which petitions God to give gladness to those devoted to him because only constant service brings full and lasting happiness. Similarly, in the Prayer over the Offerings, we ask God to accept our gifts that they may obtain the grace of being devoted to him while gaining everlasting happiness for us. The happiness-in-serving-God theme is echoed in the first optional Communion Antiphon: ". . . [F]or me

32. *Roman Missal*, 492.
33. *Roman Missal*, 493.

it is good to be near God; I have made the Lord GOD my refuge . . ." (Ps 73:28). The assurance that the prophet Jeremiah writes about is similar to the assurance given by the Markan Jesus in the second optional Communion Antiphon; he tells his disciples, ". . . [W]hatever you ask for in prayer, believe that you have received it, and it will be yours" (Mark 11:24). In the Prayer after Communion, we express our trust that by doing what Jesus commanded us to do in his memory—eating his body and drinking his blood—will enable our growth in charity.

Last Sunday in Ordinary Time, Solemnity of Our Lord Jesus Christ, King of the Universe: Anointed One[34]

The last or thirty-fourth Sunday in Ordinary Time is the Solemnity of Our Lord Jesus Christ, King of the Universe. A number of themes run through today's Mass texts, and, since they are summarized in the Preface, we will employ it as our guide. First, God anointed Jesus with the oil of gladness as eternal priest and king of all creation. The Collect explains this theme when it states that God willed to restore all things in Christ, the king of the universe. Second, by offering himself on the altar of the cross, Jesus accomplished human redemption. In the words of the Collect, he set free from slavery the whole creation. In the words of the Prayer over the Offerings, he reconciled the human race to God. Third, Christ made everything subject to his rule as king in order to render service to his Father (Collect) and to bestow unity and peace upon all nations (Prayer over the Offerings). Fourth, Christ presents a kingdom to God that is eternal and universal, one full of truth, life, holiness, grace, justice, love, and peace. This is amplified in the Communion Antiphon: ". . . [T]he LORD sits enthroned as king forever. May the LORD bless his people with peace! (Ps 29:10, 11b) It is also found in the Prayer after Communion, in which we glory in obedience to Christ the king with the hope of living eternally with him in his kingdom. Thus, we join in the Entrance Antiphon, singing, "Worthy is the Lamb that was slaughtered to receive power and wealth and wisdom and might and honor and glory and blessing! . . . [T]o him be glory and dominion forever and ever" (Rev 5:12; 1:6).

---

34. *Roman Missal*, 505–09.

Thirty-Fourth Week in Ordinary Time: Completion[35]

During the last week in Ordinary Time, we pray that God, after stirring the will of believers, will bring his divine work to completion in them. We pray that out of his kindness God will give us in greater measure his healing remedies (Collect). In the Entrance Antiphon, we state that "the LORD will speak . . . peace to his people, to his faithful, to those who turn to him in their hearts" (Ps 85:8). In the Prayer over the Offerings, we acknowledge that we offer bread and wine because God bids us to do so; we pray that our offerings will make us worthy of God's love while also granting us obedience to his commands. In the Prayer after Communion, we acknowledge that it is God who gives us the joy of celebrating the eucharist, and we pray that we may never be parted from God. In the second optional Communion Antiphon, we hear the Matthean Jesus declare, ". . . [R]emember, I am with you always, to the end of the age" (Matt 28:20b). Our only response to God's presence in the world is found in the first optional Communion Antiphon: "Praise the LORD, all you nations! For great is his steadfast love toward us" (Ps 117: 1a, 2a).

35. *Roman Missal*, 494.

7

Saints during the Liturgical Year

SAINTS DURING THE ADVENT SEASON

November 30, Feast of St. Andrew: Given Life[1]

The Entrance Antiphon for the Feast of St. Andrew, an apostle, is based on the narrative call of Peter and Andrew in Matthew's Gospel, which is itself based on the same account in Mark's Gospel (Mark 1:16–17): "While Jesus was walking along the shore of Lake Galilee, he saw two brothers. One was Simon, also known as Peter, and the other was Andrew. They were fishermen, and they were casting their net into the lake. Jesus said to them, 'Come with me! I will teach you how to bring in people instead of fish'" (Matt 4:18–19). The Communion Antiphon presents the Johannine version of the

1. *Roman Missal*, 1003.

call narrative. John the Baptist sends two of his disciples—one of them being Andrew—to Jesus. Then Andrew finds Simon and brings him to Jesus (John 1:35–42). When it is accepted, the call gives life through death; that is the meaning of fishing for people. That is why Andrew is declared a constant intercessor before God in the Collect, even though he has been dead for hundreds of years. That is why we ask God to give the life of Christ to the gifts of bread and wine in the Prayer over the Offerings. By carrying in our bodies the death of the Lord Jesus Christ, we hope to live with him in glory.

December 3, Memorial of St. Francis Xavier: Fire of Charity[2]

Francis Xavier (1506–1552) was one of the original Jesuits and a missionary to the peoples of the Far East. In the words of the Entrance Antiphon, a gloss on Psalm 18:49, he told about Jesus among the nations, and he told of his name to his brothers and sisters, a gloss on Psalm 22:22. In other words, what he heard in the dark, he proclaimed in the light; what he heard whispered, he shouted from the housetops (Matt 10:27), according to the Communion Antiphon. He is remembered burning with zeal for the faith and converting thousands to Christianity in the Collect. The same idea is presented in the Prayer over the Offerings, which remembers his journeys to distant places out of his intense desire to proclaim the gospel. And, again, in the Prayer after Communion, we ask God to kindle that same fire of charity in us which burned in Xavier. This saint, who brought many people to God through Christ, died preaching (Collect). Our prayer is that we, by our way of life, may be as effective witnesses of the gospel he preached and so bring others to join us on our eager journey towards God (Prayer over the Offerings) as we labor in the harvest.

December 6, Optional Memorial of St. Nicholas: Way of Salvation[3]

On the day that we remember St. Nicholas (+350), who in a consumer culture was turned into Santa Claus, we pray in the Collect that the way of salvation may lie open before us through his prayers. The Entrance Antiphon, taken from the Common of Pastors, II. For a Bishop, 1,[4] a gloss from verses

2. *Roman Missal*, 1007–08.

3. *Roman Missal*, 1008.

4. *Roman Missal*, 1074–75.

found in the prophet Ezekiel, emphasizes how it is the LORD who keeps the way of salvation open. "The LORD God then said: I will look for my sheep and take care of them myself," records the prophet (Ezek 34:11). He records God adding, "All of you, both strong and weak, will have the same shepherd, and he will take good care of you. . . . I will be your God" (Ezek 34:23–24). The fact that God sends shepherds to show the way of salvation is further emphasized in the Communion Antiphon, which records the words of the Johannine Jesus, who referred to himself as the good shepherd (John 10:11), declaring that we do not choose him, but he chooses us and appoints us to go and bear lasting fruit (John 15:16). That is how we give honor to God's name (Prayer over the Offerings) in imitation of St. Nicholas.

December 7, Memorial of St. Ambrose: Teacher[5]

The Entrance Antiphon, a gloss on a verse from Sirach, declares that personified wisdom exalted Ambrose (ca. 340–397) by opening his mouth to teach an understanding of the faith (Sir 15:5) in the midst of the people of Milan, Italy, where he served as bishop. The Collect refers to Ambrose as a teacher of the Catholic faith whom the Holy Spirit filled and enlightened, according to the Prayer over the Offerings. In the Prayer after Communion, we ask God to let us profit from Ambrose's teachings, which spur us to run without fear along God's paths to eternal life. Because Ambrose cooperated with God, the Holy One clothed him with a robe of glory, as stated in the Entrance Antiphon, and enabled him to yield the fruit of faith in due season, as stated in the Communion Antiphon, a gloss on Psalm 1:2, 3. The Collect petitions God to give us modern teachers, who are enlightened and filled with the wisdom of Ambrose and present a faith today that shines with the glory of God.

December 8, Solemnity of the Immaculate Conception of the Blessed Virgin Mary: Free from Sin[6]

The Immaculate Conception of the Blessed Virgin Mary celebrates the freedom from sin of the mother of Jesus. Since Jesus is the Christ, the anointed Son of God, he could not be born of anyone guilty of original sin. Thus, God, in a singular act, clothed Mary in a robe of salvation in preparation for the

---

5. *Roman Missal*, 1009.

6. *Roman Missal*, 1013–16.

fullness of grace that Christ would give (Entrance Antiphon). In the words of the Collect, she became a worthy dwelling place for God's Son. As the mother of Jesus, who is God, Mary represents the beginning of the church, the bride of Christ, according to the Preface. According to the Entrance Antiphon, a gloss on a verse from Isaiah, she is a bride adorned with her jewels (Isa 61:10), a virgin without spot or wrinkle, a woman endowed with God's own life. Because we speak glorious things of Mary on this day, according to the Communion Antiphon, and because she is our advocate of grace and model of holiness, according to the Preface, through her intercession we ask God to cleanse us of our sins (Collect), to deliver us from our faults (Prayer over the Offerings), and to heal us of the wounds of sin (Prayer after Communion) so that one day we may be admitted to God's presence (Collect), which Mary enjoys now and for eternity.

December 12, Feast of Our Lady of Guadalupe: A Great Sign[7]

The Entrance Antiphon, taken from the Book of Revelation, serves as the description of this Feast of Our Lady of Guadalupe: "Something important appeared in the sky. It was a woman whose clothes are the sun. The moon was under her feet, and a crown made of twelve stars was on her head" (Rev 12:1). The native Mexican peasant—one of the lowly ones lifted up in the first optional Communion Antiphon (Luke 1:52)—Juan Diego Cuauhtlatoatzin (1474–1548), first experienced the visionary sign on Tepeyac Hill on December 9, 1531, with three more great signs to follow. On December 12, Mary told him to gather roses in the midst of winter and place them in his cloak, which, when opened, displayed the image of pregnant Mary standing on the moon and surrounded by the sun's nimbus. The second optional Communion Antiphon emphasizes the specialness of Mexico, which received God's love (Ps 147:20) and singular protection of his Son's most holy mother (Collect). We pray for a lively faith that enables the progress of people in justice and peace (Collect) as true children of the Blessed Virgin Mary (Prayer over the Offerings), while awaiting the glorious day of the Lord's coming (Prayer after Communion).

---

7. *Roman Missal*, 1019–20.

December 13, Memorial of St. Lucy: Light[8]

Lucy (+303), whose name means *light* and who is often depicted in iconography wearing a laurel wreath crown of candles on her head, is honored as an early-church virgin and martyr. The day of her death, today, is declared by the Collect to be her heavenly birthday. She now—according to the Entrance Antiphon, a gloss on a verse in the Book of Revelation (7:17)—follows the Lamb, Jesus Christ, who himself was martyred on a cross. The Communion Antiphon quotes several phrases from Revelation 7:17: "The Lamb in the center of the throne . . . will lead [those who washed their robes and made them white in the blood of the Lamb] to springs of life-giving water." Lucy, light in the midst of the last, dark nights of fall, was sacrificed on the altar of chastity, according to the Entrance Antiphon, taken from the Common of Martyrs, IV. For a Virgin Martyr.[9] She is one of several women mentioned in Eucharistic Prayer I.[10] In the Prayer over the Offerings, we acknowledge that her suffering and death were pleasing to God, who, according to the Prayer after Communion, bestowed the crown of virginity and martyrdom upon her.

December 14, Memorial of St. John of the Cross: Boast in the Cross[11]

Because this Carmelite saint is named John of the Cross (1542–1591), the cross becomes the theme for today's Mass texts. The Entrance Antiphon quotes Paul in his Letter to the Galatians: ". . . I will never brag about anything except the cross of our Lord Jesus Christ. Because of his cross, the world is dead as far as I am concerned, and I am dead as far as the world is concerned" (Gal 6:14). The Communion Antiphon quotes Jesus in Matthew's Gospel: "If any of you want to be my followers, you must forget about yourself. You must take up your cross and follow me" (Matt 16:24). The Collect explains that the priest John was dedicated to perfect self-denial and love of the cross. In the Prayer over the Offerings, we ask God to help us imitate the mysteries of Jesus' death on the cross and Christ's resurrection which are celebrated using bread and wine. And in the Prayer after Communion, we return to the theme found in the Collect, namely, that God made

8. *Roman Missal*, 1020.

9. *Roman Missal*, 1068–69.

10. *Roman Missal*, 642.

11. *Roman Missal*, 1020–21.

known the mystery of the cross in John. Then we ask that like him we may draw our strength for living from Christ and be kept faithful while we labor for the salvation of all, which was accomplished on the wood of the cross.

SAINTS DURING THE CHRISTMAS SEASON

December 26, Feast of St. Stephen: Love of Enemies[12]

In the Collect for the feast of St. Stephen, celebrated the day after Christmas, we ask God to grant us the ability to learn to love our enemies in imitation of Stephen, whose martyrdom is described in the CB (NT) Acts of the Apostles (6:8—8:1). Stephen is modeled on Jesus in Luke's Gospel. The Entrance Antiphon is a gloss on two verses from the Acts. The author, the same one who wrote Luke's Gospel, records: ". . . Stephen was filled with the Holy Spirit. He looked toward heaven, where he saw our glorious God and Jesus standing at his right side. Then Stephen said, 'I see heaven open and the Son of Man standing at the right side of God!'" (Acts 7:55–56) The Communion Antiphon continues the story. Before Stephen was stoned to death, he prayed, "Lord Jesus, please welcome me" (Acts 7:58), the same words prayed by the Lukan Jesus before he dies an innocent martyr's death (Luke 23:46a). While celebrating the heavenly birthday of Stephen (Collect)—the glorious commemoration of his martyrdom (Prayer over the Offerings)—which gladdens us, according to the Prayer after Communion, we give thanks to God for saving us through the nativity of Jesus, who taught us to pray for and love our enemies (Matt 5:44; Luke 6:27, 35).

December 27, Feast of St. John: Word Made Flesh[13]

The celebration of the apostle and evangelist named John is, in fact, a feast of John's Gospel. The first optional Entrance Antiphon misidentifies the disciple Jesus loved (John 13:23) with John, but does focus on the celestial secrets he revealed in order to spread the word of life (1 John 1:1) throughout the world. The Communion Antiphon identifies this word of life by melding two verses from John's Gospel: "The Word became a human being and lived here with us. Because of all that the Son is, we have been given one blessing after another" (John 1:14, 16). The second optional Entrance Antiphon praises

12. *Roman Missal*, 1023.

13. *Roman Missal*, 1024–25.

116

God for unlocking the secrets of his Word through John, while the Prayer over the Offerings asks that we may draw the hidden wisdom of the Word. In the Prayer after Communion, we ask almighty God to let the Word made flesh, which was proclaimed in the prologue of John's Gospel and celebrated in the presence of Christ in bread and wine, continue to dwell among us, a clear reference to the Season of Christmas being celebrated. Thus, in the Collect, we ask God to help us grasp the words of John's Gospel which we hear with our ears.

December 28, Feast of the Holy Innocents: Faithful Witnesses[14]

This feast is based on the unique story in Matthew's Gospel about Herod having killed all the children two years old or under around Bethlehem (Matt 2:16–18), a retelling of the Exodus account of the king of Egypt's decree that all male Hebrew children should be drowned in the Nile River (Exod 1:15—2:10). The Collect explains that the holy innocents honored today bore witness to Christ not by preaching, but by dying. The Entrance Antiphon, echoing this idea, declares that they were slaughtered for Christ. The Prayer over the Offerings declares that God granted the innocents justification, even though they lacked understanding. And the Communion Antiphon seems to summarize the day by identifying the children as those who were unable to profess God's Son in speech, but were, nevertheless, crowned with divine grace on account of his birth—which ties today into Christmas. A verse from the Book of Revelation serves as the basis both for the Entrance Antiphon and the Communion Antiphon: "All of these [innocents] . . . follow the Lamb wherever he leads. They have been rescued to be presented to God and the Lamb as the most precious people on earth" (Rev 14:4). They sing forever "Glory to you, O Lord," according to the Entrance Antiphon, while, in the Collect, we ask God to let the faith we confess with our lips also speak through the way we live our lives.

14. *Roman Missal*, 1025–26.

January 1, Solemnity of Mary, Holy Mother of God: Mother of Jesus[15]

The Collect refers oxymoronically to the fruitful virginity of Mary, through whom God bestowed on us the author of life and the grace of eternal salvation. Preface I of the Blessed Virgin Mary[16] reminds us that it was by the overshadowing of the Holy Spirit that she conceived God's Son without losing her virginity. The first optional Entrance Antiphon echoes this idea declaring that holy Mary gave birth to the king, the ruler of heaven and earth. In the Communion Antiphon, a verse from the Letter to the Hebrews, king Jesus is declared to be "the same yesterday, today, and forever" (Heb 13:8). The Prayer over the Offerings sees the birth of Jesus from Mary as the new beginning of grace, the act of God sharing himself with people. Out of his kindness God begins all things and brings them to fulfillment. It is the fulfillment for which we pray in the Prayer after Communion; we ask God to grant us eternal life with rejoicing in the presence of the Blessed Virgin Mary, the mother of God's Son and the mother of the church. Thus, this eighth day of Christmas is a celebration of Mary giving birth to the One who, in the second optional Entrance Antiphon, is named "Wonderful Advisor and Mighty God, Eternal Father and Prince of Peace" (Isa 9:6b).

January 2, Memorial of Sts. Basil the Great and Gregory Nazianzen: Wisdom[17]

Both Basil (330–379) and Gregory (ca. 329–390) are honored in the Entrance Antiphon for their wisdom; thus we remember and praise them (Sir 44:15). By the fact that they are remembered this day, their names live on from one generation to the next (Sir 44:14). The Collect declares that it is God who gave light to the church by the example and teaching of these bishops and instructors of the fourth-century church. We ask God to preserve in us the integrity of the gift of faith that we may walk in salvation's path that he traces for us through the lives and teaching of Basil and Gregory in the Prayer after Communion. Like them, we continue to "preach that Christ was nailed to a cross. Our message is God's power and wisdom . . ." (1 Cor 1:23–24) (Communion Antiphon). Our prayer is that God will enable us to learn his truth and practice it faithfully in imitation of Basil and Gregory

15. *Roman Missal*, 182–83.

16. *Roman Missal*, 590–91.

17. *Roman Missal*, 801.

(Collect). The Prayer over the Offerings asks God to accept the bread and wine offered for his glory in honor of today's saints and to make them the means of our salvation.

January 4, Memorial of St. Elizabeth Ann Seton: Burning Desire[18]

While Elizabeth Ann Seton (1774–1821) is not the first U.S.-citizen saint, she is the first native-born U.S. saint. The theme of the Mass texts—true faith—center on her conversion from the Episcopal Church to the Catholic Church. The first optional Entrance Antiphon declares her to be a woman who held her family together with her wisdom and who by living right demonstrated her respect for the LORD (Prov 14:1–2). The second optional Entrance Antiphon places her in the company of those who "worship and serve the God of Jacob" (Ps 24:6). The Collect refers to her burning zeal to find God, as we pray for diligent love while seeking and finding God in daily service with sincere faith. Likewise, in the Prayer over the Offerings, we pray that we may be inserted more deeply in the mystery of faith of Jesus Christ. And in the Prayer after Communion, we ask to be inflamed with a burning desire for the heavenly table while we consecrate our lives in faithfulness here and now in imitation of Seton. The Communion Antiphon declares true faith in the eucharistic elements by quoting Jesus in John's Gospel: "I am that bread from heaven! Everyone who eats it will live forever. My flesh is the life-giving bread that I give to the people of this world" (John 6:51).

January 5, Memorial of St. John Neumann: Imitation[19]

John Neumann (1811–1860), a native of Bohemia, came to the U.S. where, after being ordained a priest in 1836, he was ordained the bishop of Philadelphia in 1852. The Communion Antiphon refers to his immigration by quoting Jesus in Matthew's Gospel: "All who have given up home or brothers and sisters or father and mother or children or land for me will be given a hundred times as much. They will also have eternal life " (Matt 19:29). However, the Prayer over the Offerings establishes the theme of the Mass texts: imitation. Neumann imitated what he celebrated at the altar. In the words of the Entrance Antiphon, "You, LORD, are all I want! You are my choice,

18. *Roman Missal*, 803.

19. *Roman Missal*, 804–05.

and you keep me safe. You make my life pleasant, and my future is bright" (Ps 16:5–6). In the Prayer after Communion, we declare that we have been refreshed in our participation in the eucharist, the memorial of Jesus' death and resurrection, and we ask that we may imitate the example of Neumann and remain in the bond of unity and truth in the church. This same idea, as expressed in the Collect, refers to the Diocese of Philadelphia, which means *brotherly love*. Neumann, again according to the Collect, is best known for his charity and pastoral service, especially in terms of educating youth, as he shepherded people in the U.S. Our prayer is that we may increase the family of God's church in imitation of Neumann.

SAINTS DURING THE SEASON OF ORDINARY TIME: PART I

January 17, Memorial of St. Anthony: Desert[20]

At the age of twenty, Anthony (251–356) heard the Matthean Jesus' words of today's Communion Antiphon: "If you want to be perfect, go sell everything you own! Give the money to the poor, and you will have riches in heaven. Then come and be my follower" (Matt 19:21). That is exactly what he did; he sold all his possessions and moved to the desert, where he lived to be one hundred five years old; he attracted many followers, making him the father (abbot) of monastic life. In the words of the Entrance Antiphon, he was a righteous man who flourished like the palm tree, and grew like a cedar of Lebanon. He was planted in the house of the LORD; he flourished in the courts of God (Ps 92:13–14). Anthony's way of life in the desert was one of self-denial so that he could love God above all things (Collect). The Prayer over the Offerings asks God to release us from our earthly attachments so that we find our riches in God alone. In the Prayer after Communion, we acknowledge the healing the eucharist brings and the victories it gave to Anthony over the powers of darkness. Our prayer is that it will enable us to escape all enemies unharmed.

January 21, Memorial of St. Agnes: Lamb of God[21]

The theme of the Mass texts for the Memorial of St. Agnes (ca. 290–305) is found in the Collect, which states that God choose the weak in the world

20. *Roman Missal*, 807.

21. *Roman Missal*, 809.

to confound the strong in the world. As a girl of twelve or thirteen, Agnes refused marriage and was decapitated. In popular iconography, she is presented with a lamb. Thus the Entrance Antiphon, taken from the Common of Martyrs, IV. For a Virgin Martyr,[22] states that Agnes followed the crucified and risen lamb as a virgin; she offered her modesty as a sacrifice on the altar of chastity. The Communion Antiphon identifies the lamb: Jesus Christ. "The Lamb in the center of the throne will . . . lead [her] to streams of life-giving water . . ." (Rev 7:17). On this day the pope blesses lambs whose wool is used to make the palliums given to archbishops. In the Prayer over the Offerings, we mention Agnes's suffering and death, while, in the Prayer after Communion, we identify her crown of virginity and martyrdom. The Collect refers to this day as Agnes's heavenly birthday; we seek to follow her constancy in faith.

January 24, Memorial of St. Francis de Sales: Inflamed[23]

The second optional Entrance Antiphon, taken from the Common of Doctors of the Church, 2,[24] states that the assembly declares a saint's wisdom, and the congregation proclaims his praise. His name lives on from one generation to the next (Sir 44:15, 14). Such is the case with Francis de Sales (1567–1622), who, in the Collect, is identified as becoming all things to all people for their salvation. Living and ministering after the Protestant Reformation in Geneva, Switzerland, where he labored for the conversion of the Calvinists for twenty years, this saint is remembered for his gentleness of charity in service of his neighbor (Collect). His gentle soul was kindled with the divine fire of the Holy Spirit, according to the Prayer over the Offerings. Our petition in the Prayer after Communion is that we may imitate de Sales's charity and meekness on earth so to attain the glory of heaven, like him. Through his spiritual direction, writing, and preaching, he proclaimed Christ crucified to be the power of God and the wisdom of God (1 Cor 1:23–24) (Communion Antiphon).

22. *Roman Missal*, 1068–69.

23. *Roman Missal*, 810.

24. *Roman Missal*, 1089–90.

January 25, Feast of the Conversion of St. Paul the Apostle: Witness[25]

The Prayer over the Offerings best presents the theme of today's Mass texts: being filled with the light of faith. The Entrance Antiphon presents Paul stating, "I thank Christ Jesus our Lord. He has given me the strength for my work because he knew that he could trust me" (1 Tim 1:12). In the Collect, Paul is identified as one who taught the whole world by his preaching; we ask God that inspired by his example we may be witnesses to God's truth in the world. According to the Prayer over the Offerings, it is the Spirit who fills and enlightens us with faith for the spreading of God's glory. This is echoed in the Communion Antiphon: Paul tells the Galatians, ". . . I now live by faith in the Son of God, who loved me and gave his life for me" (Gal 2:20b). In the Prayer after Communion, we petition God to stir in us the same fire of charity which burned ardently in Paul and was demonstrated by his concern for the churches to which he ministered as an apostle. Our faith is strengthened through our celebration of the eucharist (Prayer over the Offerings, Prayer after Communion).

January 26, Memorial of Sts. Timothy and Titus: Proclaim the Gospel[26]

The theme for the Mass which remembers the two coworkers of Paul—Timothy and Titus—is found in the Communion Antiphon, a verse spoken by the Markan Jesus and a verse spoken by the Matthean Jesus stitched together: "Go and preach the good news to everyone in the world" (Mark 16:15). "I will be with you always . . ." (Matt 28:20). The Collect acknowledges that Timothy and Titus shared in the apostolic ministry of preaching the gospel, and they can help us live justly and devoutly today as we strive to reach the heavenly homeland at which they have already arrived. In the Prayer over the Offerings, we ask God to receive our offerings and make us acceptable to him while we announce the gospel today. And in the Prayer after Communion, after being nourished with the body and blood of Christ, we ask God to fill us with the same faith taught by Timothy and Titus that we may proclaim it to the world. The Entrance Antiphon provides the reason we proclaim the good news of the death and resurrection of Jesus: "Tell every

25. *Roman Missal,* 811.
26. *Roman Missal,* 812.

nation on earth, 'The LORD is wonderful and does marvelous things! The LORD is great and deserves our greatest praise!'" (Ps 96:3–4)

January 28, Memorial of St. Thomas Aquinas: Teacher[27]

The Dominican priest, Thomas Aquinas (1225–1274), is known as a doctor or teacher in the church. That is why the first optional Entrance Antiphon, taken from the Common of Doctors of the Church 1,[28] states, he opened his mouth in the assembly of the church, and God filled him with spiritual wisdom and understanding and clothed him in glory. Today's Collect echoes that antiphon, stating that God made Aquinas great in holiness and faithful in the study of doctrine. Our prayer is to understand what he taught and wrote and to imitate his holiness. According to the first optional Communion Antiphon, he is one of those faithful and prudent stewards who served others faithfully through teaching and writing (Luke 12:42). Because of Aquinas's love of the eucharist, the Prayer after Communion is more than appropriate. Not only is Christ named the supreme teacher, whom God gives as living bread, but on the feast day of Aquinas we seek to learn divine truth and express it in our works of charity. In other words, we give ourselves over to God in words of praise (Prayer over the Offerings), as we have been taught to do by Aquinas, and then we serve our brothers and sisters.

January 31, Memorial of St. John Bosco: Youth[29]

John Bosco (1815–1888) is remembered for his love for the young. The Collect states that God gave him the fire of love and made him a father and teacher of the young. After founding the Society of St. Francis de Sales (Salesians), Bosco created a system of education that consisted of workshops for tradesmen and manual laborers, and schools of arts and sciences and liberal arts for others. The first optional Entrance Antiphon, taken from the Common of Pastors, B. For One Pastor, 2,[30] aptly describes Bosco: The Spirit of the Lord was upon him, because he anointed him to bring good news to the poor (Luke 4:18a). In the second option for the Prayer after Communion, we ask God that we, who have been nourished by the sacred meal of the

---

27. *Roman Missal*, 813.

28. *Roman Missal*, 1088.

29. *Roman Missal*, 814.

30. *Roman Missal*, 1079–80.

body and blood of Christ, may be inspired to follow the example of Bosco in serving God and neighbor. The Prayer over the Offerings acknowledges that it is God's divine power that was at work in Bosco; all we can do is implore God to impart to us the effects of salvation, like he did with this saint. In the words of the Matthean Jesus in the Communion Antiphon, he is with us until the end of the age (Matt 28:20).

February 2, Feast of the Presentation of the Lord: Praise and Light[31]

On this fortieth day since the celebration of the Lord's Nativity (Christmas), the theme of the Mass texts focus on the presentation of Jesus in the Jerusalem Temple by Mary and Joseph and the appearance of Simeon and Anna, who, enlightened by the Spirit, recognized the Christ. The Collect explains that Jesus was presented in the substance of our flesh so that one day, by God's grace, we may be presented with minds made pure. The Prayer over the Offerings explains that God's only-begotten Son, a lamb without blemish, was offered for the life of the world. In the Prayer after Communion, we seek to be made perfect with God's grace and strengthened to go forth to meet the Lord and obtain eternal life. Simeon's expectation that he would not experience death until he had seen the Christ was fulfilled, just like we believe that one day we will see him in heaven. Simeon's words form the Communion Antiphon, "With my own eyes I have seen what you have done to save your people, and foreign nations will also see this" (Luke 2:30–31). This leads to the praise of the Entrance Antiphon: "Our God, here in your temple we think about your love. You are famous and praised everywhere on earth, as you win victories with your powerful arm" (Ps 48:9–10).

or

On this day, there is also a theme of light, since candles are blessed today. The antiphon which begins the blessing of candles declares that the Lord comes to enlighten the eyes of his people. After the candles are lit, they are blessed. In the first optional blessing prayer, God, who showed Simeon that Jesus was the light for revelation to the Gentiles, is declared to be the source and origin of all light. The candles are blessed to praise God's name and to light the way for the procession from the place of blessing to the church. The second optional blessing prayer declares God to be the true light who creates eternal light; he is asked to pour perpetual light into the hearts of believers, who are brightened by the candlelight they bear, that one day they may reach

31. *Roman Missal*, 815–22.

the light of God's glory. The antiphon sung during the procession, taken from Luke's Gospel 2:29–32, is focused on Jesus as the light for revelation to the Gentiles and the glory of Israel. The Preface declares that Jesus was revealed by the Spirit to be the glory of Israel and the light of the nations. We carry the light into the world on our pilgrimage to eternal light.

February 5, Memorial of St. Agatha: Good[32]

The name Agatha means *good*. This third-century martyr found favor with God because of the courage he gave her (Collect) to undergo having her breasts cut off and being rolled over burning coals! The Prayer over the Offerings, taken from the Common of Martyrs, IV. For a Virgin Martyr,[33] refers to this as her suffering and passion. The Prayer after Communion praises God for giving good Agatha a crown among the saints because she retained her virginity while shedding her blood for her Lord. In the words of the second option for the Entrance Antiphon, she is blessed because she denied herself and took up her cross in imitation of Jesus, the spouse of virgins and the prince of martyrs. Now, the Lamb at the center of the throne is her shepherd, and he has guided her to springs of the water of life (Rev 7:17), states the Communion Antiphon. In the Collect, we ask Agatha to implore God's compassion for us, and, in the Prayer over the Offerings, graciously to accept the gifts we bring, that, like Agatha, we may bravely overcome evil and, like Agatha, attain the glory of heaven (Prayer after Communion).

February 6, Memorial of St. Paul Miki and Companions: Twenty-Six[34]

On February 5, 1597, Paul Miki and twenty-five of his companions were attached to crosses with ropes and chains before being put to death with the thrust of a lance near Nagasaki, Japan. Among the group were six Franciscans, three Japanese Jesuit catechists—including Miki—and seventeen Japanese lay Catholics. The Collect states that God called these twenty-six martyrs to life through the cross. In the first optional Entrance Antiphon, taken from the Common of Martyrs, I. Outside Easter Time, A. For Several

---

32. *Roman Missal*, 823.

33. *Roman Missal*, 1068–69.

34. *Roman Missal*, 823.

Martyrs, 2,[35] we are reminded, "The LORD's people may suffer a lot, but he will always bring them safely through. Not one of their bones will ever be broken" (Ps 34:19–20). As we commemorate this precious martyrdom of these twenty-six believers (Prayer over the Offerings), the Communion Antiphon reminds us of the Lukan Jesus' words: "My friends, don't be afraid of people. They can kill you, but after that, there is nothing else they can do" (Luke 12:4). Taking to heart these words, we ask God to give us the courage to profess our faith even if it means death (Collect) and to bravely overcome everything for the sake of Jesus, who loved us to death on his cross (Prayer after Communion).

February 10, Memorial of St. Scholastica: Pure Love[36]

Scholastica (480–547) was the twin sister of St. Benedict. From her earliest youth, in the words of the Entrance Antiphon—taken from the Common of Holy Men and Women, II. For Monks and Religious, C. For a Nun—[37]Scholastica was "like an olive tree growing in God's house, and [she could] count on his love forever and ever" (Ps 52:8). Most likely influenced by her twin brother, she demonstrated that serving God with pure love makes people happy to receive what comes from loving him (Collect). In the words of the Communion Antiphon, her "thoughts [were] filled with beautiful words for the king, and [she used her] voice as a writer would use pen and ink" (Ps 45:1). As we commemorate Scholastica, we reflect on the consolation that God gives us in this life without losing hope of what he promises us for eternal life (Prayer over the Offerings). By holding to Christ day by day, like Scholastica did, we seek to be coheirs with him and her in God's kingdom.

February 14, Memorial of Sts. Cyril and Methodius: Enlighteners[38]

The Slavic peoples were enlightened by the ministry of the brothers Cyril (827–869) and Methodius (815–885), states today's Collect. These two holy men born in Greece and baptized Constantine and Michael, respectively, says the Entrance Antiphon, became friends of God and heralds of divine

35. *Roman Missal*, 1053–54.
36. *Roman Missal*, 825.
37. *Roman Missal*, 1106–07.
38. *Roman Missal*, 826.

truth through the Slav alphabet they created in order to evangelize Moravia, Bohemia, and Bulgaria. The words of the Communion Antiphon declare that these two "preached everywhere. The Lord was with them, and the miracles they worked proved that their message was true" (Mark 16:20). After making monastic profession, Constantine took the name Cyril. After serving as a governor, Michael became a monk, taking the name Methodius, and was ordained a bishop. Our prayer in the Collect is that we may grasp the words of their teaching, like the people did to whom Cyril and Methodius preached. We seek true faith and right confession in the Collect; we seek new humanity reconciled to God in the Prayer over the Offerings; and we seek to be in one Spirit persevering in the same faith in the Prayer after Communion in order to be united in God's kingdom.

February 22, Feast of the Chair of St. Peter the Apostle: Chair[39]

The word *chair* in the title of this feast does not refer to a physical seat; chair is a synonym for authority. Thus, the Communion Antiphon presents the Matthean Jesus telling Peter, ". . . I will call you Peter, which means 'a rock.' On this rock I will build my church . . ." (Matt 16:18), after Peter tells Jesus, "You are the Messiah, the Son of the living God" (Matt 16:16). The same idea is expressed in the Entrance Antiphon, which features Jesus telling Peter, ". . . I have prayed that your faith will be strong. And when you have come back to me, help the others" (Luke 22:32). The Collect asks God to keep tempests away because he has set us on the rock of Peter's faith. In the Prayer over the Offerings, we acknowledge Peter as the shepherd of the church, leading us with his teaching. And in the Prayer after Communion, we seek unity and peace from the sharing of the body and blood of Christ—a redeeming exchange—under Peter's leadership. The authority represented by the chair of Peter, today occupied by the pope, guarantees the faith in its integrity (Prayer over the Gifts).

February 23, Memorial of St. Polycarp: Cup-Sharing[40]

The Mass texts that honor Polycarp (ca. 75–155) are focused on him sharing in the chalice of Christ's sufferings through his martyrdom (Collect). This

---

39. *Roman Missal*, 828.
40. *Roman Missal*, 829.

is explicitly stated in the Entrance Antiphon, taken from the Common of Martyrs, B. For One Martyr, 2;[41] Paul writes, "Nothing is as wonderful as knowing Christ Jesus, my Lord. I have given up everything else and count it all as garbage. All I want is to know Christ. . . . I want to suffer and die as he did" (Phil 3:8, 10). Drinking from the cup is a biblical metaphor for sharing in Jesus' sufferings through martyrdom (Mark 10:38; Matt 20:22; John 18:11). According to the Prayer over the Offerings, Polycarp professed his faith by shedding his blood. He displayed constancy, according to the Prayer after Communion. Thus, we pray through his intersession to rise to eternal life through the Holy Spirit by our sharing in the cup (Collect). While we most likely will not face martyrdom, drinking the cup may merit our eternal reward for suffering endured (Prayer after Communion).

SAINTS DURING THE SEASON OF LENT

March 7, Memorial of Sts. Perpetua and Felicity: Women Martyrs[42]

In 203, two women catechumens were imprisoned in Carthage. Perpetua, age twenty-two, with a small child, and her slave, Felicity, who gave birth while incarcerated, were baptized in prison, and afterward condemned to execution in the arena. They are honored for their martyrdom; they displayed God's love by defying their persecutors, states the Collect. The Prayer over the Offerings refers to their deaths as one of the Lord's mighty deeds because it was a heaven-sent victory of faith. They enacted in diligent service, in the words of the Prayer after Communion, the gift of faith given to them. The Communion Antiphon emphasizes this: "We face death every day because of Jesus. Our bodies show what his death was like, so that his life can also be seen in us," Paul tells the Corinthians (2 Cor 4:11). Indeed, these two women are icons of eternal life. The Entrance Antiphon says that they are rejoicing in heaven because they followed in the footsteps of Christ. Out of love for him, they shed their blood, but now they exult with Christ forever.

41. *Roman Missal*, 1060–61.

42. *Roman Missal*, 831.

March 17, Optional Memorial of St. Patrick: Missionary[43]

Patrick (385–461) was born in Britain, but is known as the missionary to Ireland, where he arrived in 432 to preach God's glory to the people of that island (Collect). Before this he was sold into slavery in Ireland in his teenage years, was converted to the Catholic faith, escaped to France, was ordained a priest and then a bishop, and was sent back to Ireland as a missionary bishop. He lived the Entrance Antiphon, taken from the Common of Pastors, V. For Missionaries, 3:[44] "Tell every nation on earth, 'The LORD is wonderful and does marvelous things! The LORD is great and deserves our greatest praise!'" (Ps 96:3–4) He fulfilled the Communion Antiphon: ". . . [T]he Lord chose seventy-two other followers and sent them out two by two to every town and village where he was about to go." They were instructed to say, "God's kingdom will soon be here!" (Luke 10:1, 9) On his first trip as a slave in Ireland, Patrick was responsible for caring for a flock of sheep. Little did he know in his teenage years that as a missionary on his second trip to Ireland that he would be responsible for caring for hundreds of sheep who glory in the name of Christ.

March 19, Solemnity of St. Joseph, Spouse of Mary: Protector[45]

Joseph, under the title Spouse of the Blessed Virgin Mary, is remembered for his faithful care in the Collect, his loving care in the Prayer over the Offerings, and his unfailing protection in the Prayer after Communion. Like Joseph's faithful care of Mary and Jesus, we ask God to make the church watchful over the mysteries of salvation. Like Joseph's loving care of God's only-begotten Son, we pray that God will make us worthy to minister with pure hearts at his altar. And like Joseph's unfailing protection of the holy family, we ask God to keep safe the gifts he has distributed among the members of the family of the church. Joseph's care is summarized in the Preface. He is called a just man, who was given as the spouse to the Mother of God, Mary, and who was established as a faithful servant charged with being the father of Jesus, who was conceived in Mary by the overshadowing power of the Holy Spirit. Thus, in the words of the Entrance Antiphon, Joseph is the

43. *Roman Missal*, 833.

44. *Roman Missal*, 1086–87.

45. *Roman Missal*, 835–38.

faithful and prudent manager whom the Lord put in charge of his household (Luke 12:42), and in the words of the Communion Antiphon, because of his care, Joseph has become the good and trustworthy servant who has entered the joy of his master (Matt 25:21).

March 25, Solemnity of the Annunciation of the Lord: Incarnation[46]

The theme of today's Mass texts is found in the Collect. We celebrate the incarnation: God, as the Word, takes on human flesh in the womb of Mary of Nazareth. The Communion Antiphon, from the prophet Isaiah, sees this as a fulfillment: "A virgin is pregnant; she will have a son and will name him Immanuel" (Isa 7:14b). This leads the church to trace its beginning mythologically to the incarnation of God's only-begotten Son in the Prayer over the Offerings. This takes place, in the words of the Preface, by the overshadowing of the Holy Spirit. Thus, today is a foreshadowing celebration of Christmas, nine months from today. Quoting two verses from the Letter to the Hebrews, the Entrance Antiphon states, "When Christ came into the world, he said to God, 'And so, my God, I have come to do what you want . . .'" (Heb 10:5, 7). In the words of the Prayer after Communion, it is a mystery of faith. We confess that Jesus, who was conceived of the Virgin Mary, is true God and true man, and we petition God that just as he shared in our humanity, we may share in his divine nature (Collect) and his resurrection (Prayer after Communion).

April 7, Memorial of St. John Baptist de la Salle: Educator[47]

Because John Baptist de la Salle (1651–1719), born in Rheims, France, was an educator of poor youths, in the Collect, we ask God to provide teachers in the church who dedicate themselves wholeheartedly to both human and Christian formation in imitation of de la Salle, who founded the Congregation of the Brothers of the Christian Schools (Christian Brothers). The Entrance Antiphon, words of Jesus from Mark's Gospel, taken from the Common of Holy Men and Women, IV. For Educators,[48] echoes de la Salle's philosophy: "Let the children come to me. Don't try to stop them. People who are like these little children belong to the kingdom of God" (Mark 10:14). In

46. *Roman Missal*, 841–44.

47. *Roman Missal*, 846.

48. *Roman Missal*, 1111–12.

commemorating the memory of de la Salle, in the Prayer over the Offerings, we ask God to accept our gifts and to enable us to reflect the pattern of his love, just like this saint did through his teaching. A similar idea is expressed in the Prayer after Communion, in which we ask God to strengthen us with the food we have received so that we can imitate de la Salle's charity and teach the light of truth. The Communion Antiphon reminds us that unless we change and become like children, we will never enter the kingdom of heaven (Matt 18:3).

April 11, Memorial of St. Stanislaus: Polish Martyr[49]

The eleventh-century bishop of Krakow, Poland, Stanislaus (1030–1079), was martyred by the king of Poland, Boleslaus II. The king responded to the bishop's excommunication—because the king had kidnapped a married woman and lodged her in his palace—by ordering the bishop's assassination. However, the king's soldiers failed three times, so the king killed Stanislaus while he was celebrating Mass on April 11, 1079. The Collect refers to this event as Stanislaus falling beneath the swords of his persecutors. We ask God to keep us strong in the faith professed by Stanislaus even until death. The Entrance Antiphon, taken from the Common of Martyrs, B. For One Martyr, 2,[50] is most fitting in remembering this bishop. He is truly a martyr, who shed his blood for Christ; he did not fear the threats of the king, but, instead, attained the real King's heavenly realm. The Prayer over the Gifts re-emphasizes our need for God's blessing to confirm us in faith, while the Prayer after Communion petitions God to help us imitate the constancy of Stanislaus and merit the eternal reward he now enjoys.

SAINTS DURING THE EASTER SEASON

April 25, Feast of St. Mark: Preacher[51]

The theme permeating the Mass texts for the Feast of Mark is preaching the gospel. The Entrance Antiphon, taken from the longer ending of Mark's Gospel (which has three endings: 16:8a; 16:8bc; 16:9–20), portrays Jesus telling the eleven disciples, "Go and preach the good news to everyone in the world"

49. *Roman Missal*, 847.

50. *Roman Missal*, 1060–61.

51. *Roman Missal*, 850.

(Mark 16:15). The Collect continues the theme by declaring that God endowed Mark with the grace to preach the good news. The Communion Antiphon, taken from the post-resurrection appearance of Christ in Matthew's Gospel, presents Jesus telling his eleven disciples, "I will be with you always, even until the end of the world" (Matt 28:20b). Thus, our prayer is that we profit from Mark's Gospel so as to follow faithfully in Christ's footsteps (Collect) and that the church persevere in preaching the gospel (Prayer over the Gifts). In the Prayer after Communion, we ask God to make us holy and strong in the faith of the gospel proclaimed by Mark. Preface II of Apostles reminds us that the church is built on the gospel, which is offered to all people.[52]

April 29, Memorial of St. Catherine of Siena: Fire[53]

Catherine (1347–1380) was born in Siena, Italy; she was the youngest of twenty-five children! At the age of six, she experienced a vision of Christ which led her to join the Dominican Tertiaries at the age of fifteen. The rest of her life was punctuated with extraordinary mystical phenomena. In the Collect, we declare that God set Catherine on fire with divine love in her contemplation of Jesus' passion and in her service to the church—one of her primary foci was the return of the pope to Rome from Avignon, France. The Entrance Antiphon declares Catherine to be a wise virgin, who went forth with a lighted lamp to meet Christ. The Communion Antiphon echoes the light theme, stating, ". . . [I]f we live in the light, as God does, we share in life with each other. And the blood of his Son Jesus washes all our sins away" (1 John 1:7). Thus, in the Collect, we pray to participate in the mystery of Christ and to exult in the revelation of his glory. In the Prayer over the Offerings, we seek to give ever more fervent thanks to God, and in the Prayer after Communion, we seek the eternal life from God's heavenly table which nourished Catherine of Siena.

May 1, Optional Memorial of St. Joseph the Worker: Laborer[54]

The Collect sets the focus for the commemoration of Joseph the Worker. We are reminded that God, the creator of all things, gave us work to do, and

52. *Roman Missal*, 596–97.

53. *Roman Missal*, 852.

54. *Roman Missal*, 854–56.

Joseph serves as an example for us to complete the work God has bestowed upon us. The Entrance Antiphon further emphasizes this: "The LORD will bless you if you respect him and obey his laws. Your fields will produce, and you will be happy and all will go well" (Ps 128:1–2). The Preface recounts Joseph's mission to be the spouse of the Blessed Virgin Mary and to provide fatherly care to God's only-begotten Son. He is referred to as a faithful servant, which further emphasizes the theme of work. The Communion Antiphon serves as an exhortation to accomplish the work God has entrusted to us: "Whatever you say or do should be done in the name of the Lord Jesus, as you give thanks to God the Father because of him" (Col 3:17). Under the patronage of Joseph, we recognize work as a sign of God's love in the Prayer after Communion.

May 2, Memorial of St. Athanasius: Champion[55]

Athanasius (295–373), bishop of Alexandria, Egypt, is remembered, according to the Collect, as a champion of the divinity of Jesus Christ. In the Prayer after Communion, we declare that we profess firmly the divinity of God's only-begotten Son. While Athanasius was still a deacon, he attended the Council of Nicaea (325) with his bishop, Alexander, in order to deal with Arius, a priest, who was teaching that the Incarnate Word was created in time by the Father. Athanasius taught that there was never a time that the Word did not exist. The first ecumenical council declared the consubstantiality of the Son with the Father. Thus, according to the Entrance Antiphon, Athanasius opened his mouth in the midst of the people (Sir 15:5), and God filled him with wisdom and understanding to declare the divinity of Christ. In the words of the Prayer over the Offerings, he witnessed to the truth, he presented an unblemished faith, and so we rejoice in his teaching and protection (Collect). The Communion Antiphon reminds us that "we must each be careful how we build, because Christ is the only foundation" (1 Cor 3:10–11).

May 3, Feast of Sts. Philip and James: Followers[56]

The holy men named Philip and James, whom the Lord chose and to whom he gave eternal glory, according to the Entrance Antiphon, are commemorated as examples of Christ's followers who shared in the passion (suffering

55. *Roman Missal,* 857.

56. *Roman Missal,* 858.

and death) and resurrection of their Lord; now they behold him for all eternity (Collect). On the feast day of the apostles Philip and James, which, according to the Collect, gladdens us each year, we ask God in the Prayer over the Offerings to bestow on us pure and undefiled religion. The Prayer after Communion asks God to purify our minds through the gifts of the body and blood of Christ so that we may contemplate God in his Son along with Philip and James and, like them, be made worthy to possess eternal life. This last point is further emphasized in the Communion Antiphon, taken from a unique dialogue between Jesus and Philip in John's Gospel: "Philip said [to Jesus], 'Lord, show us the Father. That is all we need.' Jesus replied, 'Philip, I have been with you for a long time. Don't you know who I am? If you have seen me, you have seen the Father'" (John 14:8–9abc).

May 14, Feast of St. Matthias: Number Twelve[57]

Matthias is named an apostle because he was chosen by the eleven apostles to replace Judas in the Acts of the Apostles (Acts 1:15–26). Quoting words of the Johannine Jesus, the Entrance Antiphon declares, "You did not choose me. I chose you and sent you out to produce fruit, the kind of fruit that will last" (John 15:16ab). Matthias's being given a place in the college of apostles by God, as stated in the Collect, serves as our hope to be numbered among God's elect. We need to be strengthened by God's grace, according to the Prayer over the Offerings, so that we can be admitted to a share in the lot of the saints, like Matthias, who now shares in divine light, according to the Prayer after Communion. In Preface II of Apostles,[58] we are reminded that the Father has built the church on apostolic foundations; as an apostle, Matthias's purpose was to reconstitute the Twelve in preparation for Pentecost, the beginning of the church, which is supposed to be a sign of God's holiness on earth. We participate in such holiness, according to the Communion Antiphon, when we follow Jesus' command to love one another (John 15:12).

May 26, Memorial of St. Philip Neri: Love[59]

The Mass texts honoring Philip Neri (1515–1595) carry a theme of love. The Entrance Antiphon sets the stage: ". . . God has given us the Holy Spirit, who

57. *Roman Missal*, 861.

58. *Roman Missal*, 596–97.

59. *Roman Missal*, 865–66.

fills our hearts with his love" (Rom 5:5). While still a layman, Neri founded the lay Confraternity of the Most Blessed Trinity to provide assistance for pilgrims in Rome. In the Collect, we hear how the Holy Spirit filled Neri's heart with the fire of holiness. Realizing that he could accomplish more if he were ordained, he entered the priesthood in 1551, when he was thirty-six years old. Such love prompted this saint to form the Congregation of the Oratory, which is devoted to the ministry of confessions and spiritual conferences. Neri's love prompts us to ask God to continue to raise up such faithful servants today (Collect) and to help us give ourselves cheerfully in service to his name (Prayer over the Offerings), while longing for the eucharistic food which gives us eternal life (Prayer after Communion). The Communion Antiphon returns us to the theme of love by presenting a verse spoken by Jesus in John's Gospel: "I have loved you, just as my Father has loved me. So remain faithful to my love for you" (John 15:9).

May 31, Feast of the Visitation of the Blessed Virgin Mary: Visitor[60]

This Lukan feast is commemorated in the Collect. Mary, carrying Jesus in her womb, is inspired to visit Elizabeth, who is also filled with the Holy Spirit and bears in her womb John the Baptist, who leaps for joy. Adhering to the promptings of the Holy Spirit, Mary responds to Elizabeth's greeting by magnifying God's greatness. "All who worship God, come here and listen; I will tell you everything God has done for me" (Ps 66:16), echoes the Entrance Antiphon and Mary's magnificat. The Communion Antiphon, two verses from the magnificat, further praises God's greatness: "From now on, all people will say God has blessed me. God All-Powerful has done great things for me, and his name is holy" (Luke 1:48b–49). The theme of praising God for his greatness is resumed in the Prayer after Communion. We ask God to let the church proclaim his greatness because he has done great things for his people. Mary carries in her womb the hidden presence of Christ, which causes John the Baptist in Elizabeth's womb to leap for joy. We ask God to help his church rejoice in receiving the hidden presence of Christ under the forms of bread and wine, because God has visited his people again.

---

60. *Roman Missal*, 867–68

SAINTS DURING THE SEASON OF ORDINARY TIME: PART II

Saturday after the Second Sunday after Pentecost, Memorial of the Immaculate Heart of the Blessed Virgin Mary: Heart and Grace[61]

The theme of today's Mass texts can be summarized in the words *heart* and *grace*. "I trust your love, and I feel like celebrating because you rescued me," LORD (Ps 13:5), we sing in the Entrance Antiphon. The Collect declares that God prepared the heart of the Blessed Virgin Mary to be a worthy dwelling place for the Holy Spirit, who enabled her to conceive God's only-begotten Son. And the Communion Antiphon, a verse from Luke's Gospel, states, ". . . Mary kept thinking about all this and wondering what it meant" (Luke 2:19). In the Collect, we ask God to make us a worthy temple of his glorious grace, just like he did for the Blessed Virgin Mary, and, in the Prayer after Communion, we pray that we may glory in the fullness of God's grace as it continues to increase in us toward salvation. Thus, we ask God to look favorably upon our prayers and offerings in memory of the Mother of God; we pray that they will please him and confer on us his help and forgiveness (Prayer over the Offerings), even as now we partake of eternal redemption (Prayer after Communion).

June 1, Memorial of St. Justin: Folly of the Cross[62]

Justin, who died a martyr around 166, was a layman and a philosopher. After a wise man told him to study the HB (OT), he converted to Christianity around 130 and went to Rome, where he opened a school to educate Christians in the surpassing knowledge of Jesus Christ and in the folly of the cross, according to the Collect. Justin's extensive education is referenced in the Entrance Antiphon: "Those proud people reject your teaching, [LORD,] and they dig pits for me to fall in. I have gained perfect freedom by following your teachings, and I trust them so much that I tell them to kings" (Ps 119:85, 45–46). The Communion Antiphon echoes the theme of the cross, quoting Paul and stating, ". . . I made up my mind to speak only about Jesus Christ, who had been nailed to a cross" (1 Cor 2:2). Our prayer is that we, like Justin, will reject deception and error and become steadfast in faith (Collect), and,

---

61. *Roman Missal*, 869.
62. *Roman Missal*, 870.

like Justin, defend the mysteries we celebrate (Prayer over the Offerings). By being attentive to Justin's teachings, we will find ourselves being thankful for all the gifts we have received from God (Prayer after Communion).

June 3, Memorial of St. Charles Lwanga and Companions: Twenty-Two[63]

Between the years 1886 and 1887 over one hundred Catholics and Protestants were murdered by King Mwanga of Uganda, Africa. Among these were twenty-two martyrs on May 26 and June 3, 1886, and January 27, 1887. Charles Lwanga was the leader of the group, whose blood was the seed of Christians, according to the Collect, sowed in the field of Africa and watered by the blood of Lwanga and his companions; an abundant harvest of new Christians was the result of these African martyrs' deaths. The Entrance Antiphon compares the martyrs to gold, which is purified in a furnace. It states that God tried them, and like a sacrificial burnt offering he accepted them. Now, they shine like gold because God has given them grace and mercy; they are his holy ones, over whom he watched (Wis 3:6–7a, 9cd). In mentioning a sacrificial burnt offering, the antiphon is referencing the fact that Lwanga was burned to death. The Communion Antiphon declares that the death of God's faithful people is precious in his sight (Ps 116:15). Our prayer is that God will give us the same grace to be dedicated to him alone (Prayer over the Offerings), and that he will keep us steadfast in faith and charity when we face the trials of our lives (Prayer after Communion).

June 5, Memorial of St. Boniface: Advocate[64]

Boniface was born in Wessex, England, around 673. After being educated in a monastery in Exeter, he joined the Benedictine abbey at Nursing, but was later sent to Germany to preach the gospel. He was ordained a bishop in 722, and made an archbishop in 732. The Communion Antiphon, taken from the Common of Pastors, V. For Missionaries, 1,[65] captures his episcopal responsibilities: "I promise to take care of [my sheep] and keep them safe," says the LORD God (Ezek 34:15). In 754, he and fifty-two of his companions were martyred by a hostile band as he was preparing to celebrate

63. *Roman Missal,* 871–72.

64. *Roman Missal,* 872.

65. *Roman Missal,* 1084–85.

confirmation. The Collect states that Boniface taught the faith with his lips and sealed it with his blood. The Entrance Antiphon alludes to Boniface's mission to Germany; the psalmist declares, "I will praise you, LORD, and I will honor you among the nations. . . . [W]hen your people meet, I will praise you, LORD" (Pss 18:49; 22:22). Our petition to God is that we may hold firmly to our faith and confess it with our words and deeds (Collect, Prayer after Communion), imitating what we celebrate (Prayer over the Offerings).

June 11, Memorial of St. Barnabas: Apostle[66]

While Barnabas is named an apostle in the Entrance Antiphon—"Barnabas was a good man of great faith, and he was filled with the Holy Spirit" (Acts 11:24a), worthy to be counted among the apostles—he is not one of Jesus' original apostles. The Collect helps us to understand that God chose Barnabas as a companion of Paul, filled him with faith and the Spirit, and sent him to the nations to preach the gospel of Jesus Christ. Our prayer is that like Barnabas we may be set on fire with the flame of God's love and bring the same gospel to the nations (Prayer over the Gifts) in word and deed (Collect). The Communion Antiphon, taken from a verse Jesus speaks to his apostles in John's Gospel, declares, "Servants don't know what their master is doing, and so I don't speak to you as my servants. I speak to you as my friends, and I have told you everything that my Father has told me" (John 15:15). In the Prayer after Communion, we implore God that the pledge of eternal life, which we receive in the body and blood of Christ under the signs of bread and wine on the feast of Barnabas, will be unveiled one day when, with Barnabas, we will behold God's face in heaven.

June 13, Memorial of St. Anthony of Padua: Bringer of Good News[67]

The Collect sets the theme for today's celebration in honor of Anthony. It acknowledges that God gave Anthony of Padua (1195–1231) to us as an outstanding preacher. This theme is emphasized in the Entrance Antiphon, taken from the Common of Pastors, B. For One Pastor, 2:[68] "The Lord's Spirit has come to me, because he has chosen me to tell the good news to the poor"

66. *Roman Missal*, 874–75.
67. *Roman Missal*, 875.
68. *Roman Missal*, 1079–80.

(Luke 4:18a). Anthony began his life in Lisbon, Portugal, with the name of Ferdinand. After joining the Augustinians for nine years, he transferred to the Franciscans and took Anthony as his religious name. Later, after meeting Francis of Assisi, he was ordained a priest and began a preaching ministry that took him to northern Italy and southern France. In 1227, he went to Padua, where he died in 1231 at the age of thirty-six. Our prayer in the Collect is that with Anthony's intercession we may follow the teachings of the Christian life and know God's help in every one of our trials. Likewise, in the Prayer after Communion, we petition God to make us faithful servants, like he made Anthony a saintly steward.

June 21, Memorial of St. Aloysius Gonzaga: Penitent[69]

The theme permeating the Mass texts that remember Aloysius Gonzaga (1568–1591), a Jesuit seminarian, is penitence and innocence. During his short life, he was known for his austerity and self-imposed mortification; he knew that he was a sinner. He was also known for his innocence; at the age of ten he consecrated himself to God with a vow of virginity. The Collect states that this saint joined penitence to innocence, referred to as being clothed in his baptismal or wedding garment in the Prayer over the Offerings. "Who may climb the LORD's hill or stand in his holy Temple? Only those who do right for the right reasons . . . (Ps 24:3–4a); the Entrance Antiphon also emphasizes Gonzaga's innocence, which was maintained through his regular participation in the eucharistic mystery (Prayer over the Offerings). According to the Prayer after Communion, he was fed with the food of angels, which enabled him to serve God in purity all the days of his life. "From heaven [God] sent grain that they called manna. He gave them more than enough, and each one of them ate this special food " (Ps 78:24–25), states the Communion Antiphon. In the Collect, we pray that we, who have failed in innocence, may imitate Gonzaga's penitence.

69. *Roman Missal*, 876.

June 24, Solemnity of the Nativity of St. John the Baptist: Precursor[70]

Vigil

John the Baptist, who was called to a singular honor among human kind (Preface), is referred to as the precursor of our Lord Jesus Christ (Collect) and the herald of the Lamb of God (Preface), who took away the sins of the world (Prayer after Communion). The Entrance Antiphon, taken from Luke's Gospel, portrays the angel Gabriel telling John's father, Zechariah: "His birth will make you very happy, and many people will be glad. Your son will be a great servant of the Lord" (Luke 1:14–15a). The Communion Antiphon, taken from Zechariah's hymn of praise after John is born, states, "Praise the Lord, the God of Israel! He has come to save his people" (Luke 1:68). In marking the birth of John, near the summer solstice when the days begin to decrease in length of light, we pray that God will enable us to walk the path of salvation in order to reach safely the One he foretold (Collect). Our hope is that along the way we will demonstrate our faith with deeds of service (Prayer over the Offerings) while we get our strength from the sacrificial feast of the Lamb of God.

During the Day

The Entrance Antiphon, a gloss on two verses from John's Gospel and one from Luke's Gospel, states the role of John the Baptist: "God sent a man named John, who came to tell about the light and to lead all people to have faith" (John 1:6–7). "That is how John will get people ready for the Lord" (Luke 1:17d). The Collect echoes this theme by declaring that God sent John to make a nation ready for Christ. Not only did John foretell the coming of the Savior, but he pointed to him when he came (Prayer over the Offerings), even baptizing the author of baptism and making holy the flowing waters of the Jordan River (Preface). Our prayer is that God will fill us with spiritual joys as he directs us along the way of salvation and peace. Even though we honor the birth of John the Baptist, we eat and drink the body and blood of the heavenly Lamb, finding joy in knowing the author of rebirth whose coming was foretold by John. According to the Communion Antiphon: "God's love and kindness will shine upon us like the sun that rises in the sky" (Luke 1:78).

70. *Roman Missal*, 878–82.

June 28, Memorial of St. Irenaeus: Truth and Unity[71]

Irenaeus (ca. 120/140–202/203) is a second-century bishop and martyr who is known for preaching the truth, in terms of doctrine, and for his focus on unity. The Entrance Antiphon emphasizes his love of truth: "He taught the truth and never told lies, and he led a lot of people to turn from sin, because he obeyed [God] and lived right" (Mal 2:6). The Communion Antiphon, words of the Johannine Jesus, emphasizes his focus on unity: "Stay joined to me, and I will stay joined to you. . . . [Y]ou cannot produce fruit unless you stay joined to me" (John 15:4a, 5). The Collect states that God called Irenaeus, whose name means *peaceful*, to confirm the doctrine and peace of the church. On this heavenly birthday of Irenaeus, we ask God to keep us focused on unity and concord. In the Prayer over the Offerings, we ask God to fill us with a love of the truth so that we may preserve unity. And in the Prayer after Communion, we seek an increase in faith and the strength to maintain that same faith through death to justification in God's sight.

June 29, Solemnity of Sts. Peter and Paul: Foundations[72]

Vigil

The Collect refers to Peter and Paul as the instruments through whom God gave the foundations of the church's heavenly office. In the Preface, Peter is declared foremost in professing faith in Jesus and the apostle who was the foundation of the church in Israel. The Communion Antiphon, taken from John's Gospel, illustrates Peter's confession of faith: "[Jesus asked Simon,] 'Simon son of John, do you love me more than the others do?' [Simon Peter] told Jesus, 'Lord, you know everything. You know I love you'" (John 21:15a, 17c). The solemn blessing for this solemnity also mentions Peter's saving confession along with the keys entrusted to him by Jesus. Our prayer is that God will bring us to the heavenly homeland which Peter entered through the cross.[73] We ask God to sustain us through the intercession of Peter (Collect) and that we will doubt our ability to save ourselves while rejoicing that God saves us through his loving kindness (Prayer over the Offerings). In the Prayer after Communion, we ask God to strengthen us with the eucharist even as we are enlightened by Peter's teaching.

71. *Roman Missal*, 883.

72. *Roman Missal*, 885–89.

73. *Roman Missal*, 682.

During the Day

The Entrance Antiphon declares Peter and Paul to be the saints who planted the church through their martyrdom. We petition God to grant us adherence to their teaching. In the Preface, Paul is named teacher, master of the Gentiles, and an outstanding preacher. The solemn blessing refers to him as an instructor, from whom we may be taught by his words and example.[74] We ask God on this day of holy joy to help us follow Paul's teaching (Collect). We also ask God to hear Paul's intercession to make us more devoted to God, and to give us perseverance in breaking bread and keeping the teaching of the apostle Paul (Prayer after Communion). The goal, according to the Prayer after Communion, is to keep us one in heart and soul and steadfast in God's love. As the Preface states, both Peter and Paul, each in his own way, gathered together the one church from Jews and Gentiles. The Communion Antiphon, taken from Matthew's Gospel, echoes this: "Simon Peter spoke up [and said to Jesus], 'You are the Messiah, the Son of the living God.' [Jesus told him], '. . . I will call you Peter, which means "a rock." On this rock I will build my church . . .'" (Matt 16:16, 18).

July 3, Feast of St. Thomas: Faith[75]

While Thomas is usually known as a doubter of Christ's resurrection—illustrated in the Communion Antiphon, words of Jesus to Thomas: "Put your finger here and look at my hands! Put your hand into my side. Stop doubting and have faith!" (John 20:27)—his feast day is a celebration of his faith. The Entrance Antiphon sets that theme: "The LORD is my God! I will praise him and tell him how thankful I am. I praise the LORD for answering my prayers and saving me" (Ps 118: 28, 21). In the Collect, we ask God to give us firmness of faith through Thomas's intersession and to turn our faith into life in the name of Jesus, whom Thomas declared to be Lord. In the Prayer over the Offerings, we honor Thomas's confession while asking God to preserve the gifts he has given us through our sacrifice of praise. And in the Prayer after Communion, we pray that we will always recognize God's only-begotten Son by faith in the elements of bread and wine and proclaim him both in our deeds and our life.

---

74. *Roman Missal*, 682.

75. *Roman Missal*, 890–91.

July 4, Optional Memorial of Independence Day: Peace and Justice[76]

Peace and justice permeate all the Mass texts for this celebration. The Entrance Antiphon, a gloss on two verses from the OT (A) book of Sirach, asks God to give peace to those who wait for him, to hear the prayer of his servants, and to guide them in the ways of justice (Sir 36:21–22). The God of justice, the Father of truth, is addressed in the first optional Collect and asked to let peace rule our hearts and justice to guide our lives. In the second optional Collect, we name God as the Father of nations and seek his help for the work of peace and justice that remains to be done in our own country. It is the gospel that leads us to true justice and lasting peace, according to the first optional Prayer over the Offerings. In the second option, we seek to be instruments of God's peace. The first Preface identifies Jesus as a messenger of peace, while the second records how Jesus bore witness to justice and truth. In the first option of the Prayer after Communion, we ask God to help us work together to build a city of lasting peace, while in the second option we seek God's will for our nation. We seek peace and harmony in the Solemn Blessing, along with wisdom, grace, and love—all of which lead us to justice.

July 11, Memorial of St. Benedict: Holy Living[77]

The Entrance Antiphon identifies Benedict (480–547), the father of Western Monasticism, as a practitioner of holy living. It declares that he was blessed by grace and name—his name means *blessed*—and called by God to leave his home and inheritance to practice living for God alone. The Collect names Benedict as a master of the school of divine service; this means that the saint sought to please God by seeking him (Prayer over the Offerings), by putting nothing before the love of God (Collect), and by faithfully serving his designs (Prayer after Communion). After studying in Rome, at the age of twenty Benedict left the world and lived an eremitical life. However, he attracted followers; he founded a monastery and wrote a rule of life for the monks, identified as a school for the service of the Lord. The Communion Antiphon calls him the faithful and prudent servant whom his master put in charge "of giving the other servants their food supplies at the proper time" (Luke 12:42). Our prayer is that God will fill us with the same love with

---

76. *Roman Missal*, 892–98.

77. *Roman Missal*, 901.

which he filled Benedict (Collect) that we may merit the gifts of unity in his service and peace (Prayer over the Offerings).

July 14, Memorial of St. Kateri Tekakwitha: Native American[78]

Kateri (Catherine) Tekakwitha (1656–1680), known as the Lily of the Mohawks, is the first Native North American to be canonized. The Collect states that she flowered among her people in a life of innocence. It needs to be noted that she was captured during an Iroquois raid and taken to what is now New York to be the wife of a Mohawk chief; from this union two children were born, but neither survived. Later, after being catechized, she was baptized in 1676, made a vow of virginity in 1679, and died in 1680. Except for the Collect, all the Mass texts are taken from the Common of Virgins, II. For One Virgin, 2.[79] The Entrance Antiphon exhorts us to rejoice and exult over the love God has shown to this holy woman. The Prayer over the Offerings identifies her as an example of one renewed by growth in the life of heaven. We seek to grow in the same sincere love of God in imitation of Tekakwitha in the Prayer after Communion. The Communion Antiphon identifies this saint as one of the wise bridesmaids who "took along extra oil for their lamps. [I]n the middle of the night someone shouted, 'Here's the groom! Come to meet him!'" (Matt 25:4, 6) Our prayer is that those gathered to meet Christ from every nation, tribe, and tongue may sing a song of praise to God (Collect).

July 15, Memorial of St. Bonaventure: Doctor[80]

Bonaventure (1217/18–1274) is identified as a bishop and doctor of the church. This Franciscan saint served as bishop of Albano, Italy, and, before being named a bishop, as a professor (doctor) in the University of Paris. In the Collect, we declare that we celebrate his heavenly birthday and pray that we may benefit from his learning. The rest of the Mass texts are taken from the Common of Doctors of the Church, 1.[81] The Entrance Antiphon is very appropriate for this day: He opened his mouth in the midst of the people (Sir

---

78. *Roman Missal*, 902.

79. *Roman Missal*, 1093–94.

80. *Roman Missal*, 903.

81. *Roman Missal*, 1088–89.

15:5), and God filled him with wisdom and understanding. The Prayer over the Offerings mentions how Bonaventure teaches us to give ourselves entirely to God in praise, and the Prayer after Communion, after naming Jesus as the supreme teacher, asks God to help us learn his truth and practice it in works of charity—a minor theme mentioned in the Collect. The Communion Antiphon identifies this saint as one whom the law of the LORD made happy, and he thought about it day and night. He succeeded in everything he did (Ps 1:2, 3b).

July 22, Feast of St. Mary Magdalene: Apostle to Apostles[82]

Mary Magdalene is honored as the apostle to the apostles in the Preface.[83] It mentions how she sought Jesus as he lay dead in his tomb. Then, Christ appeared to her in a garden, and she adored him after his resurrection. He honored her with the responsibility of serving as an apostle to the apostles so that the gospel might reach everyone on the earth. The Collect states that Christ entrusted to her the message of his resurrection, saying to her, ". . . [T]ell my disciples that I am going to the one who is my Father and my God, as well as your Father and your God" (John 20:17) (Entrance Antiphon). The Preface also declares that Mary Magdalene loved Jesus in life; this note is called persevering love in the Prayer after Communion and the homage of charity in the Prayer over the Offerings, and it is echoed in the Communion Antiphon: "We are ruled by Christ's love for us. And Christ did die for all of us. He died so we would no longer live for ourselves, but for the one who died and was raised to life for us" (2 Cor 5:14a, 15). Thus, our prayer is that we might imitate the example of Mary Magdalene by proclaiming the living Christ in the hope of one day seeing him in all his glory (Collect).

July 25, Feast of St. James: Drinking the Cup[84]

The theme of drinking the cup of suffering—which permeates the Mass texts for this celebration of James, son of Zebedee, who, with his brother John, was in "a boat with their father, mending their nets," when Jesus called him to follow him (Matt 4:21) (Entrance Antiphon)—refers to his death by martyrdom; according to the Acts of the Apostles (12:2–3), he was the first of the

---

82. *Roman Missal*, 905–06.

83. "Preface for the Feast."

84. *Roman Missal*, 907–08.

apostles to share in the baptism of Jesus' passion (Prayer over the Offerings). The Collect calls the blood of James the first fruits among the apostles and prays that his confession of faith to his beheading somewhere between the years 42 and 44 will both strengthen the church and protect her. The Communion Antiphon declares that James drank the Lord's cup and became a friend of God. In the Prayer over the Offerings, we pray that God will cleanse us through Jesus' suffering and death and accept our sacrifices of bread and wine in the same way he accepted the sacrifice of James, whose intercession we seek as we receive the holy gifts of the body and blood of Christ with joy on James's feast day (Prayer after Communion).

July 26, Memorial of Sts. Joachim and Anne: Grandparents[85]

Although the couple of Joachim and Anne appear in no biblical text, this husband and wife are considered to be the parents of Mary, mother of Jesus, according to tradition. The Collect confirms this tradition by stating that God bestowed the grace of being the parents of the mother of Jesus on Joachim and Anne, the grandparents of Jesus, who was born of humankind that people might be born again from him (Prayer over the Offerings). The Entrance Antiphon, a gloss on two verses from the OT (A) book of Sirach, declares that we sing the praises of this famous couple, our ancestors in faith. The Lord brought them forth and they found favor in the sight of all; they were beloved by God and people (Sir 44:1, 23b—45:1). The Communion Antiphon continues this praise, stating, "The LORD God, who saves them, will bless and reward them" (Ps 24:5). We pray that we may share in the salvation God promised to his people (Collect), that we may merit to share in the blessings promised to Abraham, Sarah, and their heirs (Prayer over the Offerings), and that God in his kindness may confirm with the spirit of adoption those he feeds with the body and blood of his Son (Prayer after Communion).

July 29, Memorial of St. Martha: Hospitality[86]

Martha appears in Luke's Gospel and in John's Gospel. In Luke's Gospel, she is identified as "a woman named Martha" who welcomes Jesus "into her home" (Luke 10:38) (Entrance Antiphon); she has a sister named Mary. In

85. *Roman Missal*, 908–09.
86. *Roman Missal*, 909–10.

John's Gospel, she has a sister named Mary and a dead brother named Lazarus. She tells Jesus, "I believe that you are Christ, the Son of God. You are the one we hoped would come into the world" (John 11:27) (Communion Antiphon). The Collect states that Jesus was pleased to be welcomed as a guest into Martha's home. In the Prayer over the Offerings, we proclaim the deed of Martha's hospitality and ask God to let our service find favor with him, just as Martha's love was pleasing to his Son. In the Prayer after Communion, we seek to learn from Martha's example to grow in love of God now in order to behold his presence in heaven. This latter idea is also found in the Collect; we pray that we may imitate Martha by showing hospitality to Christ in all our brothers and sisters, even as he shows hospitality to us by feeding us his body and blood at his table (Prayer after Communion).

July 31, Memorial of St. Ignatius of Loyola: Name of Jesus[87]

Ignatius of Loyola (1491–1556) founded the Society of Jesus, better known as the Jesuits, in 1534. The Jesuits, an order of priests, are missionaries and educators. The motto of the society is *For the greater glory of God*. This is expressed in the Collect, which states that God raised up this saint to glorify his name. The Entrance Antiphon also emphasizes this theme: ". . . [A]t the name of Jesus everyone will bow down, those in heaven, on earth, and under the earth. And to the glory of God the Father everyone will openly agree, 'Jesus Christ is Lord!'" (Phil 2:10–11) This saint's life illustrates the words of Jesus in the Communion Antiphon: "I came to set fire to the earth, and I wish it were already on fire" (Luke 12:49). Thus, our prayer is that we may imitate Ignatius in our good fight on earth in order to merit to share with him a heavenly crown (Collect) and exalt God's goodness without end (Prayer after Communion). Here and now we are strengthened by the body and blood of Christ, the font of all holiness and sanctification in the truth (Prayer over the Offerings).

August 1, Memorial of St. Alphonsus Liguori: Wisdom[88]

Alphonsus Liguori (1696–1787), founder of the Congregation of the Most Holy Redeemer (Redemptorists) in 1732, is best known, among other things, for his wisdom as a preacher and a teacher. This saint demonstrated

---

87. *Roman Missal*, 911.
88. *Roman Missal*, 912.

his intellectual wisdom at the age of seventeen by earning two doctorates. The Entrance Antiphon, taken from the Common of Doctors of the Church, 2,[89] emphasizes his wisdom: "Everyone who has been wise will shine as bright as the sky above, and everyone who has led others to please God will shine like the strars" (Dan 12:3). The Communion Antiphon, words of Paul, reflects on wisdom: We preach Christ crucified. Christ is the power of God and the wisdom of God (1 Cor 1:23–24). We ask God to kindle the fire of his Spirit in our hearts that we, like Liguori, may offer ourselves to him as a holy sacrifice. The Prayer after Communion refers to the saint as a steward and preacher of the eucharistic mystery; we pray that we who receive it will praise God without end for his great gift. It is the body and blood of Christ that enables us to follow closely in Liguori's footsteps and maintain our zeal until we reach the joys of heaven (Collect).

August 4, Memorial of St. John Vianney: Zeal[90]

According to the Collect, John Vianney (1786–1859), a parish priest better known as the *Curé* of Ars, demonstrated pastoral zeal for his parishioners for forty-two years. The Entrance Antiphon, taken from the Common of Pastors, III. For Pastors, B. For One Pastor, 2,[91] states that his zeal came from God: "The Lord's Spirit has come to me, because he has chosen me to tell the good news to the poor" (Luke 4:18). He brought good news to the poor by serving them and being available for their confessions. He won sisters and brothers for Christ (Collect), wearing himself out through his tireless religious education of his people. He bore witness to divine power effecting salvation in those to whom he ministered (Prayer over the Offerings). We pray that we can follow Vianney's example in serving others with zeal and untiring charity (Prayer after Communion), knowing that Christ is with us always, to the end of the age (Matt 28:20) (Communion Antiphon). Our hope is to attain eternal glory (Collect).

89. *Roman Missal* 1089–90.
90. *Roman Missal*, 914.
91. *Roman Missal*, 1079–80.

August 6, Feast of the Transfiguration of the Lord: Transfiguration[92]

This biblical feast, found in the synoptic gospels (Mark 9:2–8; Matt 17:1–8; Luke 9:28–36), refers to the complete change of the appearance of Jesus with the corresponding appearance of Moses and Elijah—referred to in the Collect as the witness of the fathers—in glory. The Preface states that Jesus revealed his glory to Peter, James, and John—three apostles he chose to accompany him—filling his body with the radiant splendor of his divinity (Prayer over the Offerings). The author of Matthew's Gospel records: ". . . [T]he shadow of a bright cloud passed over [Peter, James, and John]. From the cloud a voice said, 'This is my own dear Son, and I am pleased with him. Listen to what he says!'" (Matt 17:5) Our prayer is that we will listen to him (Collect), be cleansed of our sins (Prayer over the Offerings), and, through our reception of his body and blood, be transformed into his likeness (Prayer after Communion) and merit to share in his resurrected life. The words of the Communion Antiphon declare: ". . . [W]hen Christ returns, we will be like him, because we will see him as he truly is" (1 John 3:2b).

August 8, Memorial of St. Dominic: Champion[93]

Dominic Guzman (1170–1221) founded the Order of Preachers in 1217–1218. The mission of the friars was, obviously, preaching, after studying Scripture and doctrine, in order to save people. According to the Prayer after Communion, the church flourished because of Dominic's preaching. The Collect refers to him as an outstanding preacher of truth. He opened his mouth in the midst of the church (Sir 15:5) and "[t]he Spirit of the LORD" gave "him understanding, wisdom, and insight" (Isa 11:2), and God placed a robe of glory on him, states the Entrance Antiphon. This is what made him a champion of the faith (Prayer over the Offerings). In the Communion Antiphon, he is identified as that "faithful and wise servant" whose "master . . . put in charge of giving the other servants their food supplies at the proper time" (Luke 12:42). We pray that Dominic will continue to help the church through his teaching (Collect) and his intercession (Collect, Prayer after Communion). In the Prayer over the Offerings, we ask God to strengthen all who champion the faith with the protection of his grace.

92. *Roman Missal*, 917–20.
93. *Roman Missal*, 921.

August 10, Feast of St. Lawrence: Deacon[94]

The Entrance Antiphon names Lawrence blessed because he sacrificed himself for the poor, the treasure of the church; the result was martyrdom as he made his way with joy to Christ in 258. As a deacon, Lawrence was the manager of the material treasures of the church. According to the tradition, he was burned to death on a gridiron after refusing to hand over the non-existent material treasure that the authorities claimed he had. Instead, he presented the poor, whom he considered to be the real treasure. The Collect states that Lawrence was faithful in service, responding to the ardor of love God gave to him. In the Prayer after Communion, we ask God to bless our service with an increase of his grace. In the Preface,[95] we are reminded that Lawrence's blood was shed like Jesus' both to glorify God's name and to demonstrate how God gives strength for bearing witness to feeble people, like Lawrence. The words of Jesus in the Communion Antiphon summarize this saint's diaconal service and martyrdom: "If you serve me, you must go with me. My servants will be with me wherever I am" (John 12:26ab).

August 11, Memorial of St. Clare: Poverty[96]

There has been no one who has ever put into practice St. Francis of Assisi's love of poverty better than Clare (1193/4–1253). That is why the Collect states that God led Clare to her love of poverty. The Entrance Antiphon, taken from the Common of Holy Men and Women, II. For Monks and Religious, C. For a Nun,[97] states that Clare despised the world with its finery for the love of Christ, whom she saw, loved, believed, and in whom she found delight. She had met Francis numerous times; after she came to him, he placed her in a house attached to the church of San Damiano and named her the abbess, an office she held for forty years. Many women, including her sister and mother, joined her in living absolute poverty. She believed what the Communion Antiphon states: ". . . [O]nly one things is necessary. [She] has chosen what is best, and it will not be taken away from her" (Luke 10:42). In the Collect, we pray that God will enable us to follow Christ in poverty of spirit; in the Prayer after Communion, we ask God to help us to follow Christ every day so as to merit being coheirs in eternity.

94. *Roman Missal*, 922–23.
95. *Roman Missal*, 602–03.
96. *Roman Missal*, 923.
97. *Roman Missal*, 1106–07.

August 14, Memorial of St. Maximilian Kolbe: Neighborly Love[98]

Maximilian Kolbe (1894–1941), a Franciscan priest, demonstrated neighborly love by offering himself as a replacement for one man condemned to death in the Nazi concentration camp in Auschwitz, Poland. While he was not killed immediately, he died of starvation later. The Communion Antiphon, words of the Johannine Jesus, emphasizes his love: "The greatest way to show love for friends is to die for them" (John 15:13). The Collect mentions Kolbe's love for the Immaculate Virgin Mary along with his love of neighbor. We pray that through our service of neighbor, we may be conformed to the image of Jesus, even if it means death (Collect). Kolbe serves as an example of how we can offer our lives to God (Prayer over the Offerings). He was strengthened with the body and blood of Christ to offer his life in exchange for another (Prayer after Communion). Like him, we hope one day to hear the words of the Matthean Jesus: "My father has blessed you! Whenever you did it for any of my people, no matter how unimportant they seemed, you did it for me" (Matt 25:34a, 40) (Entrance Antiphon).

August 15, Solemnity of the Assumption of the Blessed Virgin Mary: Raised to Life[99]

Vigil

Jesus is raised from the dead, and his mother, Mary, is assumed into heaven. Because she bore the Son of God in her womb and nursed him at her breasts, she is declared blessed (Luke 11:27) (Communion Antiphon). In the words of the Collect, the lowly Virgin Mary gave birth to the only-begotten Son of the Father according to the flesh, and because of this singular grace she was raised from the dead to share in her child's glory. On this day, in the words of the Entrance Antiphon, glorious things are said in honor of Mary, who entered into eternal triumph with Christ. The Preface identifies her as both the beginning of the church—the first member as a follower of her Son—and an image of what the church is called to be—a model of holiness through her cooperation with God. She is presented as a sign of hope and comfort to us as we continue our journey to God. Our prayer is that we who have been saved by Christ's redemption may be protected from all harm

98. *Roman Missal*, 925.

99. *Roman Missal*, 927–30.

and one day share in her exaltation (Collect, Prayer over the Offerings, Prayer after Communion).

During the Day

The Blessed Virgin Mary's body was preserved from corruption because she gave birth to the incarnate Son of God, states today's Preface. The author of all life raised her from the dead, that is, assumed her into heaven. The Collect emphasizes this by stating that God assumed the Immaculate Virgin body and soul into the glory of heaven. The second optional Entrance Antiphon exhorts us to rejoice as we celebrate this feast, and the Communion Antiphon, words of Mary's song in Luke's Gospel, declares: "From now on, all people will say God has blessed me. God All-Powerful has done great things for me . . ." (Luke 1:48b–49). On this day we pray that we may one day share in her glory (Collect), that our hearts may be on fire with the same longing love of Mary (Prayer over the Offerings), and that we may be raised from the dead just like Christ was, and after him, just like his mother was (Prayer after Communion). The first optional Entrance Antiphon, taken from the CB (NT) book of Revelation, summarizes the focus of this day: "Something important appeared in the sky. It was a woman whose clothes were the sun. The moon was under her feet, and a crown made of twelve stars was on her head" (Rev 12:1).

August 20, Memorial of St. Bernard: Inspirited[100]

The Entrance Antiphon declares that Bernard (1090–1153) was filled with the spirit of understanding, and from him issued streams of clear teaching to God's people. This Cistercian monk and abbot demonstrated his burning zeal for the church, states the Collect; he was like a light shining in the Dark Ages. He stood out of the ordinary in word and deed as he worked to bring order and concord to the church in a time of chaos (Prayer over the Offerings). In the words of the Johannine Jesus, despite the darkness and chaos Bernard abided in Jesus' love just as Jesus abided in his Father's love (John 15:9) (Communion Antiphon). Eucharistic food strengthened Bernard and worked its effects in him, according to the Prayer after Communion, and so we ask God to help us learn from his example how to be caught up in love of the incarnate Word. We seek to be on fire with the

---

100. *Roman Missal*, 932.

Spirit and walk as children of light in the darkness and chaos of our world (Collect). Bernard shows us the way and intercedes for us as a member of the communion of saints.

August 21, Memorial of Pope St. Pius X: Restoration[101]

The words of the Collect about restoring all things in Christ summarize the reign of Pope Pius X (1903–1914). Born Joseph Sarto in 1835, Pius X reformed the liturgy and sought more active participation from those celebrating it. The Collect states that God filled him with wisdom and fortitude which were demonstrated in his pastoral work of teaching, restoring church law, and formation of the clergy, among many others. Using the words of the Entrance Antiphon, taken from the Common of Pastors, I. For a Pope or for a Bishop, 1,[102] we say that Pius X was a great priest, who pleased the God who gave him growth for all his people. As a good shepherd, he laid down his life—dying in office—for his sheep (Communion Antiphon). In the Prayer over the Offerings, we pray that we may celebrate the eucharist with sincere reverence and in a spirit of faith, following the teachings of this saint. By imitating his example, and by the unity enacted at the altar, we seek constancy in our faith and love from God (Prayer after Communion).

August 22, Memorial of the Queenship of the Blessed Virgin Mary: Queen[103]

The Entrance Antiphon establishes the theme for this celebration: ". . . [Y]our [queen] bride stands at your right side, wearing a wedding gown trimmed with pure gold" (Ps 45:9). The Collect confirms it stating that God made the mother of Jesus our mother and queen. Her queenship flows from the celebration of her assumption into heaven (August 15), which in turn flows from her cooperation with God in giving birth to the humanity of Christ, who made an unblemished offering of himself to God on the cross (Prayer over the Offerings). The Communion Antiphon, words of Elizabeth to Mary in Luke's Gospel, emphasizes Mary's faithfulness: "The Lord has blessed you because you believed that he will keep his promise" (Luke 1:45). Thus, our prayer is to be sustained by the Queen's intercession in order to

101. *Roman Missal*, 933.

102. *Roman Missal*, 1071–72.

103. *Roman Missal*, 934.

share in heavenly glory (Collect). We, who receive the heavenly sacrament of the body and blood of Christ, hope to merit participation in his heavenly banquet (Prayer after Communion) with his queen mother.

August 24, Feast of St. Bartholomew: Kingdom[104]

Because we know little to nothing about the apostle Bartholomew, the Mass texts are general statements concerning salvation in God's kingdom. The theme of kingdom is best stated in the Communion Antiphon, words of Jesus to his apostles during their Passover celebration: ". . . I will give you the right to rule as kings, just as my Father has given me the right to rule as a king. You will eat and drink with me in my kingdom . . ." (Luke 22:29–30). The Entrance Antiphon exhorts us: "Day after day announce, 'The LORD has saved us!' Tell every nation on earth, 'The Lord is wonderful and does marvelous things!'" (Ps 96:2b–3a) In the Collect, after naming Bartholomew's faith, we ask that God let his church become the sacrament of salvation for all the nations of the world. In the Prayer after Communion, the eucharist, our help now and in the life to come, is referred to as the pledge of eternal salvation. In John's Gospel (1:45–51; 21:2), Nathanael may be Bartholomew named in the synoptics (Mark 3:18, Matt 10:3, Luke 6:14) because he is paired with Philip (John 1:45) and the names Philip and Bartholomew follow each other in the synoptic gospels.

August 27, Memorial of St. Monica: Tears[105]

The Collect establishes the theme concerning the memory of Monica (332–387); it states that God accepted the tears she shed for the conversion of her son, Augustine. The Entrance Antiphon, taken from the Common of Holy Men and Women, V. For Holy Women, 2,[106] declares Monica to be a wise woman who built her house and walked uprightly in fear of the LORD (Prov 14:1–2). She built her house by following her teenage son from Tagaste, Africa, to Milan, Italy, to Ostia—outside Rome—Italy. She walked uprightly in the fear of God, knowing that only he could hear her prayerful tears and turn Augustine away from his passions and heresy. She is one of those identified by the Matthean Jesus who does the will of his Father in heaven and is his

---

104. *Roman Missal*, 935–36.

105. *Roman Missal*, 937.

106. *Roman Missal*, 1114–15.

brother and sister and mother (Matt 12:50) (Communion Antiphon). In the Prayer over the Offerings, we join with Monica in asking God to give our offerings of bread and wine the power to save us, and in the Prayer after Communion, we seek to be purified by their effects. In the Collect, we pray that God, who consoles the sorrowful, like Monica, may enable us to regret our waywardness and discover his pardoning grace.

August 28, Memorial of St. Augustine: Seeker[107]

Augustine (354–430), son of Monica, was a seeker of truth. At first, he did not realize that by seeking truth he was seeking God. The Collect states this very clearly; God filled Augustine with spirit and made him thirsty for the only font of true wisdom: God. The Communion Antiphon also emphasizes this: Jesus says, "The Messiah is your only leader. You have only one teacher, and all of you are like brothers and sisters" (Matt 23:10b, 8). Likewise, the Entrance Antiphon reflects on how Augustine, once he was ordained a bishop in 395 for Hippo, opened his mouth to teach the members of his church; God filled him with the spirit of wisdom and understanding, and after his death, he clothed him in a robe of glory. Thus, we pray that God will renew the spirit in the church with which he endowed Augustine. Filled with that spirit, then we may seek God, the author of love, like Augustine did (Collect). By sharing at the Lord's table, we become what we already are: members of the body of Christ (Prayer after Communion), a sign of unity bound together in charity (Prayer over the Offerings).

August 29, Memorial of the Passion of St. John the Baptist: Decrease[108]

The words of John the Baptist in the Communion Antiphon give us the meaning of this memorial: "Jesus must become more important, while I become less important" (John 3:30). According to the Preface, John's decreasing culminated in his supreme witness to Jesus by the shedding of his blood: He was beheaded. The Prayer over the Offerings states that he went before Jesus to prepare the way for him by being a voice shouting in the desert, decreasing as Jesus increased. Both the Prayer over the Offerings and the Collect declare that his final decrease was dying a martyr, shedding his

---

107. *Roman Missal*, 938.

108. *Roman Missal*, 939–40.

blood for truth and justice. On this day, according to the Prayer after Communion, we celebrate the heavenly birthday of John the Baptist; we pray that we may be as strong as he was in confessing God's truth (Collect), and that we may be the voice crying in the desert today (Prayer over the Offerings). Then, like John, we can declare to God: ". . . I trust [your teachings] so much that I tell them to kings. I love your commands! They bring me happiness" (Ps 119:46–47) (Entrance Antiphon).

September 3, Memorial of St. Gregory the Great: Contemplation and Action[109]

Gregory (540–604) was the first monk to become a pope (590–604), even turning his family home into a monastery. According to the Entrance Antiphon, he was raised to Peter's throne, from where he sought the Lord's beauty through contemplation and responded in action by living God's love. In the Collect, we pray that God will endow shepherds, like Gregory, with wisdom to govern the sheep. Contemplation leads to action, that is, the flourishing of the flock becomes the joy of the shepherd. Like God, Gregory cared for the sheep with gentleness, and he ruled the church in love (Collect). The Communion Antiphon declares Gregory to be the faithful and prudent manager whom God put in charge of his sheep to give them their allowance of food at the proper time (Luke 12:42). This shepherd knew that Christ the teacher fed the sheep with living bread (Prayer after Communion). Thus, we pray that we may learn God's truth or wisdom and put it into practice with works of charity (Prayer after Communion).

September 8, Feast of the Nativity of the Blessed Virgin Mary: Birth[110]

Celebrating with joy the birth of the Blessed Virgin Mary, according to the Entrance Antiphon, is grounded in her giving birth to the Son of God, referred to as the sun of justice. The theme that Mary's birth is marked because she gave birth to Jesus permeates the Mass texts. We seek deeper peace from God for those of us for whom the birth of Jesus was the dawning of salvation for the world (Collect). In the Prayer after Communion, we rejoice in marking Mary's birthday, which is the daybreak of salvation for the world.

109. *Roman Missal*, 941–42.
110. *Roman Missal*, 942–43.

In the first optional Prayer over the Offerings, we seek the aid of the Son of God, who, being born of the Virgin, consecrated her integrity while taking away our wickedness. In the second optional Prayer over the Offerings, we seek strength through the humanity of Jesus, who took flesh from Mary. The Communion Antiphon, pieced together from two biblical verses, reinforces the theme of the two births, stating, "A virgin is pregnant; she will have a son and . . . he will save his people from their sins" (Isa 7:14b; Matt 1:21).

September 9, Memorial of St. Peter Claver: Charity[111]

If there is a single word that describes the priest Peter Claver (1580–1654), it is charity. This Jesuit saint heard the call to leave Spain and go to Cartagena, Colombia, South America, and minister to the slaves. The Collect declares that God made him a slave of slaves and strengthened him with charity towards them. The second optional Entrance Antiphon, found in the Common of Holy Men and Women, III. For Those Who Practiced Works of Mercy,[112] presents Claver's charity: "[He] will always be remembered and greatly praised, because [he was] kind and freely gave to the poor" (Ps 112:9). In the Prayer over the Offerings, we pray that Christ's work of boundless charity, exemplified by Claver, be confirmed in our love of God and neighbor. The theme of love of neighbor demonstrated in charity is further illustrated in either of the two Communion Antiphons (John 15:13, 13:35). In both the first and second optional Prayer after Communion, we pray to receive divine grace to imitate the example of Claver, who honored God with his surpassing charity to slaves and his love of neighbor demonstrated in deeds and in truth (Collect).

September 13, Memorial of St. John Chrysostom: Eloquence[113]

Chrysostom is not the last name of this saint. It is a description of his eloquence; Chrysostom means *golden-mouthed*. The Collect states that John Chrysostom (344/49–407) was illustrious by his eloquence. He was known for his pastoral and catechetical style of preaching. Using words from the HB (OT) book of Daniel, the Entrance Antiphon declares John to be one of those

---

111. *Roman Missal,* 943.

112. *Roman Missal,* 1110–11.

113. *Roman Missal,* 945.

"who has been wise [and] shine[s] as bright as the sky above, [and] who has led others to please God [and] shine[s] like the stars" (Dan 12:3). His eloquence consisted in proclaiming Christ crucified to be the power of God and the wisdom of God (1 Cor 1:23–24) (Communion Antiphon). We pray to be instructed by his teaching and strengthened by his example (Collect), to imitate him in giving ourselves to God (Prayer over the Offerings), and to be enabled to confess God's truth faithfully (Prayer after Communion).

September 14, Feast of the Exaltation of the Holy Cross: Cross[114]

The themes focused on the cross are found in the Preface. First, the salvation of the world, Jesus Christ, was placed on the cross by God. The Collect echoes this by stating that God willed that his Son undergo the cross to save humankind. The Communion Antiphon also echoes this first point, quoting the Johannine Jesus: "If I am lifted up above the earth, I will make everyone want to come to me" (John 12:32). Second, the instrument of death was also the means for life to spring forth. The Entrance Antiphon emphasizes this point: "I will never brag about anything," states Paul, "except the cross of our Lord Jesus Christ. Because of his cross, the world is dead as far as I am concerned, and I am dead as far as the world is concerned" (Gal 6:14); from the cross came salvation, life, and resurrection. Third, just as the evil one conquered Adam and Eve on a tree, on a tree Jesus conquered him. The Prayer over the Offerings echoes this point; it refers to Jesus as the oblation on the altar of the cross who canceled the offenses and sins of the world. Our prayer is that we, who have been redeemed by the wood of the life-giving cross, may merit a share in the grace of redemption and the glory of the resurrection (Prayer after Communion, Collect).

September 15, Memorial of Our Lady of Sorrows: Suffering[115]

The Entrance Antiphon takes us back to Luke's Gospel in which Simeon says to Mary: "This child of yours will cause many people in Israel to fall and others to stand. This child will be like a warning sign. Many people will reject him, and you, Mary, will suffer as though you had been stabbed by a

114. *Roman Missal*, 946–48.
115. *Roman Missal*, 949.

dagger" (Luke 2:34–35). Simeon's words are fulfilled in the Collect, which states that when Jesus was lifted up on the cross, his mother, Mary, stood by and shared in his suffering (John 19:25b–27). The unique story in John's Gospel mentions that Jesus gave his mother to his beloved disciple and the beloved disciple to his mother. The Prayer over the Offerings states that God gave Mary to us as a mother, too. The suffering endured by a Mother watching her Son be executed is mentioned in the Prayer after Communion; the prayer is based on a verse found in the Letter to the Colossians in which the author states, "I am glad that I can suffer for you. I am pleased also that in my own body I can continue the suffering of Christ for his body, the church" (Col 1:24). The Communion Antiphon prepares us for that prayer: "Be glad for the chance to suffer as Christ suffered. It will prepare you for even greater happiness when he makes his glorious return" (1 Pet 4:13). By joining Our Lady of Sorrows in participating in Jesus' passion, we hope one day to share in his resurrection (Collect).

September 16, Memorial of Sts. Cornelius and Cyprian: Guardian[116]

God as guardian is the theme of the Mass texts for this memorial of the martyrs Cornelius (+253) and Cyprian (+258). It is expressed in the first optional Entrance Antiphon, taken from the Common of Martyrs, I. Outside Easter Time, A. For Several Martyrs, 2:[117] "The LORD's people may suffer a lot, but he will always bring them safely through. Not one of their bones will ever be broken" (Ps 34:19–20). These diligent shepherds (Collect)—Cornelius, a pope for three years, and Cyprian, a bishop for nine years—found courage through the eucharist (Prayer over the Offerings) to bear witness to the gospel (Prayer after Communion) when persecuted and put to death. They are examples of those who follow the words of the Lukan Jesus: "My friends, don't be afraid of people. They can kill you, but after that, there is nothing else they can do" (Luke 12:4) (Communion Antiphon). We pray that God will strengthen us in faith and constancy so that we can foster church unity (Collect). Being steadfast through our trials (Prayer over the Offerings), we need fortitude that comes from the Spirit (Prayer after Communion).

---

116. *Roman Missal*, 950.

117. *Roman Missal*, 1053–54.

September 20, Memorial of Sts. Andrew Kim Tae-gon, Paul Chong Ha-sang, and Companions: Seed[118]

Between 1839 and 1867 one hundred thirteen Korean Christians were martyred; among the laity were three bishops and seven priests. The Collect declares that God made the blood of these men and women the fruitful seed of Christianity in Korea. The Entrance Antiphon explains how the blood of these holy martyrs was poured upon the earth in imitation of Jesus; through their martyrdom, these men and women gained everlasting life, just like Christ did through his resurrection. This truth is found in the Entrance Antiphon, words of the Matthean Jesus: "If you tell others that you belong to me, I will tell my Father in heaven that you are my followers" (Matt 10:32). We seek to be defended by the one hundred thirteen Korean martyrs and to learn from their example (Collect). Like them, we pray that we may become an acceptable sacrifice for the salvation of the world (Prayer over the Offerings). By clinging faithfully to Jesus Christ, we are nourished by the same eucharistic food that strengthened these men and women to labor for the salvation of all (Prayer after Communion).

September 21, Feast of St. Matthew: Tax Collector[119]

Matthew, called a tax collector in today's Collect, was chosen by Jesus to be one of his apostles (Matt 9:9). In Mark's Gospel and in Luke's Gospel, he is called Levi (Mark 2:13–14; Luke 5:27), even though the name Matthew appears in the list of the twelve apostles (Mark 3:18; Luke 6:15); only in Matthew's list is Matthew identified as "the tax collector" (Matt 10:3). At Jesus' time, a tax collector was a Jew who worked for the Roman occupation forces; he made his living by raising the set amount of the tax and pocketing the difference. He was considered to be a sinner as the words of Jesus forming the Communion Antiphon and the mention made in the Prayer after Communion make clear: "I didn't come to invite good people to be my followers. I came to invite sinners" (Matt 9:13b; Mark 2:17b; Luke 5:32). The Prayer after Communion mentions that Matthew welcomed Jesus to his home (Matt 9:10–13); similarly, Mark and Luke record that Levi welcomed Jesus to his home (Mark 2:15–17; Luke 5:29–32). Matthew is one of the eleven disciples who hear the risen Jesus tell them: "Go to the people of all nations . . . . Baptize them . . . and teach them to do everything I have told you" (Matt

118. *Roman Missal*, 952.
119. *Roman Missal*, 953.

28:19–20) (Entrance Antiphon). Our prayer is to be firm in following Christ (Collect) in the faith preached by the apostles (Prayer over the Offerings).

September 23, Memorial of St. Pius of Pietrelcina: Stigmatic[120]

Pius of Pietrelcina (1887–1968) is better known as Padre Pio, a Capuchin—a reformed branch of the Franciscans—priest. In 1918, Padre Pio had a vision of Jesus and received the stigmata, the visible marks of Jesus' crucifixion in his hands, feet, and side, which remained until his death. The Collect mentions that God gave this priest a share in the cross of Jesus. It goes on to refer to the priest's ministry in the confessional up to ten hours a day as a display of the wonders of God's mercy. Except for the Collect the rest of the Mass texts are taken from the Common of Holy Men and Women, II. For Monks and Religious, D. For Religious, 1.[121] The first optional Entrance Antiphon may be a prayer Padre Pio prayed often: "You, LORD, are all I want! You are my choice, and you keep me safe" (Ps 16:5). Likewise, the second optional Communion Antiphon could have been a part of his prayer: "Deep in my heart I say, 'The LORD is all I need; I can depend on him!' The LORD is kind to everyone who trusts and obeys him" (Lam 3:24–25). Our prayer is that, like Padre Pio, we may be united to the suffering of Jesus and brought to the glory of Christ's resurrection.

September 27, Memorial of St. Vincent de Paul: Poor[122]

Not only was "[t]he Spirit of the Lord upon" Vincent de Paul (1581–1660), God also anointed him "to bring good news to the poor" and to heal the broken-hearted (Luke 4:18a) (Entrance Antiphon). The Collect refers to de Paul's mission as bringing relief to the poor. The Prayer over the Offerings states that this priest put into practice what he celebrated in the eucharist. And the Prayer after Communion asks God to help us imitate the example of de Paul, who himself imitated Jesus, in preaching the gospel to the poor. Besides the charity shown to the poor, de Paul also founded the Congregation of the Mission, known as Vincentians, whose responsibility was to preach parish missions among the poor and uneducated; to this was added

120. *Roman Missal*, 954.

121. *Roman Missal*, 1107–08.

122. *Roman Missal*, 956.

the formation of the clergy, mentioned in the Collect. There is no doubt that de Paul was on fire with the Spirit of love. This is echoed in the Communion Antiphon: "You should praise the LORD for his love and for the wonderful things he does for all of us. To everyone who is thirsty, he gives something to drink; to everyone who is hungry, he gives good things to eat" (Ps 107:8–9).

September 29, Feast of Sts. Michael, Gabriel, and Raphael: Archangels[123]

An archangel is a heavenly being who ranks above an angel and usually has a name that has something to do with God (El). Thus, Michael means *who is like God*; Gabriel means *God is strong*; and Raphael means *God heals*. The names indicate the ministries of God on earth, while the word *angel* itself refers to God as a messenger who defends, watches over (Collect), and protects us (Prayer after Communion). The Entrance Antiphon expresses this well: "All of you mighty angels, who obey God's commands, come and praise your LORD!" (Ps 103:20) The Preface reminds us that by honoring angels we honor God's glory. Their dignity and splendor display how great God is; he is to be exalted above all. In the Prayer over the Offerings, we acknowledge that angels bring our gifts into the divine presence, an echo of a line in Eucharistic Prayer I which asks God to command that our gifts be borne by the hands of his angel to his altar on high.[124] The action of God sending himself to defend, protect, and accept our gifts is what we name *angel*, best thought of as a verb instead of a noun. Thus, the Communion Antiphon states, "With all my heart I praise you, LORD. In the presence of angels I sing your praises" (Ps 138:1).

September 30, Memorial of St. Jerome: Scripture[125]

The Communion Antiphon summarizes the theme of the memorial of Jerome (ca. 347–419/20): "When you spoke to me, I was glad to obey, because I belong to you, the LORD All-Powerful" (Jer 15:16). This saint is responsible for translating the Bible from Hebrew, Aramaic, and Greek into Latin; it is known as the Vulgate. The Collect states that God gave this priest both a living and a tender love for the Scriptures. Blessed is he whom "the Law

---

123. *Roman Missal*, 959–61.

124. *Roman Missal*, 641.

125. *Roman Missal*, 962.

of the LORD makes . . . happy, and [he] think[s] about it day and night" (Ps 1:2), states the Entrance Antiphon. Like a tree planted near running water, Jerome has yielded fruit. In the Prayer over the Offerings, we declare that we follow Jerome's example of meditating on the Word before we offer the body and blood of Christ—the sacrifice of salvation—to God. Our prayer is that we will be nourished by God's Word and find in it the fountain of life (Collect). In the Prayer after Communion, we ask God to stir up our hearts so that we can be attentive to the Bible, which offers us the path to follow to everlasting life.

October 1, Memorial of St. Therese of the Child Jesus: Little Way[126]

Therese (1873–1897), often called the Little Flower, is known for her teaching about the little way. The Collect explains that the little way means that God's kingdom is open to the humble and to little ones. The Communion Antiphon also emphasizes this point, presenting words of the Matthean Jesus: "I promise you this. If you don't change and become like a child, you will never get into the kingdom of heaven" (Matt 18:3). The Entrance Antiphon, a gloss on three verses from the HB (OT) book of Deuteronomy, states that the LORD shielded her, cared for her, and guarded her "as though [she] were his own eyes. The LORD was like an eagle teaching its young to fly, always ready to swoop down and catch them on its back" (Deut 32:10b–12). As we remember Therese, we proclaim God's wonders in her short life (Prayer over the Offerings). This Carmelite saint understood her vocation to be love; thus in the Prayer after Communion, we ask God to kindle that same love in us and to instill in us a longing for divine mercy. Thus, just as Therese's merits pleased God, we ask God to find our service pleasing in his sight (Prayer over the Offerings).

October 2, Memorial of the Holy Guardian Angels: Guardians[127]

The Collect establishes the theme of the Mass texts: God sends angels to guard us. The concept is based on the words of the narrator of the HB (OT) book of Exodus before the Israelites cross the Sea of Reeds: ". . . God's angel

126. *Roman Missal*, 963.
127. *Roman Missal*, 964–65.

had gone ahead of Israel's army, but now he moved behind them" (Exod 14:19a). In other words, one aspect of God's mercy is defending and protecting his people (Collect). The Prayer over the Offerings acknowledges that it is only with the angels' constant protection that we can be free from any dangers. And one aspect of such ministry is directing us in the way of salvation and peace (Prayer after Communion). All we can do in awareness of God's unfathomable providence is to give thanks to God and sing his praises before the angels (Ps 138:1) (Communion Antiphon). In the Entrance Antiphon, we declare: "Bless the Lord, you angles of the Lord; sing praise to him and highly exalt him forever" (NRSV, Sg Three :37 [Dan 3:58]).

October 4, Memorial of St. Francis of Assisi: Poor[128]

The Entrance Antiphon declares Francis Bernardone (1181/2–1226) to be a man of God who left all his wealth behind, abandoning his inheritance, and became poor, but God raised him up in holiness. After renouncing his possessions and consecrating himself to God, he gathered a small group of men to be itinerant preachers to follow the gospel as literally as possible. Thus, he founded the Order of Friars Minor (Franciscans) in 1209. The Collect declares that God conformed Francis to Christ in both poverty and humility. We celebrate the mystery of the cross embraced by Francis in bearing the stigmata—the marks of Jesus' crucifixion in his hands, feet, and side—two years before his death at the age of forty-five (Prayer over the Offerings). We pray that we may walk in his footsteps and imitate his joyful charity (Collect) and apostolic zeal, experiencing the effects of God's love and spreading that love to all, especially the poor (Prayer after Communion). The Communion Antiphon brings together Francis's life of poverty and his concern for the poor: "God blesses those people who depend only on him. They belong to the kingdom of heaven" (Matt 5:3).

October 7, Memorial of Our Lady of the Rosary: Grace[129]

The theme of the Mass texts for this memorial of the Blessed Virgin Mary is grace, which is God's free and undeserved gift of himself enabling us to participate in divine life. The Entrance Antiphon, a compilation of two verses from Luke's Gospel—one consisting of words of Gabriel to Mary, and the

128. *Roman Missal*, 966.
129. *Roman Missal*, 968.

other consisting of words of Elizabeth to Mary—establish the theme: "You are truly blessed! The Lord is with you. God has blessed you more than any other woman! He has also blessed the child you will have" (Luke 1:28, 42). We recognize that this is the first part of the Hail, Mary, prayer said repeatedly in the Rosary. In the Collect, we ask God to pour grace into our hearts. In the Prayer over the Offerings, we seek grace to be conformed to the bread and wine, which become the body and blood of Christ, which we offer. The Communion Antiphon goes back to Gabriel's words to Mary: ". . . [Y]ou will have a son. His name will be Jesus" (Luke 1:31). Keeping in mind that all Mariology flows from Christology, the Collect declares that the incarnation of Christ was made known to us by Gabriel, but it is through his passion and cross that he attained the glory of the resurrection, in which we hope to receive the grace to share (Collect, Prayer after Communion).

October 15, Memorial of St. Teresa of Jesus: Prayer[130]

Teresa of Jesus (1515–1582), better known as Teresa of Avila, Spain, not only reformed the Carmelites, but wrote extensively on prayer. With the help of St. John of the Cross she created the discalced (barefoot or wearing sandals) branch in distinction to the calced (with shoes) branch. The Entrance Antiphon sets the theme of prayer for her memorial: "As a deer gets thirsty for streams of water, I truly am thirsty for you, my God. In my heart, I am thirsty for you, the living God" (Ps 42:1–2a). Through his Spirit, God raised up Teresa to show the way to perfection in prayer, states the Collect. The Prayer over the Offerings declares her service to be pleasing to God in great measure. In the Prayer after Communion, we seek to follow Theresa's example in singing of God's mercies forever. This last note is echoed in the Communion Antiphon: "Our LORD, I will sing of your love forever. Everyone yet to be born will hear me praise your faithfulness" (Ps 89:1). Our prayer is that God will fire us with longing for holiness through our prayer (Collect), just as he filled Teresa of Jesus with his Spirit.

October 17, Memorial of St. Ignatius of Antioch: Wheat[131]

Ignatius (ca. 50–107), an early bishop and martyr, wrote letters to seven churches on his way from Antioch to Rome, where he was led to the

---

130. *Roman Missal*, 970–71.

131. *Roman Missal*, 972–73.

amphitheater and devoured by lions. In one of his letters, he writes about being the wheat of Christ which will be ground by the teeth of the lions into pure bread (Communion Antiphon). In the Prayer over the Offerings, we remember that God accepted this saint as the wheat of Christ through his suffering and martyrdom. Just as the eucharist is a memorial of the suffering and death of Jesus, Ignatius understood his imminent death as a participation in Christ's. The words of Paul in the Entrance Antiphon further emphasize this: "I have been nailed to the cross with Christ. I have died, but Christ lives in me. And I now live by faith in the Son of God, who loved me and gave his life for me" (Gal 2:19b–20). In the Collect, we remember that God decorates the body of Christ, the church, with the confession of martyrs, like Ignatius. As we remember his suffering and death, which brought him eternal glory (Collect), we pray that the eucharist we receive may make us Christians both in name and in deed (Prayer after Communion).

October 18, Feast of St. Luke: Gospel[132]

The English word *gospel* is the equivalent of the Greek word *euangelion*, which means *good news*. The theme for the feast of Luke is good news. It is proclaimed in the Entrance Antiphon: "What a beautiful sight! On the mountains a messenger announces to Jerusalem, 'Good news! You're saved. There will be peace'" (Isa 52:7). According to the Collect, God chose Luke to reveal his good-news love for the poor through Luke's preaching and writings. Through his gospel and the Acts of the Apostles, Luke accepted Jesus' commission: ". . . [T]he Lord chose . . . other followers and sent them . . . to every town and village where he was about to go. [He told them to say:] 'God's kingdom will soon be here!'" (Luke 10:1, 9). In the Prayer after Communion, we ask God to sanctify us and to make us strong in the faith of the gospel Luke proclaimed. In the Collect, we ask God to help us persevere in announcing the gospel of Jesus so that all the nations of the world will see the salvation that, in the words of the Prayer over the Offerings, brings healing to us and gives glory to us.

132. *Roman Missal*, 973–74.

October 19, Memorial of Sts. John de Brebeuf, Isaac Jogues, and Companions: Eight[133]

Between 1642 and 1649, eight French Jesuits, missionaries from what is now Nova Scotia, Canada, to Maryland, United States, were martyred by the Iroquois and Huron native North Americans. John de Brebeuf (+1649), Isaac Jogues (+1646), Charles Garnier (+1649), Anthony Daniel (+1648), Gabriel Lallemant (+1649), Noel Chabanel (+1649), John de Lalande (+1646), and Rene Goupil (+1642) were chosen by God, in the words of the Collect, to manifest the hope of his eternal kingdom by the shedding of their blood. The Entrance Antiphon, taken from the Common of Martyrs, III. For Missionary Martyrs, A. For Several Missionary Martyrs,[134] is composed of two verses from Paul's letters and describes what the Jesuit missionaries did: ". . . I will never brag about anything except the cross of our Lord Jesus Christ. The message about the cross . . . for those of us who are being saved . . . is God's power at work" (Gal 6:14a; 1 Cor 1:18). In the Prayer over the Offerings, we acknowledge venerating the suffering and death of the martyrs while proclaiming the suffering and death of Jesus, who strengthened them by word and example. The first optional Communion Antiphon reminds us that among the blessed are "those who are treated badly for doing right. They belong to the kingdom of heaven" (Matt 5:10). In the words of the Prayer after Communion, we hope to enjoy perpetual peace by following the example of Jesus and the eight martyrs.

October 28, Feast of Sts. Simon and Jude: Unknown Apostles[135]

These holy men, according to the Entrance Antiphon, were chosen by the Lord in perfect love; he gave them eternal glory. The theme of love is found also in the words of the Johannine Jesus in the Communion Antiphon: "If anyone loves me, [he] will obey me. Then my Father will love [him], and we will come to [him] and live in [him]" (John 14:23). Because we know nothing about these two apostles, all the Collect can state is that the apostles collectively have enabled people to acknowledge God's name. In the Prayer over the Offerings, we state that we venerate the glory of Simon and Jude, and in the Prayer after Communion, we honor them and ask God to keep us

133. *Roman Missal*, 974.
134. *Roman Missal*, 1066–67.
135. *Roman Missal*, 977.

ever in his love. In Mark's Gospel and Matthew's Gospel, Simon is identified as a Cananaean (Mark 3:18; Matt 10:4), but in Luke's Gospel he is called the Zealot (Luke 6:15). Only Luke lists an apostle named Judas son of James (Luke 6:16); in Mark and Matthew there is an apostle named Thaddaeus (Mark 3:18; Matt 10:3). Thus, in order to avoid confusion between Judas son of James and Judas Iscariot, in tradition this apostle is named Jude Thaddaeus, a name which nowhere appears in the CB (NT)! Our prayer is that through the intercession of these two apostles—whatever their names—the church will continue to grow and increase the number of people who believe in God.

November 1, Solemnity of All Saints: Festival[136]

The Solemnity of All Saints is a festival day. The Preface refers to the festival of the heavenly Jerusalem, where our brothers and sisters praise God eternally. The Entrance Antiphon calls upon everyone to rejoice in the Lord on this day of celebration; at this festival even the angels rejoice and praise the Son of God. We remember all the saints, who are illustrated in the words of the Matthean Jesus in the Communion Antiphon: "God blesses those people whose hearts are pure. They will see him! God blesses those people who make peace. They will be called his children! God blesses those people who are treated badly for doing right. They belong to the kingdom of heaven" (Matt 5:8–10). In the Preface, we declare that we are on pilgrimage toward Jerusalem, our mother, honoring the glory that God has bestowed upon the saints of the church who have been assured already of immortality (Prayer over the Offerings); they give us strength to continue our journey and provide examples of holy living. We ask God to bestow on us the reconciliation we long for with him (Collect), and we implore his grace to make us perfect in holiness that we may one day pass from the pilgrim table to the heavenly festival table (Prayer after Communion).

---

136. *Roman Missal*, 979–82.

November 2, Commemoration of All the Faithful Departed (All Souls' Day): Death and Life[137]

1

The theme of death and life is modeled best by Jesus Christ, states the Entrance Antiphon: "We believe that Jesus died and was raised to life. We also believe that when God brings Jesus back again, he will bring with him all who had faith in Jesus before they died. Adam brought death to all of us, and Christ will bring life to all of us" (1 Thess 4:14; 1 Cor 15:22). In the Collect, we state that our faith in Christ, raised from the dead, is deepened, and we hope that resurrection belongs to all God's departed servants. Likewise, in the Prayer over the Offerings, we ask God to take into glory with his Son all his departed servants, and in the Prayer after Communion, we pray that all God's departed servants will find a dwelling place of light and peace. We receive comfort from the Johannine Jesus' words to Martha, which form the Communion Antiphon: "I am the one who raises the dead to life! Everyone who has faith in me will live, even if [he] die. And everyone who lives because of faith in me will never really die" (John 11:25–26a). The Prayer over the Offerings reminds us that all of us—living and deceased—are united in God's mystery of love.

2

The theme of death and life is illustrated by two verses from the OT (A) book of 4—usually called 2—Esdras. The Entrance Antiphon states: "Wait for your shepherd; he will give you everlasting rest, because . . . perpetual light will shine on your forevermore" (NRSV, 4 [2] Esd 2:34–35). The Communion Antiphon states: ". . . [Let] perpetual light . . . shine on [them] forevermore" (NRSV, 4 [2] Esd 2:35) for God is merciful. It is by the paschal mystery—the death and resurrection of Christ (Prayer after Communion)—that we are redeemed, states the Collect and the Prayer after Communion. We are immersed in the paschal mystery through baptism, which also washes away our sins in the blood of Christ (Prayer over the Offerings). Thus, we ask God to forgive the sins of the departed, to bestow his merciful forgiveness upon them, and bring them through death to life. Just as the deceased professed their faith in the resurrection of Christ, we state in the Collect, so we

---

137. *Roman Missal*, 982–85.

ask God to give them the joys of eternal happiness, the gift of resurrection (Prayer after Communion), perpetual light.

3

The theme of death and life is illustrated in Preface I for the Dead;[138] it states that for God's faithful people life is changed not ended. The Entrance Antiphon echoes this theme using words from Paul's Letter to the Romans: ". . . God raised Jesus to life! God's Spirit now lives in you, and he will raise you to life by his Spirit" (Rom 8:11). The Collect picks up the theme in stating that God willed that Jesus conquer death and pass over to new life. The Prayer over the Offerings asks God to accept our offering on behalf of all who sleep in Christ. The Communion Antiphon, taken from Paul's Letter to the Philippians, states, ". . . [W]e are citizens of heaven and are eagerly waiting for our Savior to come from there. Our Lord Jesus Christ has power over everything, and he will make these poor bodies of ours like his own glorious body" (Phil 3:20–21). Our prayer for our departed is that they may gaze on God, who is their creator and redeemer (Collect), that they may be set free from the bonds of death and enjoy eternal life (Prayer over the Offerings), and that they may receive God's mercy, since they have been endowed with the grace of baptism to inherit eternal life (Prayer after Communion).

November 4, Memorial of St. Charles Borromeo: Renewal[139]

The theme of renewal best describes the Mass texts on the memorial of Charles Borromeo (1538–1584), a bishop and church reformer following the Council of Trent in the sixteenth century. The Collect asks God to continue to fill people with the same spirit he gave to Borromeo for constant renewal of the church into the image of Christ in order to display his face to the world. The first optional Entrance Antiphon, taken from the Common of Pastors, II. For a Bishop, 2,[140] applies the words of the LORD, the God of Israel, delivered by a man of God to Eli in the HB (OT) First Book of Samuel to Borromeo: "I have chosen someone else to be my priest, someone who will be faithful and obey me" (1 Sam 2:35). The first optional Communion Antiphon applies the words of the Johannine Jesus to Borromeo's ministry:

138. *Roman Missal*, 622.

139. *Roman Missal*, 986–87.

140. *Roman Missal*, 1075–76.

"I came so that everyone would have life, and have it in its fullest" (John 10:10b). The Prayer over the Offerings calls Borromeo an attentive pastor outstanding in virtue. In the Prayer after Communion, we ask God to give us the same determination that this saint possessed so that we might be faithful in our ministries and fervent in our charity as we continue the renewal of the church in these post-Vatican II days.

November 9, Feast of the Dedication of the Lateran Basilica: House and Mother[141]

Every bishop has a cathedral in which is located his chair, called a cathedra, a sign of his pastoral authority to teach and govern the people entrusted to his care. The pope, the bishop of Rome, has his cathedra in his cathedral: St. John Lateran. One of the themes for this feast of the dedication of the pope's cathedral is house and temple. The second optional Entrance Antiphon states this theme: "God's home is now with his people. He will live with them, and they will be his own. Yes, God will make his home among his people" (Rev. 21:3). In the Prayer over the Offerings, we declare that people come to the church to seek God's favor to receive the sacraments and answers to their prayers. The Preface declares that God is pleased to dwell in a house of prayer, a temple of the Holy Spirit—called a temple of grace in the Prayer after Communion—supported with his grace and displaying lives acceptable to him. The first optional Collect compares the lives of God's people to living and chosen stones that form a dwelling place for him. The Communion Antiphon exhorts, ". . . [N]ow you are living stones that are being used to build a spiritual house. You are also a group of holy priests . . ." (1 Pet 2:5). In the house of living stones, we pray for an increase of grace for the church so that new growth may take place (first optional Collect).
or

Every bishop has a cathedral in which is located his chair, called a cathedra, a sign of his pastoral authority to teach and govern the people entrusted to his care. The pope, the bishop of Rome, has his cathedra in his cathedral: St. John Lateran. One of the themes for this feast of the dedication of the pope's cathedral is mother Jerusalem and bride. The first optional Entrance Antiphon begins the theme of Jerusalem as a mother and bride. John of Patmos states: ". . . I saw New Jerusalem, that holy city, coming down from God in heaven. It was like a bride dressed in her wedding gown and ready to meet her husband" (Rev 21:2). In the first optional Collect, we seek

141. *Roman Missal*, 987–90.

to build up the heavenly Jerusalem, while in the second optional Collect, we acknowledge that God calls the church his bride; thus, we pray that the bride may revere her husband, love him, and follow him to heaven. The Preface refers to the church as Christ's bride signified by visible buildings; she is also the mother of countless children, who seek the heavenly Jerusalem. The Prayer after Communion reiterates the same idea, stating that the heavenly Jerusalem is foreshadowed on earth in the sign of the church. We ask God to make us a temple of his grace and to admit us to his glorious dwelling place.

November 10, Memorial of St. Leo the Great: Defender[142]

Pope Leo I (+461), better known as Leo the Great, is remembered as a defender of the church; this theme is present in the Mass texts for this memorial. As pope for twenty-one years, he stressed the foundation of the papacy on St. Peter. The Communion Antiphon, words of the Matthean Jesus to Peter, states: "Simon Peter spoke up [to Jesus], 'You are the Messiah, the Son of the living God.' [And Jesus answered him,] 'So I will call you Peter, which means "a rock." On this rock I will build my church, and death itself will not have any power over it'" (Matt 16:16, 18). The Collect states that God never allows the gates of hell to prevail against the church, which is founded on the rock of Peter. We pray to stand firm in truth and know lasting peace through the intercession of Leo, with whom, in the words of the Entrance Antiphon, a covenant of friendship was established by God with him so that he could be the leader of the sanctuary and of his people and have the dignity of the priesthood forever (Sir 45:24). In the Prayer over the Offerings, we pray that the church may prosper under God's guidance and that leaders be pleasing to him, so that she may enjoy freedom and persevere in integrity of religion (Prayer after Communion).

November 11, Memorial of St. Martin of Tours: Least[143]

Martin of Tours (317–397) is primarily remembered for giving half of his cloak to a beggar in 334, while he was enlisted in the imperial guard. Later, Christ appeared to him in a dream wearing the same half of the cloak. This faithful priest and bishop whom God raised up for himself, according to what was in his heart and in his mind (1 Sam 2:35) (Entrance Antiphon),

142. *Roman Missal*, 991–92.
143. *Roman Missal*, 992–93.

fulfilled the words of the Matthean Jesus in the Communion Antiphon: "Whenever you did it for any of my people, no matter how unimportant they seemed, you did it for me" (Matt 25:40). After being elected bishop of Tours, France, in 371, he focused his efforts on evangelization. According to the Prayer after Communion, this saint submitted himself totally to God both in life and death (Collect), both in tribulation and prosperity (Prayer over the Offerings). We pray for an increase in grace so that neither life nor death can separate us from God's love (Collect), that our lives will always be directed to God (Prayer over the Offerings), and that we will find harmony with God's will for us in all things in order to glory in being truly God's people (Prayer after Communion).

November 12, Memorial of St. Josaphat: Unity[144]

Josaphat (1580–1623) was born into an Orthodox family but joined the Uniate Ruthenian Church. After becoming a monk in 1604 and the bishop of Polotsk in Belarus in 1617, he spent the rest of his life working toward Ruthenian unity of the Latin Church in union with Rome, the Orthodox Greek Church, and the Greek Uniate Church. The Entrance Antiphon emphasizes how he persevered in loving brotherhood, acknowledging that there was but one Spirit and one faith. His efforts brought opposition from almost every social level and resulted in his death. The Collect states that the Spirit filled this saint, who was attempting to bring his sheep to unity. Josaphat's martyrdom illustrates the Matthean Jesus' statement in the Communion Antiphon: ". . . [I]f you give [your life] up for me, you will surely find it" (Matt 10:39). Our prayer is that God will strengthen us with his Spirit so that we are not afraid to give our lives for others (Collect), that God will confirm us in faith (Prayer over the Offerings), and that following the example of Josaphat we may spend our lives working for the unity of the church (Prayer after Communion).

November 13, Memorial of St. Frances Xavier Cabrini: Servant of Immigrants[145]

Frances Xavier Cabrini (1850–1917), the first canonized U.S. citizen, began the Missionary Sisters of the Sacred Heart and immigrated to the U.S. in

---

144. *Roman Missal*, 993–94.

145. *Roman Missal*, 994.

1889 to minister to Italian immigrants. The Collect states that God called her from Italy to serve immigrants in the U.S., where she would found sixty-seven charitable institutions and houses of her congregation during her lifetime. The Entrance Antiphon, taken from the Common of Holy Men and Women, III. For Those Who Practiced Works of Mercy,[146] illustrates her philosophy concerning immigrants: "My father has blessed you! When I was sick, you took care of me .... Whenever you did it for any of my people, no matter how unimportant they seemed, you did it for me" (Matt 25:34a, 36b, 40). Our prayer is that we will imitate the example of Cabrini by having concern for the strangers, the sick, and all in need in order to see Christ in all men and women (Collect, Prayer over the Offerings). "If you love each other, everyone will know that you are my disciples," states the Johannine Jesus in the Communion Antiphon (John 13:35). In the first optional Prayer after Communion, we ask God to help us imitate the tireless devotion and love of Cabrini in being of service to his people.

November 17, Memorial of St. Elizabeth of Hungary: Giving Freely[147]

The second optional Entrance Antiphon, taken from the Common of Holy Men and Women, III. For Those Who Practiced Works of Mercy,[148] accurately summarizes the life of Elizabeth of Hungary (1207–1231): ". . . [S]he will always be remembered and greatly praised, because [she was] kind and freely gave to the poor" (Ps 112:9). Elizabeth, a Hungarian princess, was promised in marriage when she was only four years old and married when she was fourteen! She gave birth to three children and was left a widow when she was twenty. Before she died at the age of twenty-four, she founded a hospital in honor of St. Francis, became a Franciscan Tertiary, and worked in her hospital until her death, giving freely of herself to the poor and afflicted. We ask God to help us serve with charity the needy and afflicted in imitation of this saint (Collect, Prayer after Communion) and be confirmed in love of him and of our neighbor (Prayer over the Offerings). Elizabeth's short life illustrates the words of the Johannine Jesus in the first optional Communion Antiphon: "The greatest way to show love for friends is to die for them" (John 15:13). Giving freely, Elizabeth reverenced Christ in the poor (Collect).

146. *Roman Missal*, 1110–11.

147. *Roman Missal*, 996.

148. *Roman Missal*, 1110–11.

November 21, Memorial of the Presentation of the Blessed Virgin Mary: Memory[149]

In the Collect, we declare that we venerate the memory of the holy Virgin Mary, who, according to apocryphal sources, was presented in the Jerusalem Temple. The Entrance Antiphon, taken from the Common of the Blessed Virgin Mary, I. Ordinary Time, 5,[150] focuses on remembering her holiness: "You are truly blessed! The Lord is with you. God has blessed you more than any other woman! He has also blessed the child you will have" (Luke 1:28, 42). Being God's favored one means that Mary was given the fullness of God's grace in which we desire to share (Collect). The memory aspect of this celebration is found in the Communion Antiphon formed from glosses on two biblical texts. ". . . [W]onderful things are told about you," O Virgin Mary (Ps 87:3), for "God All-Powerful has done great things for [you]" (Luke 1:49). In the Prayer over the Offerings, we seek to remember and imitate the example of the Virgin of Nazareth in order to be confirmed in our love of God and neighbor. In the Prayer after Communion, we ask God to guide our steps to the vision of peace which Mary, his handmaid, already enjoys eternally in glory.

November 22, Memorial of St. Cecilia: Gladdened[151]

The Collect states that God gladdens us each year with the memory of his handmaid Cecilia (+230 or +250), about whom we know very little. Most people venerate this virgin martyr as the patroness of sacred music, but that attribute only dates from the fifteenth century. Except for the Collect, in which we pray to imitate Cecilia in what has been given to us by tradition, all the Mass texts are taken from the Common of Martyrs, IV. For a Virgin Martyr.[152] The theme of the first optional Entrance Antiphon and the Communion Antiphon comes from the CB (NT) book of Revelation. In the Entrance Antiphon, we declare that this saint, powerful in virginity, follows the crucified Lamb, making herself a martyr on the altar of chastity. The Communion Antiphon declares, "The Lamb in the center of the throne will . . . lead [her] to streams of life-giving water" (Rev 7:17). In the Prayer over the Offerings, we declare that Cecilia's suffering and passion were pleasing to

149. *Roman Missal*, 998.

150. *Roman Missal*, 1043–44.

151. *Roman Missal*, 999.

152. *Roman Missal*, 1068–69.

God, and in the Prayer after Communion, we acknowledge the crown God bestowed on her for the triumph of virginity and martyrdom.

November 24, Memorial of St. Andrew Dung-Lac and Companions: One Hundred Seventeen[153]

Often referred to as the Vietnamese martyrs, only ninety-six of the one hundred seventeen were Vietnamese; eleven were Spaniards, and ten were French. They include eight bishops, fifty priests, and fifty-nine laity who were burned alive, had limbs hacked off joint by joint, had their flesh torn from their bones, were drugged, were branded on the face, or were beheaded by Vietnamese authorities in the eighteenth and nineteenth centuries. Dung-Lac (1795–1839), a priest, represents the other one hundred sixteen martyrs, who, in the words of the Collect, were faithful to Christ even to the point of shedding their blood. The Communion Antiphon declares their holiness: "God blesses those people who are treated badly for doing right. They belong to the kingdom of heaven" (Matt 5:10). To each of these martyrs is attributed the Entrance Antiphon: ". . . I will never brag about anything except the cross of our Lord Jesus Christ. The message about the cross . . . for those of us who are being saved . . . is God's power at work" (Gal 6:14; 1 Cor 1:18). We pray for the ability to spread God's love among all people in order to demonstrate that we are his children in name and in truth (Collect), that when dealing with the trials of life, we may be found faithful (Prayer over the Offerings), and that by abiding in God's love we may endure our trials to eternal life (Prayer after Communion).

Fourth Thursday in November: Optional Memorial of Thanksgiving Day: Gratitude[154]

Gratitude, being thankful, to God is the theme of the Mass texts. The Entrance Antiphon firmly establishes it: "When you meet together, sing psalms, hymns, and spiritual songs, as you praise the Lord with all your heart. Always use the name of our Lord Jesus Christ to thank God the Father for everything" (Eph 5:19–20). In the Collect, we acknowledge God's countless gifts of love and goodness, and we declare that we come to him with gratitude for his kindness. In the Prayer over the Offerings, again we acknowledge God's

153. *Roman Missal*, 1001.

154. *Roman Missal*, 1004–06.

generous gifts which have been given so we can share them in gratitude. The Preface expresses gratitude to God for freedom, which calls us to responsibility and commitment to the fundamental dignity of all people before him. In the first optional Communion Antiphon, each of us declares: "With all my heart I praise you, LORD. When I asked for your help, you answered my prayer . . ." (Ps 138:1, 3). In the second optional Communion Antiphon, we ask: "What must I give you, LORD, for being so good to me? I will pour out an offering of wine to you, and I will pray in your name because you have saved me" (Ps 116:12–13). We pray that God will help us to reach out in loving service to people and share with them in gratitude the gifts of time and eternity (Collect, Prayer after Communion).

Bibliography

Contemporary English Version, The. Nashville, TN: Thomas Nelson, 1995.

"General Instruction of The Roman Missal." In *The Roman Missal: Study Edition*, 17–87. Collegeville, MN: Liturgical, 2011.

O'Day, Gail R., and David Peterson, eds. *The Access Bible: New Revised Standard Version with the Apocryphal/Deuterocanonical Books.* New York: Oxford University Press, 1999.

"Preface for the Feast of Saint Mary Magdalene." Washington, DC: United States Conference of Catholic Bishops, 2019. http://usccb.org/about/divine-worship/liturgical-calendar/saint-mary-magdalene.cfm.

Roman Missal, The: Study Edition. Collegeville, MN: Liturgical, 2011.

"Universal Norms on the Liturgical Year and the General Roman Calendar." In *The Roman Missal: Study Edition*, 105–135. Collegeville, MN: Liturgical, 2011.

White, David. "Liturgical Spirituality and the Rooted Heart." *Worship* 91:3 (2017) 244–50.

Recent Books by Mark G. Boyer

(all Wipf and Stock unless otherwise noted)

Nature Spirituality: Praying with Wind, Water, Earth, Fire

A Spirituality of Ageing

Caroling through Advent and Christmas: Daily Reflections with Familiar Hymns (Liguori)

Weekday Saints: Reflections on Their Scriptures

Human Wholeness: A Spirituality of Relationship

The Liturgical Environment: What the Documents Say (third edition, Liturgical Press)

A Simple Systematic Mariology

Praying Your Way through Luke's Gospel and the Acts of the Apostles

Daybreaks: Daily Reflections for Advent and Christmas (Liguori)

Daybreaks: Daily Reflections for Lent and Easter (Liguori)

An Abecedarian of Animal Spirit Guides: Spiritual Growth through Reflections on Creatures

Overcome with Paschal Joy: Chanting through Lent and Easter—Daily Reflections with Familiar Hymns

Taking Leave of Your Home: Moving in the Peace of Christ

A Spirituality of Mission: Reflections for Holy Week and Easter (Liturgical Press)

An Abecedarian of Sacred Trees: Spiritual Growth through Reflections on Woody Plants

Divine Presence: Elements of Biblical Theophanies

Fruit of the Vine: A Biblical Spirituality of Wine

Names for Jesus: Reflections for Advent and Christmas

Talk to God and Listen to the Casual Reply: Experiencing the Spirituality of John Denver

Christ Our Passover Has Been Sacrificed: A Guide through Paschal Mystery Spirituality—Mystical Theology in The Roman Missal

Rosary Primer: The Prayers, The Mysteries, and the New Testament

From Contemplation to Action: The Spiritual Process of Divine Discernment Using Elijah and Elisha as Models

Love Addict

Shhh! The Sound of Sheer Silence: A Biblical Spirituality that Transforms

What is Born of the Spirit is Spirit: A Biblical Spirituality of Spirit

Lightning Source UK Ltd.
Milton Keynes UK
UKHW021412070223
416619UK00023B/602